LATIN AND GREEK TEXTS 5

Series editor Francis Cairns. ISSN 0951-7391

SENECA'S PHAEDRA

D1554678

SENECA'S PHAEDRA

Introduction, Text, Translation and Notes

A. J. BOYLE

FRANCIS CAIRNS

Published by Francis Cairns (Publications) Ltd
PO Box 296, Cambridge, CB4 3GE, Great Britain

First published 1987
Reprinted 2010

British Library Cataloguing in Publication
A catalogue record for this book is available from the British Library

ISBN 978-0-905205-66-3 (paperback)

Printed in Great Britain by
Antony Rowe Limited, Chippenham, Wiltshire

CONTENTS

FOR MY PARENTS THERESA AND ARTHUR

★

Sed qualescumque sunt, tu illos [libros] sic lege, tamquam uerum quaeram adhuc, non sciam, et contumaciter quaeram.

Whatever the quality of my works is, read them as if I were still seeking, but were not possessed of, the truth—and seeking it with defiance.

Seneca *Epistle* 45

PREFACE

This edition and translation of Seneca's *Phaedra* are intended to be of use to students of Senecan drama in translation and to students of Latin. The introduction and the notes have been designed with both kinds of reader in mind. As in my earlier *The Eclogues of Virgil* (Melbourne 1976), I have attempted in the translation to produce a text suitable for serious study. A high level of verbal and stylistic accuracy has been sought, and attention has been given to the changing verse-forms of the play, to significant verbal and imagistic repetition, and to the order of words and phrases in the original Latin line. The Latin text itself, edited and punctuated by me, is based on recent consultation of the main manuscripts, and contains 51 different readings from the Zwierlein Oxford text of 1986 (listed in Appendix III). A selective critical apparatus has been provided for the benefit of more advanced Latin students together with an appendix on Senecan metre. Scholarly readers should also find material of interest in this edition.

Much of the work for this book was done in Cambridge in 1985, when I was a Visiting Fellow of Clare Hall. I am grateful to Clare Hall and its president, Sir Michael Stoker, for the provision of a stimulating and agreeable environment in which to conduct research. Several friends and colleagues have read through parts of this book and offered advice: Marcus Wilson of Sydney University; Saul Bastomsky, William Dominik, John Penwill, Marianne Westbrook and Bronwyn Williams of Monash; Peter Davis of the University of Tasmania, who also generously allowed me to see his own translation of the play; and Guy Lee and Ruth Morse of Cambridge University, who discussed the whole translation with me at an early and crucial stage. To them and to my research assistant, Mrs. Betty Williams, I am much indebted. My thanks are also due to the four libraries which supplied photographs or microfilms of the major Senecan manuscripts and in two cases provided facilities for examining the manuscripts *in situ*: Corpus Christi College Library, Cambridge; Biblioteca Medicea-Laurenziana, Florence; Bibliothèque Nationale, Paris; Biblioteca Real, Escorial. Help of various kinds was given by Judy, James and Kathryn Boyle. A lifelong debt is acknowledged elsewhere.

Monash University, Melbourne, July 1986   A.J.B.

INTRODUCTION

1. LIFE AND WORKS

> Quasi in tutte le sue tragedie, egli avanzò (per quanto a me ne
> paia) nella prudenza, nella gravità, nel decoro, nella maiestà,
> nelle sentenze, tutti i Greci che scrissero mai.
>
> In almost all his tragedies he surpassed (in my opinion) in
> prudence, in gravity, in decorum, in majesty, in epigrams, all the
> Greeks who ever wrote.
>
> Giraldi Cintio, Discorsi (1543)

Seneca *tragicus* has received a variable press. Tragic idol of the
Renaissance, *bête noire* of a century and a half of British and German
classical scholarship, the enigmatic author of the Senecan plays still
evokes responses both of approbation and of censure. The tendency
to unqualified vilification, so marked in the nineteenth and early
twentieth centuries, has however largely disappeared, replaced by a
growing attention to the nature of the plays and their intellectual and
cultural context. Replaced too by augmented respect for our
dramatic forebears. Seneca's attested influence on French and
Elizabethan tragedy, on dramatists of the distinction of Corneille,
Racine and Shakespeare, is in the latter part of the twentieth century
not likely to be dismissed simply as a bizarre historical accident.
Important recent studies of the plays reveal not the pseudo-
tragedian, hackneyed rhetorician or Stoic propagandist of Seneca's
detractors, but a dramatist interested in drama—in the careful
shaping of dramatic action, in the interrelationship between chorus
and act, in dramatic movement, pace, impetus, in the structuring and
unfolding of dramatic language and imagery, in the spectacular and
thematic use of "theatre", in human psychology emblematic and
imaged. The considerable variation evidenced in such standard
matters as prologue composition, choral length and sequence, the
number of choruses and actors, the messenger's speech, the five or six
act division, discloses in fact a dramatist interested in dramatic
experimentation. And interest in form in Seneca is wedded inextricably to interest in what is dramatically efformed, the themes,
ideas, problems, issues, which his tragedies realise, which constitute

1

their world. A world neither simply Stoic nor simple. Neither formal nor ideological simplicity determines Senecan drama. Its hallmarks are intricacy of language, structure, image, thought— and human centrality of theme. As *Phaedra* demonstrates, Seneca's seminal position in European drama is well merited.

Lucius Annaeus Seneca was born in 1 B.C. or shortly before in Corduba (modern Cordova) in southern Spain, the second of three sons to the cultivated equestrian, Annaeus Seneca (c.55 B.C. to c.A.D. 40—*praenomen* probably also Lucius), author of a lost history of Rome and a surviving (but badly mutilated) work on Roman declamation, *Controuersiae* and *Suasoriae*. The youngest son, Mela, was the father of the epic poet Lucan. Brought to Rome as a young child and given the standard education in rhetoric, Seneca had become by the early years of Tiberius' principate (A.D. 14-37), while still in adolescence, a passionate devotee of philosophy. The focus of his ardor was an ascetic, locally taught form of Stoic-Pythagoreanism with a strong commitment to vegetarianism. Before long he had been dissuaded from it by his father (*Ep.* 108. 17-22). During his youth and throughout his life Seneca suffered from a tubercular condition, and was impelled on one occasion to contemplate suicide when he despaired of recovery. He records that only the thought of the suffering he would have caused his father prevented his death (*Ep.* 78.1f.).

Ill health presumably delayed the start of his political career, as did a substantial period of convalescence in Egypt during the twenties under the care of his maternal aunt. He returned to Rome from Egypt in A.D. 31 (surviving a shipwreck in which his uncle died), and entered the senate via the quaestorship shortly afterwards, as did Gallio his elder brother. By the beginning of Claudius' principate (A.D. 41) he had also held the aedileship and the office of tribune of the people (*tribunus plebis*). During the thirties too he married (although whether it was to his wife of later years who survived him, Pompeia Paulina, is uncertain), and he achieved such fame as a public speaker as to arouse the attention and jealousy of the emperor Gaius (Suetonius *Gaius* 53.2, Dio 59.19.7f.), better known as Caligula. By the late thirties Seneca was clearly moving in the circle of princes, among "that tiny group of men on which there bore down, night and day, the concentric pressure of a monstrous weight, the post-Augustan empire" (Herington). His presence in high places was initially short-lived. He survived Caligula's brief principate (A.D. 37-41) only to be exiled to Corsica in the first year of Claudius' reign

2

(A.D. 41). The charge was adultery with Caligula's sister, Julia Livilla, brought by the new empress, Claudius' young wife, Messalina.

Seneca's exile came at a time of great personal distress (both his father and his son had recently died—*Helv.* 2.4f.), and, despite pleas for imperial clemency (see esp. *Pol.* 13.2ff.), lasted eight tedious years. In A.D. 48 Messalina was executed. In the following year Seneca, through the agency of Agrippina, Claudius' new wife, was recalled to Rome and designated praetor for A.D. 50. His literary and philosophical reputation were now well established (Tac. *Ann.* 12.8.3), and he was appointed tutor to Agrippina's son, Nero. This appointment as Nero's tutor not only placed Seneca again at the centre of the Roman world, but brought him immense power and influence when Agrippina poisoned her emperor-husband and Nero acceded to the throne (A.D. 54). Throughout the early part of Nero's principate Seneca (suffect consul in A.D. 56) and the commander of the praetorian guard, S. Afranius Burrus, acted as the chief ministers and political counsellors of Nero, whom they increasingly became unable to control. Nero's matricide in A.D. 59, to which it is probable that neither Seneca nor Burrus was privy, but for which nevertheless Seneca wrote a *post factum* justification (Tac. *Ann.* 14.11), signalled the weakening of their power. When Burrus died (perhaps poisoned—Tac. *Ann.* 14.15.1) in A.D. 62, Seneca went into semi-retirement. In A.D. 65 he was accused of involvement in the Pisonian conspiracy against Nero and was ordered to kill himself. This he did, leaving to his friends "his one remaining possession—and his best—the pattern of his life" (*quod unum iam et tamen pulcherrimum habeat, imaginem uitae suae*, Tac. *Ann.* 15.62.1).

Although Seneca was born only a few years after Horace's death he inhabited a different world. Horace (65-8 B.C.) lived through Rome's momentous and bloody transformation from republic to empire; he fought with Brutus and Cassius at Philippi (42 B.C.). Seneca never knew the republic. Born under Augustus and committing suicide three years before Nero's similar fate, he lived through and was encompassed by the Julio-Claudian principate. Throughout Seneca's lifetime—despite the preservation of Rome's political, legal, moral, social and religious forms—power resided essentially in one man, the *princeps* or emperor, sometimes (as in the case of Caligula) a vicious psychopath. Political and personal freedom were nullities. In Rome and especially at the court itself, on which the pressure of empire bore, nothing and no one seemed secure, the Roman world's controlling forms used, abused and nullified by the *princeps'* power. Servility, hypocrisy, corrupting power indexed this Julio-Claudian world. Or so at least the ancient historians would have us believe, especially Tacitus, whose *Annales*, written in the first decades of the second century A.D., documents the hatreds, fears, lusts, cowardice, self-interest, self-abasement, abnormal cruelty, extravagant vice, violent death, inversion and perversion of Rome's efforming values and institutions—and, more rarely, the nobility and the heroism— which to his mind constituted the early imperial court. Tacitus' indictment of Nero's principate is as emphatic as it is persuasive. Nero's debauchery (*Ann.* 15.37), fratricide (*Ann.* 13.16-18), matricide (*Ann.* 14.8-10), sororicide (*Ann.* 14.60-64) are emblematically portrayed. Witness the murder of Octavia, ex-wife and step-sister (A.D. 62):

> restringitur uinclis uenaeque eius per omnes artus exsoluuntur; et quia pressus pauore sanguis tardius labebatur, praeferuidi balnei uapore enecatur. additurque atrocior saeuitia, quod caput amputatum latumque in urbem Poppaea uidit. dona ob haec templis decreta quem ad finem memorabimus? quicumque casus temporum illorum nobis uel aliis auctoribus noscent, praesumptum habeant, quotiens fugas et caedes iussit princeps, totiens grates deis actas, quaeque rerum secundarum olim, tum publicae cladis insignia fuisse.

> She was bound in chains and her veins were opened in every limb; but her blood, congealed by terror, flowed too slowly, so she was suffocated by the steam of a boiling bath. A more appalling cruelty followed: her head was cut off and taken to Rome to be viewed by Poppaea. How long shall I go on recounting the thank-offerings in temples on such occasions? Every reader of the history of that period, in my work or in others', should assume that the gods were thanked each time the emperor ordered an exile or a murder, and that what formerly signalled rejoicing now indicated public disaster.

> (*Ann.* 14.64)

Or the black farce of Roman servility (A.D. 65):

> sed compleri interim urbs funeribus, Capitolium uictimis; alius filio, fratre alius aut propinquo aut amico interfectis, agere grates deis, ornare lauru domum, genua ipsius aduolui et dextram osculis fatigare.

> Funerals abounded in the city, thank-offerings on the Capitol. Men who had lost a son or brother or relative or friend gave thanks to the gods, bedecked their houses with laurel, and fell at the feet of Nero kissing his hand incessantly.

> (*Ann.* 15.71)

4

Tacitus' account of Rome's distemper is prejudicial, in part myopic. The author of the *Annales* had experienced at first hand the human degradation at the centre of the early principate, the paralysing nightmare of a tyrant's (in his case Domitian's) court. As had Seneca. And, as in Tacitus, it shows. The themes of Seneca's tragedies—vengeance, madness, power-lust, passion, irrational hatred, self-contempt, murder, incest, hideous death, fortune's vicissitudes and savagery—were the stuff of his life. Those who think them merely rhetorical commonplaces have never stared into the face of a Caligula (see *Ira* 3.18-19.5).

Omitting a body of epigrams handed down under Seneca's name (most of which are certainly spurious) Seneca's writings can conveniently be divided into the prose works and the tragedies. The prose works comprise a scientific work, *Naturales Quaestiones* ("Natural Questions"), a satire on Claudius' deification, *Apocolocyntosis* ("The Pumpkinification"), and a series of texts more or less philosophical in content: the ten so-called *Dialogi* ("Dialogues"), *De Beneficiis* ("On Benefits"), *De Clementia* ("On Clemency"—addressed to Nero on his accession), and *Epistulae Morales ad Lucilium* ("Moral Epistles"). These so-called "philosophical" works are infused to a greater or lesser extent with Stoic ethical ideas: the advocation of virtue, endurance, self-sufficiency, true friendship; the condemnation of evil, emotions and the false values of wealth and power; the praise of reason, wisdom, poverty; contempt for the fear of death. The prose works cover a considerable period of time—from the thirties A.D. to Seneca's death. Among the earliest to be written was *Consolatio ad Marciam*, composed under Caligula (A.D. 37-41); among the last were *Naturales Quaestiones* and *Epistulae Morales*, written during the years of Seneca's retirement (A.D. 62-65).

At least seven complete tragedies can be assigned to Seneca: *Hercules* [*Furens*], *Troades*, *Medea*, *Phaedra*, *Oedipus*, *Agamemnon* and *Thyestes*. Such are their titles in the E branch of the ms. tradition. In the A branch *Hercules* is given the augmented title *Hercules Furens*, *Troades* is called *Tros*, and *Phaedra* is called *Hippolytus* (*Phaedra* is also the title used by the sixth century grammarian, Priscian, quoting *Pha.* 710). An eighth play, *Phoenissae* (*Thebais* in A) is also accepted by most modern scholars as Senecan, but it possesses no choral odes and is thought by some to be incomplete. A ninth play, *Hercules Oetaeus*, is almost twice as long as the average Senecan play and is generally agreed to be—at least in its present form—non-Senecan. A tenth play, the *fabula praetexta* or historical drama, *Octauia*, in which Seneca appears as a character and which seems to refer to events which took place after Seneca's death, is missing from A and is certainly not by Seneca.

The date of the composition of the plays is not known. Most modern commentators accept a *terminus ante quem* of A.D. 54 for *Hercules Furens* on the grounds that the *Apocolocyntosis* (securely dated to A.D. 54) seems to parody it. But the first unambiguous reference to any of Seneca's plays is by Quintilian (*Inst.* 9.2.8), writing a generation after Seneca's death. Seneca in fact makes no mention of his tragedies in his prose works. Many commentators allocate them to the period of exile on Corsica (A.D. 41-49); others regard it as more likely that their composition, like that of the prose works, was spread over a considerable period of time. Recent stylometric studies of the plays seem to support the latter position.

The relationship between the tragedies and the philosophical works continues to be debated. Although the tragedies are not mentioned in the prose works, it is perhaps still conventional to regard them as the product of Stoic convictions and the dramatisation of a Stoic world-view. Certainly they abound in Stoic moral ideas (many traceable to the *Epistulae Morales*) and their preoccupation with emotional pathology and with the destructive consequences of passion, especially anger, is deeply indebted to the Stoic tradition (see especially *De Ira*). But this Stoicism is no outer ideological clothing but part of the dramatic texture of the plays. And to many, including the present editor, the world-view of most of the plays is decidedly unstoic, the Stoic ideology itself being critically exhibited within a larger, more profound, more disturbing vision.

2. THE LITERARY BACKGROUND

Roman Tragedy

Graecia capta ferum uictorem cepit et artis
intulit agresti Latio.

Enslaved Greece enslaved her savage victor and brought
The arts to rustic Latium.

Horace Epistle 2.1.156f.

Product of the Hellenisation of Rome in the third and second centuries B.C., when Rome sought to enhance its own self-image and Greek literary and artistic forms were adopted and adapted by the Roman world, Roman tragedy in the late republic was a vital literary force. The first tragedy known to have been written in Latin was the adaptation of a Greek play by the early translator of Homer's *Odyssey*, the ex-slave, Livius Andronicus; it was performed at the *Ludi Romani* of 240 B.C. Thence until the end of the republic the writing and the performance of Roman tragedies were active industries. Most of such tragedies took their themes and plots from existing Greek plays (but the process was nothing at all like "translation"), and a new kind of tragedy also emerged, the historical drama or *fabula praetexta* (Horace *Ars Poetica* 288), which took its theme from Roman history. Four major figures stand out, whose works, however, survive only in fragments: Naevius (died c. 200 B.C.), Ennius (239-169 B.C.), Pacuvius (220-130 B.C.) and Accius (170-c.85 B.C.). The first of these to devote himself entirely to tragic drama was Pacuvius—erudite, allusive, Alexandrian. But it was "soaring" Accius (Horace *Ep.* 2.1.55), famed for his rhetorical skills, especially the emotive force of his speeches, who dominated the late republic. His output was immense. So too his popularity, nor only in his lifetime. Revivals of Accius' plays—sometimes performed with contemporary political overtones—are attested for the years 57 B.C. (*Eurysaces* and *Brutus*), 55 B.C. (*Clytemnestra*), 54 B.C. (*Astyanax*), and 44 B.C. (*Tereus*). Other second century tragedians too had their work performed at this time, but Accius' popularity seems to have been unmatched. Even Cicero, who judged Pacuvius supreme in tragedy (*Op. Gen.* 1.2), admired him greatly (see, e.g., *Sest.* 119ff.).

Like that of Athens, Roman tragedy was constituent of a social context. During the late third and second centuries B.C. *ludi scaenici*,

7

"theatrical shows", including comedies, tragedies, music and dancing, were incorporated into the annual festivals held at Rome in honour of Jupiter, Apollo, Magna Mater, Flora and Ceres. At the same time the practice arose of performing plays at the triumphs or funerals of distinguished citizens and at the consecration of temples. The *ludi scaenici* were organised by Roman magistrates, who used them— among other things—to impress their peers, clients and the citizen body as a whole, and (especially where the *praetexta* was concerned) for specific political goals. Initially it was to the magistrate who commissioned the *ludi* that the bulk of the credit for a performance went. The early playwrights themselves were accorded little social status, being regarded as paid employees of the magistrate, if they were not his actual slaves. This situation began to change during the second century B.C., and by the first century the early writers of Roman tragedy were being regarded as the fathers of an important indigenous literature. They were sometimes even thought to excel their Greek counterparts (see, e.g., Cic. *Tusc.* 2.49).

As to how these early Roman tragedies were staged much remains obscure. It is clear that the lyric sections of the plays, which took up a far greater proportion of the drama than in fifth-century Greek tragedy or in Seneca, were musically accompanied (by a piper or flute-player, *tibicen*), and certainly by the first century B.C. actors were wearing the tragic mask (Cic. *De Orat.* 3.221) and buskins. Moreover, at Rome until 55 B.C. all plays were staged on temporary wooden structures, erected for the duration of the *ludi scaenici*. Both the stage and the stage-building with its three doorways would have been of wood. The wealthier Greek cities of southern Italy and Sicily had stone theatres dating from the fifth century (the theatre of Syracuse was dedicated c.460 B.C.) and by the end of the second century several Italian towns had acquired their own permanent stone-built theatre (the large theatre of Pompeii dates from c.200 B.C.). But the conservative moralists at Rome prevented the capital itself from acquiring its first stone-built theatre until the construction of the Theatre of Pompey in 55-52 B.C. The wait was perhaps worthwhile. A revolutionary concrete and marble structure, in which stage-building, semicircular orchestra and tiered concave auditorium were united into a closed, holistic space, the Theatre of Pompey provided the model and the standard for the theatres of the capital and the empire to come. Even in the fourth century A.D. it was still heralded as one of the outstanding monuments of Rome (Ammianus Marcellinus 16.10.14).

But if the physical context of Roman tragedy improved after the death of Accius, the same cannot automatically be said about tragedy itself. Many maintain that Accius was the last great Roman tragedian and that after his death tragedy became the plaything of aristocratic litterateurs, composing tragedies for diversion, not for the stage. Cicero's brother, Quintus, for example, composed four tragedies in sixteen days (Cic. *Q.Fr.* 3.5, 6.7); Julius Caesar wrote an *Oedipus* and Augustus attempted an *Ajax* (Suetonius *Julius* 56.7, *Augustus* 85.2). But although the second half of the first century B.C. seemed to produce no tragedian of the stature of an Accius, notable tragedies were written by Asinius Pollio, praised by Virgil (*Ecl.* 8.9f.) and Horace (*Odes* 2.1.11f.), by Varius Rufus, whose *Thyestes* was performed at the Actian Games of 29 B.C., and by Ovid. Varius' *Thyestes* and Ovid's *Medea* were held in high esteem at least by Quintilian (*Inst.* 10.1.98—cf. also Tac. *Dial.* 12.5). During the early empire (first century A.D.) the *ludi scaenici* became increasingly dominated by "popular theatre", in the form of mime (coarse and indecent) and pantomime, and by spectacle, but some tragedy continued to be written and publicly performed. There is evidence too of "political" tragedy. Aemilius Scaurus, for example, wrote a tragedy, *Atreus*, which angered Tiberius (Dio 58.24; Tac. *Ann.* 6.29), and in Tacitus' *Dialogus* Curiatius Maternus is credited with a tragedy, *Cato*, which may have offended Vespasian (*princeps* A.D. 69-79), and with another political tragedy, *Thyestes*. Maternus is also described as reciting his tragedies in public (Tac. *Dial.* 2.3, 11.2), but that tragedies were still being written for the stage in the mid-to-late first century A.D. is clear from the example of Seneca's contemporary Pomponius Secundus, a distinguished dramatist (Tac. *Dial.* 13.7) who, according to Quintilian, excelled in "learning", *eruditio*, and "brilliance", *nitor* (*Inst.* 10.1.98), and who definitely wrote for the stage (*is carmina scaenae dabat*, Tac. *Ann.* 11.13; see also Pliny *Ep.* 7.17.11). Pomponius Secundus figured in fact in a celebrated argument with Seneca on tragic diction (Quint. *Inst.* 8.3.31).

The following complex picture emerges of the theatrical conditions of Seneca's day. Throughout Italy and the empire theatres abound (three in Rome itself)—Roman, not Greek. Their concrete structures, marble revetments, socially stratified seating, holistic design, their deep stages, on which all the action takes place (the small orchestra having been given over to senatorial seating), richly decorated stage-curtains (including in Seneca's day the "drop-curtain"), baroque stage-buildings adorned with statues, scene-paintings, masks and

9

garlands — index their *romanitas*. Mime, pantomime, spectacle predominate, but comedy (Suetonius *Nero* 11) and high tragedy are still regularly performed in the theatre and probably also in private houses (*intra domum*—see Suetonius *Domitian* 7.1; cf. Sen. *NQ* 7.32.3). Tragedies too are often "recited" (by a single speaker). The recitation takes place in a private house or recitation-hall, *auditorium* (both for its own sake and as a preliminary to theatrical performance and/or publication—see Pliny *Ep.* 7.17.11), or in the theatre itself as a virtuoso individual recital of a tragic speech, episode or monody. To the last category belong Nero's own performances (Suetonius *Nero* 21.3) of "the tragedies of heroes and gods wearing the tragic mask (*personatus*)". Some have also assigned Senecan tragedy to the category of recitation-drama—generally on the basis of (unjustified) naturalistic assumptions about the conventions of the imperial stage. But Seneca's exhibited "stage-craft" in the construction of scenes, his thematic use of stage-setting, the stage-directions in the text itself indicate that his plays were designed for dramatic performance— whether the performance envisaged was in the theatre or in a private house to a coterie audience (or both). Senecan tragedy belongs, if anything does, to the category of performance drama.

But while an intricate but clear picture emerges of the continuing existence and developing complexity of Roman tragedy as both social institution and literary form, little is known of its dramaturgical practices and conventions. Contemporary witnesses of republican tragedy mention such matters as the presence of the flute-player, the wearing of tragic masks and the predominance of spectacle (as in the gala performance of Accius' *Clytemnestra* in 55 B.C. to celebrate the opening of the Theatre of Pompey—Cic. *Fam.* 7.1.2), but provide little detailed dramaturgical information. The Augustan picture is a little clearer. Vitruvius' comments in *De Architectura* 5.6, although confined essentially to theatre design and construction, include important remarks on stage-scenery and the different functions of the two stage-exits; and Horace in the *Ars Poetica* (189-92) draws attention to the five act rule, the three actor rule and the *deus ex machina*. The evidence however remains largely internal. And what the fragments of the early Roman tragedians suggest is that even in the republic there had been a fusion of classical and Hellenistic techniques. Certainly the tragedies of Seneca, while they reveal and exploit an obvious counterpoint with the plays of the fifth-century Attic triad, especially in respect of divergent treatments of the same myth (see below p. 15), display many dramaturgical features—the five act structure (*Phaedra* and *Oedipus* are exceptions here), the use of extended asides (e.g. *Pha.* 424ff., 592ff.) including entrance monologue-asides (*HF* 332ff., *Med.* 177ff.), choral exit and re-entry (see *Pha.* 405n.), miscellaneous stage-practices (see *Pha.* 601n.)—derived from the conventions of Hellenistic drama, particularly New Comedy of the fourth and third centuries B.C. It is not unreasonable to suppose that by the Augustan period, when the Hellenistic influence on Roman poetry was at its height, many of these features were standard Roman practice. Seneca is certainly indebted to Augustan tragedians for their refinement of the crude iambic dialogue line (the *senarius* or "sixer") of the earlier playwrights (Horace *Ars Poetica* 251ff.) and probably also for aspects of his tragic language. It seems likely that the debt extended to dramaturgy too.

Postclassicism

> oratio certam regulam non habet; consuetudo illam ciuitatis, quae numquam in eodem diu stetit, uersat.
>
> Style has no fixed rules; the usage of society changes it, which never stays still for long.
>
> Seneca Epistle 114.13

Indebted to earlier tragedy both Roman and Greek, Senecan drama is also product and index of an age—the age of the baroque in Roman architecture and the "pointed", declamatory style in poetry. The age is improperly understood. The change which took place in Roman poetry between the early Augustan period and that of Nero, between the "classicism" of Virgil and Horace and the "postclassicism" of Seneca and Lucan, is conventionally described as the movement from Golden to Silver Latin. The description misleads on many counts, not least because it misconstrues a change in literary and poetic sensibility, in the mental sets of reader and audience, and in the political environment of writing itself, as a change in literary value. What in fact happened awaits adequate description, but it seems clear that the change began with Ovid (43 B.C. to A.D. 17), whose rejection of Augustan classicism (especially its concept of *decorum* or "appropriateness"), cultivation of generic disorder and experimentation (see, e.g., *Ars Amatoria* and *Metamorphoses*), love of paradox, absurdity, incongruity, hyperbole, wit, and focus on extreme emotional states, influenced everything that followed. Ovid also witnessed and suffered from the increasing political repression of the principate; he was banished for—among other things—his words, *carmen*. And political repression seems to have been a signal factor, if difficult to evaluate, in the formation of the postclassical style.

After Ovid political and literary repression accelerated. The trial and suicide of the historian Cremutius Cordus and the burning of his books in A.D. 25 showed what could and did happen (Tac. *Ann.* 4.34ff.; for other victims see *Ann.* 3.49ff., Sen. Rhet. *Con.* 10 Pref.3 and 5ff., Dio 57.22.5). And no major Roman poet emerges before Seneca and the Neronians. During the reigns of Tiberius and Gaius, though occasional tragedies, for example, are written, poetry is confined essentially to such literary kinds as fable (Phaedrus— himself a victim of Tiberius' minister, Sejanus, *Fabulae* 3. Prol. 41ff.) and scientific didactic (Manilius and possibly the author of *Aetna*), or else occupies the attention of aristocratic amateurs like Germanicus and Tiberius himself. The middle of the first century (primarily the Neronian era) witnessed a literary renaissance. Epic (Lucan), satire (Persius), pastoral (Calpurnius), the prose-verse novel (Petronius) erupted onto the scene—together with renascent tragedy (Seneca)— saturated with the imagery, diction, commonplaces, narratology and character-analysis of Augustan literature, indebted above all to the triad of Virgil, Horace and Ovid (the *Aeneid* and the *Metamorphoses* especially inform Neronian texts), but operating in a post-Ovidian, non-Augustan mode. Augustan literary forms returned but subject to new energies and new stylistic modes. Individual styles varied, but what specifically characterised this new postclassical mode was the cultivation of paradox, discontinuity, antithesis and point, the adoption of declamatory structures and techniques, and the striking mixture of compression, elaboration, epigram and hyperbole.

Several factors seem involved in the evolution of this style. One was Ovid. Another was the emphasis on rhetoric in the schools. During the early empire training in *declamatio* in a school run by a professional declaimer or *rhetor* was the final and indispensable constituent of a young Roman's formal education. This was in itself nothing new. What however had occurred from the early Augustan period onwards was a rise in the number of such schools, and (more significantly) an increasing focus in them on the skills of declamation as ends in themselves and an increasing detachment of the decla- matory exercises from any exterior practical function. Another important innovation was the "display" declamation of a practising *rhetor*. Public declamations by rival professors and declamatory "debates" between them became a social institution and a regular form of public and imperial entertainment (for the latter see Sen. Rhet. *Con.* 2.4.12, 10.5.21, *Suas.* 3.7). The *Controuersiae* and *Suasoriae* of Seneca's father, which were probably written in the thirties A.D. and must have had a profound impact on Seneca himself, document such declamations and indicate the kind of training the schools provided.

There were essentially two kinds of speech in which students were practised: deliberative (*suasoriae*) and disputatious (*controuersiae*). In the former students purported to "advise" mythological or historical characters at critical points in their lives ("Agamemnon deliberates whether to sacrifice Iphigenia", *Suas.* 3; "Cicero deliberates whether to beg Antony's pardon", *Suas.* 6); in the latter they played the role of litigants or advocates in imaginary law-suits, debating intricate and generally far-fetched moral and legal issues. An armoury of rhetorical techniques was the progeny of such training. Students were taught the declamatory employment of antitheses and conceits, of descriptive set-pieces and historical *exempla*, of moralising commonplaces (*loci communes*) and rhetorical flourishes. They were taught the use of apostrophe, alliteration, assonance, tricolon, anaphora, asyndeton, homoeoteleuton, polyptoton, *figura etymologica*, *commutatio*; the use of synonyms, antonyms, oxymora, paradox, innuendo (*suspicio*), epigram, point; above all, declamatory structure. The watchwords of the new rhetoric, as proclaimed by Marcus Aper at Tacitus *Dialogus* 20ff., give the essence of the instruction: "brilliance", *nitor*; "elegance", *cultus*; "elevation", *altitudo*; "colour", *color*; "luxuriance", *laetitia*; "splendour", *aliquid inlustre*; "memorability", *dignum memoria*; "epigram", *sententia*. The schools were later much criticised—for the unreality of the declamatory themes and the unsuitability of the "education" they provided for the rigours of law-court life (Sen. Rhet. *Con.* 3 Pref., 9 Pref., Petron. *Sat.* 1ff., Quint. *Inst.* 2.10.4ff., Tac. *Dial.* 35). But their popularity was considerable, as was that of the virtuoso public declamations of the *rhetores* themselves. And, whatever the new rhetoric's success in preparing pupils for public careers (and Seneca's own life indicates that not all pupils failed), it played a substantial role in changing the mental sets of the Roman reader and audience, and the Roman world's verbal and literary modes.

Style is function of an age. The educational system of early

13

imperial Rome generated minds formed by rhetoric. Rhetoric taught and was structure. Postclassical literary modes accord with the changed mental sets of reader and audience, with the contemporary passion for rhetoric and the contemporary fullness of response to rhetoric, to declamation, dialectic, verbal brilliance and ingenuity. But the style was also the style of shock, index of an age of political repression and moral lethargy, an age which began to express itself in painting, sculpture, architecture and literature in increasingly hyperbolic forms. For those who had something compelling to say the declamatory, "pointed" style of postclassical Roman verse was a powerful, shocking mode. As Seneca *tragicus*, its master, shows.

3. THE MYTH

And it came to pass after these things, that his master's wife cast her eyes upon Joseph; and she said, Lie with me. But he refused...As she spake to Joseph day by day, he hearkened not unto her, to lie by her, or to be with her...And she caught him by his garment, saying, Lie with me; and he left his garment in her hand, and fled, and got him out...She called unto the men of her house, and spake unto them, saying, See, he hath brought in an Hebrew unto us to mock us; he came in unto me to lie with me, and I cried with a loud voice: And it came to pass, when he heard that I lifted up my voice and cried, that he left his garment with me, and fled, and got him out. And she laid up his garment with her, until his lord came home...And it came to pass, when his master heard the words of his wife, which she spake unto him, saying, After this manner did thy servant to me; that his wrath was kindled. And Joseph's master took him, and put him into the prison...

Genesis 39.7-20

The story of a married woman who falls in love with a young man, finds her advances rejected and pre-empts denunciation by accusing him to her husband is a common folk-tale theme. Joseph's encounter with Potiphar's wife (see above) is well known. In the Graeco-Roman mythopoeic tradition the theme occurs in several variants, among which are the stories of Bellerophon and the wife of Proetus (Anteia according to Homer *Iliad* 6.160, Sthcneboea according to others, e.g. Juvenal 10.327), and Peleus and the wife of Acastus (Hippolyte according to Pindar *Nemean* 4.56ff., 5.25ff., Astydamea according to others). The story of Hippolytus and Phaedra proved the most popular. In the second century A.D. Pausanias could write (1.22.1f.) that the story was known to all who had learnt Greek. Its main elements are clear: the married woman, Phaedra, is the young man's, Hippolytus', stepmother; he rejects her advances (or another's on her behalf); Phaedra accuses him to her husband; the husband curses Hippolytus and invokes Poseidon's (Neptune's) aid; Hippolytus is killed, while driving his chariot, by a monstrous bull from the sea; Phaedra kills herself.

The legend probably originated at Troezen, a town in the north-east Peloponnese on the southern shore of the Saronic gulf, where Poseidon was the most important local god and Hippolytus the central figure of a major cult. By the sixth century B.C. the legend may already have been appropriated by the Athenians and incorporated into an epic poem, *Theseis*, concerned with the exploits of Athens' national hero, Theseus. Certainly by the fifth century the myth was well established and became the subject of three plays by Attic tragedians, one by Sophocles, *Phaedra*, and two by Euripides, both entitled *Hippolytus*. The Sophoclean play and Euripides' first *Hippolytus* (referred to in Greek as the *Hippolytos Kalyptomenos*, "Hippolytus Covered") survive only in fragments. Euripides' second *Hippolytus* is extant. It was produced in 428 B.C. and won for Euripides one of the few first prizes of his long dramatic career. Each of the plays provided a fresh reshaping of the myth; each is likely to have influenced Seneca. Because of the accident of survival only the counterpoint between Seneca's *Phaedra* and Euripides' second *Hippolytus* can be seen. Not that Seneca's indebtedness to Greek dramatisations of the myth is limited to the fifth-century tragedians. It was observed above that Seneca is likely to have derived several aspects of his dramaturgical practice from the Hellenistic theatre (even if only by way of Augustan tragedy), and it is more than possible that Seneca was influenced by lost Hellenistic plays on the Phaedra theme, such as the *Hippolytus* of the prolific tragedian, Lycophron (fl. c.280 B.C.).

In Roman tragedy there is no record of a dramatisation of the Phaedra myth until Seneca. The story was of course well known:

> notus amor Phaedrae, nota est iniuria Thesei:
> deuouit natum credulus ille suum.

> Famous is Phaedra's love, famous Theseus' wrong:
> Credulous he cursed his son to death.
>
> Ovid *Fasti* 6.737f.

And was alluded to often. Virgil refers to the story twice in the *Aeneid* (6.445, 7.761ff.), placing the dead Phaedra in the "fields of mourning", *lugentes campi*, among those whom "hard love (*durus amor*) has consumed with cruel wasting" (*Aen.* 6.440ff.). Horace makes Hippolytus a paradigm of futile chastity (*Odes* 4.7.25f.); Ovid, following Virgil's lead (*Aen.* 7.761ff.), restores him to life (*Fasti* 6.737ff., *Met.* 15.497ff.). To Ovid in fact Seneca is especially indebted. Mention was made above of the influence of Ovidian poetic modes on the style of postclassical Roman verse and the probable influence of Ovidian and Augustan dramaturgy on Seneca. But Seneca was also indebted to Ovid in matters of motif, theme and characterisation, and one Ovidian text influenced Seneca's *Phaedra* above all else, Phaedra's imagined verse epistle to Hippolytus, *Heroides* 4.

Whatever the precise date of *Phaedra*'s composition, Seneca could look back on a long and rich tradition of the poetic and dramatic presentation of the Phaedra-Hippolytus myth. The counterpoint with Ovid's treatment is the most immediate and overt. But since Greek literature was still an active and formative ingredient in Roman culture (see, for example, the authors that Statius' father, a *grammaticus*, was teaching in the second half of the first century A.D.—Statius *Siluae* 5.3.146ff.), Seneca could expect a significant part of his audience to appreciate something of the interplay between *Phaedra* and earlier Greek presentations of the myth. Much of this intertextuality is now lost; but where it can be gauged, as in the cases of Euripides' second *Hippolytus* and Ovid *Heroides* 4 (see the Notes for details), it demonstrates a potent, creative use of a tradition which, as Racine in the seventeenth century and Robinson Jeffers and Eugene O'Neill in the twentieth century have shown, is not yet ended.

4. THE PLAY

Quid enim aliud est natura quam deus et diuina ratio toti
mundo partibusque eius inserta?

For what else is nature but god and divine reason inserted into
the universe and its parts?

Seneca De Beneficiis 4.7.1

Natura Vindex: Claimant Nature

Phaedra is a play which meditates on "nature". *Thyestes* dramatises
the beast in man, *Medea* civilisation endemically flawed; *Phaedra*
focusses on *natura* and human impotence. Enshrined on stage is
Diana, the play's emblematic and central divinity, mistress of forest,
mountain, beast and hunt, goddess of the moon. Associated both
with the movement of the planets and stars (309ff., 410ff., 785ff.) and
with that part of earth's domain still free of man's "civilising" hand
(55ff., 406f.), she appears "nature's" goddess par excellence; she is
paradoxically conjoined, as will be seen, with the goddess of sexual
love, in turn associated directly with *natura* (352). The play's main
image is the hunt, activity of Diana, Venus, *natura*; it operates with
structurally pervasive and ironic effect. But other images too—
images of fire, sea, storm, winter, summer, planets, stars, images of
"nature's" violence, order, beauty—reflect the concern with *natura*.
The action of the play, the dramatisation of its major figures,
and—often the index in Senecan tragedy of where a play's attention
lies—the preoccupations of the chorus sustain the focus on "nature"
and its relationship to the human world.

   The play begins in the murky half-light of dawn with an address by
Hippolytus—lively, energetic, full of verve, vitality and feeling (1-
84)—to his huntsmen and his goddess. The monody heralds much.
The contradictory aspects of Diana's kingdom, nature's uncivilised
realm, are barely concealed: order, beauty, perceptual richness and
life (1-30); destruction, fear, violence and death (31-53). The
ambivalence of Hippolytus' attitude is patent. Evidencing a deep,
emotional response to the countryside and the wild, a felt sense of its
beauty, grandeur, its aesthetic richness and variety (1-30), Hippolytus
is yet far from Wordsworth's "priest". As the instructions for the
hunt (31-53) especially reveal—with their emphasis on the controlled
manipulation of violence, reaching vigorous climax in the final

18

"victory" (*victor*, 52), the knifing of the innards from the prey (52f.)—Hippolytus, unlike the primitives of *Epistle* 90 who receive "nature's" gifts (*Ep*. 90.36-38), seeks to control the world he inhabits, seeks to attack, ensnare, kill, plunder. Important in this regard is the prayer to the huntsman's own goddess at 54ff. For Diana, to whom Hippolytus prays, is exhibited by her worshipper as a goddess not of life but of death. The kingdom she rules is one of fear (esp.72); the beasts who owe her allegiance she terrifies and kills (54-72). Mistress of "earth's secret parts" (55), she appears to connote something in *natura* of irresistible power and irresistible violence—a power and a violence unconsciously (and ironically) sexualised in Hippolytus' description (55ff.), and which Diana's worshipper imagines can be transferred to himself (73-80). The military imagery of the monody is overt and telling—the victor (52), the spoils (*praeda*, 77), the triumph (*triumpho*, 80)—imagery which, suggesting an analogy between Hippolytus' confident aggression, his urge to control, to dominate, his worship of destructive power and that of Rome's triumphant military, underscores the former and intimates its contemporary relevance. Signally, the geographical bounds of Diana's kingdom (67-71) suggest those of Rome itself. Not only in the case of Hippolytus is the issue of human power and its reality or illusion paramount.

Conspicuous in Senecan tragedy at large, the *potentia* theme, the issue of man's desire to assert control over the universe he inhabits, over his destiny, his life, is especially prominent in *Phaedra*. Its presence in the opening monody and its association there with imagery of hunting, pursuit, snares, entrapment, violence preface theme, action and imagery to come. Certainly the issue of human power and its relationship to "nature" pervades the following scene between Phaedra and the Nurse (85ff.), as Phaedra, self-exhibited victim of forces political, domestic, moral, emotional, biological, historical, divine, shows herself driven towards a love which repulses her (112ff.), which seems as unnatural and as monstrous as her mother's monstrous love. The Nurse's abstract moralising and interrogatory rhetoric (129ff., 195ff.) serve only to allow Phaedra to become more confirmed in her sense of helplessness until she moves into wish-fulfilment (Theseus will not return, 219-21) and fantasy (Theseus will pardon her, 225), as the urge for the hunt, described with alarm in her opening soliloquy (110-12), explodes into a fantasy image of an erotic hunt for Hippolytus in the wild (233ff.), Phaedra seeking to take control, if only in fantasy, of her life. When Phaedra's fragile optimism, her fantasies and delusions founder on the Nurse's emotional appeal (246-49), her talk of shame, honour and death (250ff.) only succeeds in drawing the Nurse into the fantasy of a successful Hippolytan hunt.

The choral ode on sexual passion which follows at 274ff.—the first choral ode of the play—is crucial. It serves to place in a larger metaphysical framework not only Phaedra's dilemma and the inevitability of her destruction but Hippolytus' sex-excluding commitment to Diana and its deluded basis. Delineating the universality of love's power, its irresistibility, its devastation, its violence, the ode confirms Phaedra's position as to her own impotence (cf. esp. 186-94 and 294ff.) and suggests an analogy between Venus and Cupid, on the one hand, and Diana, on the other, the huntsman's own goddess. The analogy seems less than casual, linked as the divinities are by identity of weapons (the bow, 72, 278), analogous destructive power and violence, analogous irresistibility (cf. esp. *certis telis*, "unerring shafts", 56f., *certo arcu*, "unerring bow", 278), analogous universality. The chorus' description of love's kingdom (285-90) echoes that of Diana's before (66-72), confirming the relationship between the divinities. Indeed Diana's kingdom of deer, tiger, lion and forest, like Diana herself, who left the heavens for love of Endymion (309-16), is subject to the power of love (341-50). The divinities of sexual love and the goddess of the moon, wilderness and the hunt seem to represent in fact complementary aspects of nature's power, savagery and violence; for it is with *natura* that the ode seems concerned. Controlling gods (294ff.), animals (338ff.) and humankind (290ff.), sea (335ff., 351f.), land (285ff.) and sky (294ff., 338), directing the movements of the planets themselves (309ff.), imaged in terms of nature's element par excellence, fire (276, 309, 330, 337, 338, 355), sexual passion is presented as a manifestation of *natura* itself (350-52):

> amat insani
> belua ponti Lucaeque boues.
> uindicat omnes natura sibi.

> Raging ocean's
> Beast and Luca-bulls love.
> Nature for itself claims all.

Venus uindex (124f.) become *natura uindex* ("claimant nature"—see 352n.) with pointed paradox. In Phaedra's initial, perceptive analysis, in the Nurse's subsequent rejoinder, the Cretan princess' love for Hippolytus was presented as monstrous passion, a perversion of nature (esp. 173-77); from the perspective of the first choral ode it is *natura* itself, which claims its victims like the goddess of the hunt. Ironically the ode's opening address to the daughter of the ungentle sea (*diua non miti generata ponto*, 274) has foreshadowed whence nature's "vindication" will come. The realm which Cretan might thought its own (85) will prove instrument of a higher and more enduring power.

In Act Three the hunt for Hippolytus begins, preceded appropriately by a picture of the deranged huntress, Phaedra, attempting to make her fantasy world reality (387-403), and by a prayer from the Nurse to Diana to assist in the ensnaring of her hunter (406-23). Significantly the prayer to Diana is to her in her dual "nature" role as goddess of the moon (410-12, 418-22) and of the wild (406-9). Diana will indeed ensnare her hunter, but not in the way the Nurse prays for. In the ensuing confrontation with Hippolytus (431-582), in fact, the Nurse's cunning rhetoric fails to ensnare despite its general position—that Hippolytus' mode of life is essentially a violation of the code he claims to follow, viz. *natura* (see esp. 481)—being, as the first chorus had underlined, in an important sense correct. Hippolytus' asexual idealisation of the wild (483ff.), contradicted by the exhibited violence, latently sexual (see esp. 55ff.) of the monody, is made to seem in context less the product of noble vision than of a deranged psychology, as its connection with a ferocious misogynism reveals (556-64)—the irrationality of which is virtually acknowledged by Hippolytus himself (566-68)—and it leads inevitably to a condemnation of Phaedra as unnatural monstrosity when the revelation of her love and appeal for compassion are made (671-97). The climax of the revelation scene at 704ff. as Hippolytus, the hunter, sword in one hand, Phaedra's hair twisted back in the other, about to plunge the steel in her throat, turns to ask the enshrined Diana, "goddess of the bow" (*arquitenens dea*, 709), to accept the just sacrifice of Phaedra as if hunted beast, is not only brilliant theatrics, but, reinforcing the helplessness of Phaedra and the delusion of Hippolytus, focusses once more on the issue of the larger framework of things in which the human scene is set. The delusion of Hippolytus, the hunter hunted, and hunted not only by Phaedra, is cardinal. Diana, as the first choral ode revealed, has felt love's pangs and, as the next ode will disclose, is enamoured of and watching Hippolytus himself. The world of *siluae* and *ferae* to which the young prince flees at 718 is more ambiguous and more complex than he thinks.

Little doubt is expressed on this matter by the chorus which
follows (736-823), concerned as it is with and for Hippolytus,
concerned too with that larger scheme of things, *natura*, to which
Hippolytus seems blind. Uniting diverse aspects of nature's operation
—the movement of the planets and stars (736-52), the ravaging
process of summer (764ff.), the ravishing of beauty by time (770ff.),
the fragility and ambiguity of beauty itself, the moral imperative that
enjoins (774), the treachery and violence of the wild (777-84), the
blush and delay of the moon (785-94), Diana's Hippolytan and
amatory gaze (785, 793f.)—the ode creates an atmosphere of
foreboding and menace embracing Diana's "favourite". The atmosphere is not diminished by recollection of the first choral ode's
attention to the "ravages" (*populante*, 280) of *amor/natura*. Committed to a neurotic fantasy of innocent communion with the wild
(Hippolytus' idealised view of the wilderness as voiced to the Nurse is
specifically undermined by this chorus—cf. esp. 519-21 and 777-84),
ignorant of its sexual entrapment and of himself as object of Diana's
erotic gaze (785-94), ignorant of nature's sexual imperative articulated
by this and the preceding choral ode (352, 774), Hippolytus seems
destined prey to the wilderness, Diana and *natura*. Ironically
Hippolytus' deathly skill as hunter, his surrogate embodiment of
Diana's violence and power, are recalled (812-19) just prior to the
final hunt, in which the world he thought he controlled rips the flesh
from his limbs and the limbs from his body.

A final party needs to be embroiled in nature's "vindicatory" hunt
before the denouement itself: the deserter of Ariadne (245, 665, 760),
the murderer of Hippolytus' mother, Antiope (226ff., 926ff.), the
despised husband of Phaedra (89ff.), the violator of covenants moral
and natural (89ff., 835ff.), Theseus. The short fourth act (835-958)
serves to give Theseus the dubious privilege of accelerating the
movement towards nature's vindication, intensifies too the concern
with human impotence and delusion. Falling victim to Phaedra's
deceptive ambiguities (891ff.), trapped too by his own self-image,
appealing (903-14) to the covenants of morality and nature (910,
914), of which he is singularly in breach, Theseus joins the hunt for
Hippolytus (see esp. 929ff.). It is little wonder that the ode to *natura*
which follows at 959, parading Hippolytus as test-case for the moral
machinery of the universe, is one of unrelieved despair. Drawing an
explicit contrast between, on the one hand, the physical order of the
cosmos governed by *natura* and, on the other, the moral chaos of
man's experience governed by blind *fortuna*, the third chorus sees the

world of human affairs, *res humanae*, not simply as amoral, but as morally perverse. But what this third choral ode ignores in this severe contrast between the cosmic order of *natura* and blind *fortuna* are those aspects of *natura* to which the first two choral odes drew arresting attention: the violent, destructive, transformational aspects of *natura*, the violence of the wild, the universal tyranny and ravage of love, forces intrinsic to the world of this play, and not only the world of this play, forces which, albeit morally perplexing and perhaps from man's point of view amoral *simpliciter*, may yet be far from blind, may be closely linked in fact—in a way the chorus will come to acknowledge—to the very cosmic order it sees as paradigm. *Natura* and the world of human action and history are not so easily separated. There is *natura* in the fall of a sparrow.

There is certainly *natura* in the fall of Hippolytus and the collapse of the Athenian royal house, as Acts Five and Six exhibit. With devastating speed and finality *Phaedra*'s closing scenes show *natura uindex* in triumphant and irresistible operation, as Theseus' curse, Phaedra's monstrous love and Hippolytus' denial of Venus' covenant and nature's rule generate a monster from Venus' native realm, the sea (cf. 274), and Hippolytus, ensnared by his own instruments of control (1085-87), is "ravaged" (1093ff.; esp. *populatur*, 1095) by the *natura* he had worshipped, just as Phaedra was earlier "ravaged" (*populatur*, 377) by love. The chorus' earlier pronouncements on the "ravages" of Cupid/Venus/*natura* (274ff.; esp. *populante*, 280), on nature's plunder of beauty (761ff.) and the sexual violence and entrapment of the wild (777ff.) prove tragically veridical in Hippolytus' gruesome death, as the hunter of the play's first scene, confident then with his armoury of snares, nets, spears and dogs, falls victim to the "gripping snares" (*laqueo tenaci*, 1086; cf. 46, 75) and "clinging knots" (*sequaces...nodos ligat*, 1087; cf. 36f.) of a far more powerful huntress and Diana's kingdom of field, rock, bramble, bush and tree tears his flesh and his body apart in a grotesque and unambiguous orgy of sexual violence (1093ff.). The irresistibility and destructiveness of Diana's erotic gaze (785ff.) and of *Venus/natura uindex* receive dreadful confirmation. The goddess and the landscape he had unwittingly sexualised (see esp. 55ff.) in *Phaedra*'s opening act now works its sexual violence on him. One final irony awaits. Hunted by Phaedra, the Nurse, Theseus and the bull from the sea (1077ff.), hunted by Diana, Venus, *natura* to his death, Hippolytus becomes victim of an even more macabre hunt, as the messenger describes (1105ff.) how Hippolytus' own hunting dogs and servants track the fields for remnants of their master's body.

Theseus cannot be indifferent. *Natura* binds as well as separates. It involves Theseus in the catastrophe he has in part caused (1114-16):

> O nimium potens,
> quanto parentes sanguinis uinclo tenes,
> natura, quam te colimus inuiti quoque.

> O too potent
> Nature, with what bond of blood you tether
> Parents; we serve you even against our will.

Endeavouring to make sense of all this the final chorus on human reversals (1123-53) dissolves the *natura-fortuna* contrast of the preceding ode and presents fortune's operations in Theseus' case as evidencing an ironic cosmic justice, a paradoxical pattern and order reflective of, and by implication originating from, the order of nature itself. Hippolytus' death is seen as payment for the debt incurred by Theseus' breach of natural law in returning from the world of death (1150ff.). The numbers now tally (1153) and Pluto's "greed" (*patruo rapaci*, 1152) seems but an instance of the rapacity of *natura* itself (764ff.), great mother of gods, *natura parens deum* (959).

There is no comfort in this. Phaedra, burdened with guilt, shame and a life bereft of purpose, suicides (1159-98) and Theseus is left (1199ff.) not only with the experience of catastrophic reversal but with the unendurable knowledge of his own role in the perversion and irreversible dismemberment of his world (esp. 1208ff., 1249ff.). Ironically his final description of Hippolytus at 1269f.—

> haecne illa facies igne sidereo nitens,
> inimica flectens lumina? huc cecidit decor?

> Is this the face that shone with starry fire,
> Turned hostile eyes aside? This that beauty set?

—echoes earlier cosmic imagery associated with him (736ff., 1111f., 1173f.) and presents the spectacle of Hippolytus' downfall as part of nature's inexorable processes. The play ends in ritual and order (1275-80), as Hippolytus' opening instructions to his fellow-hunters are echoed in those of Theseus to the same huntsmen (1277-79). The framework, the structure of things, *rerum natura*, remains constant.

Power and Delusion

About human impotence and delusion, especially delusion about power, the play seems unambiguous. Used in connection with each of the play's main figures—Hippolytus (1-84, 708f., 812-19, 1077-87, 1105-8, 1277-79), Phaedra (110ff., 233-35, 240f., 387ff., 700ff., 1179f.), the Nurse (271ff., 406ff.), Theseus (938ff., 1210, 1277ff.)—the hunting imagery serves as pointer to this theme. Associated right from the start of the play (1-84) with the issue of control, dominance, power, the imagery articulates each character's attempt in fantasy or in fact to control the forces that shape their lives, articulates too the failure of that attempt. Hippolytus, the confident hunter of the first scene, becomes hunted beast and prey; Phaedra and the Nurse, joint partners in the erotic hunt for Hippolytus, reveal themselves instruments of a larger, more sinister hunt; Theseus, the great male hero, returned alive from the world of the dead, initiates too a Hippolytan hunt only to be manifest instrument and victim of the huntress par excellence, *natura*. Deluded *uindex* (1210) Theseus signals where real "vindication" lies.

The focus on delusion is emphatic. The movement of Phaedra and the Nurse from realism to fantasy in Act Two has already been noted; Theseus' delusion too—about his marriage to Phaedra, about the relationship of his behaviour to the values he professes (esp.903ff.), about his ability to effect, shape, control—is dramatically evident. But it is the dramatisation of Hippolytus' self-deception which perhaps most intrigues because of its particularising and percipient blend of moral rejectionism, psychological trauma, and the human aspiration towards freedom, self-sufficiency, power over self. The scene with the Nurse in Act Three is most important in this regard. Hippolytus' golden age reverie (483ff.), conspicuous for the contradictions it exposes between vision and personal practice (cf. esp. 542-49 and 31-80; 498f., 547f., and 706-09) and conjoined as it is with the most neurotic, frenetic misogynism (555-79), seems product not of primeval innocence or Stoic wisdom but of self-deceived, pathological idealism, idealism which, the play suggests, has its origins in Theseus' murder of Hippolytus' mother, Antiope (578f.; cf. 226f., 926-29), whose life-style he has adopted, and whose replacement, Phaedra, he loathes and through her womankind (238f., 558). Phaedra's dramatic entrance after Hippolytus' Antiope pronouncement (578f.)—

> Solamen unum matris amissae fero,
> odisse quod iam feminas omnes licet.

> I've one consolation for my mother's loss:
> That I may now detest all womankind.

25

—signals the complex nexus of circumstances from which Hippolytus' self-validating fantasy derives.

As in other plays, the theme of delusion is also crystallised in *Phaedra* in the prayer motif, which Seneca skilfully employs at crucial moments in the action. All the prayers uttered in this play—and there are many (54-80, 406-23, 671-81, 945-58, 1159-63, 1201-07, 1223-42)—are either unfulfilled or fulfilled in the most ironic and perverse manner, one which inverts the original and patent intention of the prayer—all prayers, that is, except apparently one ("apparently" is important), Theseus' prayer to Neptune at the end of Act Four (945ff.), the aberrant prayer for punishment upon one who had not sinned. The characters themselves sometimes see signs of imminent or actual fulfilment of their prayers (e.g. 81f., 424ff.), but the play and its action show them to be not indices of efficacious prayer but the quiet, cynical laughter of things, nature's reflection of Cupid's lascivious smile (277).

There are of course moments when at least partial understanding and insight seem displayed by the figures of the drama, most conspicuously by Phaedra (113ff., 698f.,880), who recognises at times the forces acting upon her, their power, irresistibility, monstrosity, and even by Theseus (1201ff., esp. 1242f., 1249), who in the final act comes to see the vanity of his previous belief in his own power and judgment, the absurdity of his earlier vision of the world, and comes to appreciate part at least—though by no means the most signal part (Theseus' final judgment of Phaedra at 1279f. shows how little in the end he has understood)—of his role in Hippolytus' death. But even such moments of insight as do occur serve but to reinforce the notion of man's impotence, man's existential status as victim, victim not simply of his own deficiencies or delusions, not simply of chance events, but of the inbuilt structure of things, *rerum natura*, which works itself out irresistibly.

This is why paradox, irony and dramatic reversal are so important in Senecan tragedy, and especially in *Phaedra*. They are signal dramatic instruments for the presentation of the tragedian's fatalism. The sense of an inner patterning of events, an ironic, paradoxical, at times perverse, efforming structure permeates the action: Hippolytus the hunter of the opening scene becomes the hunted of the close, as the instructions he gave his companions to search the fields for prey are given by Theseus to the same comrades to search the fields for remnants of a different prey, Hippolytus himself; Phaedra, the indecisive, oppressed victim of the politico-military world, of

Theseus, of love's raging tyranny, of an inherited family curse and an irrepressible moral consciousness, achieves in her final hour a supreme moment of control and performs the act which partially atones for her sin and consummates her desire for Hippolytus—ironically her only moment of control over her destiny resides in the implementation of the suicide intention voiced in her opening scene and the ending of her destiny and herself; Theseus returns from Hades expecting to find light but discovers darkness (1217), and in the final act's ironic reversal of his opening speech asks to return to hell (the great punisher asking to be punished) but cannot do so, condemned to live a hell worse than that he has escaped—the place in Hades which he occupied at the start of the play now taken by his son. Ironic reversal, ironic patterning, an ironic and dramatic cycle, a cycle of history too in which the structure of things remains constant, in which fate revolves (1123).

This notion of the cycle of history in and through which fate revolves deserves more attention than can be given here. Like *Thyestes*, *Medea*, *Agamemnon* and *Troades*, *Phaedra* is studded with analogies with the past, articulating a compelling sense of history and nature's cyclicity, of *semper idem*. Analogies between Phaedra and her mother, Pasiphae (see esp. 112ff., 169ff., 242, 688ff., 698f.), between Hippolytus and the bull that Pasiphae loved (cf. esp. 116-18 and 413-17, and note the sustained application of "wild animal" epithets to Hippolytus, eg., "wild", *ferus*, 240, 272, 414, "savage", *saeuus*, 273, "ungentle", *immitis*, 231, 273, "fierce", *toruus*, 416, 798, "ferocious", *ferox*, 416, 1064), between the Minotaur (122, 171ff., 649f., 688ff., 1067) and the bull from the sea (1015ff.), the latter product of Phaedra's love as the former was product of her mother's love (note esp. the pregnancy imagery of 1016 and 1019f.), and other analogies too (e.g. between Hippolytus and the Minotaur) seem to assert the imperatives of history, the dispassionate cyclic order of things, the circle of fate, fortune, nature. Time past becomes time present; time present becomes time future. The world changes to remain the same:

> constat inferno numerus tyranno.
>
> For hell's king the numbers tally.   (1153)

Always. Even the delusion of human power recycles to stay constant, as the Roman analogy of the opening act shows. To *natura* belong the power and the glory.

Emblem and Image

The human intelligibility and signification of *Phaedra*'s tragic world arrest. Some of course have denied this "humanness"—and not only to *Phaedra*. Confusing manner with matter, idiom with intent, they have seen in Senecan drama at large only constructs of rhetoric and/or Stoic abstractions. And yet both the emblematic quality of Senecan tragedy, its status as dramatic representation, as symbol of the world outside itself, and the inner logic, the human "convincingness" of its presentation of event, action, character—Senecan tragedy's function as image, as dramatic realisation of human psychology, behaviour, experience—seem self-evident. Often indeed what might be regarded as purely formal features of drama in Seneca seem designed, in part at least, to underscore tragedy's function as emblem and image.

Phaedra is our text. Necessary building blocks of the play's internal world, many of *Phaedra*'s formal features seem constitutive too of the play's emblematic and imagistic function. The ironies and paradoxes of the play's action and structure, its dramatic reversals and cycles, suggest not only the revolutions of fate, nature and fortune, their power, irresistibility and apparent perversity, but the ironies and paradoxes constitutive of and indicative of human impotence and the human world. Other aspects of the bonding of the play, the close thematic and linguistic interrelation between chorus and act, the tightly woven serial effect of repeated language, imagery, analogies, connecting action with action, thought with thought, speech with speech, event with event, seem also related to the concern with *natura* and fate, the inexorable order of things, the unbreakable chain of cause and effect. There is an oppressiveness about *Phaedra*, which comes in part from its unbreakable form, an oppressiveness emblematic it seems of the world beyond the play. The asymmetry and dramatic pace of the play similarly discomfort—lengthy opening song, long second act and chorus, followed by even longer third act and chorus, followed by short fourth act and minuscule chorus. The effect is of speed and devastating finality. The complex issues of the play and the positions of its human figures, laid out and played out at considerable dramatic length, are resolved suddenly, finally, violently. Prayer to Neptune, short ode of despair, Hippolytus' dismemberment as history. No time for reflection; inexorable swiftness.

Even the impressive theatrics of the play seem in part emblematic in import. The power-impotence, freedom-incarceration issue clearly underlies the arresting juxtaposition of the crowded scene of the opening, with its energy, life, animation, action, openness, and the monolithic, brooding, introspective speech of the cabined Phaedra. The climactic horror of Theseus' attempt to piece together the bloody remnants of Hippolytus' body (1247ff.) provides dramatic enactment not only of the terror of the acknowledgement of delusion, impotence, futility, but in a larger sense the terror too of nature's dismembering finality. Like Diana in Hippolytus' opening song, *natura* terrifies and it kills. Similarly the theatrics of the Phaedra-Hippolytus confrontation have emblematic as well as spectacular function. The whole scene in fact is organised around a series of theatrical "high-spots"—Phaedra's entrance after the Antiope pronouncement (578f.), her fainting into Hippolytus' arms (585ff.), her prayer for compassion ("pity a lover", *miserere amantis*, 671), Hippolytus' demand for cosmic reversal (671ff.), and the latter's manic prayer to Diana, sword in one hand, Phaedra's hair twisted back in the other, to accept the sacrifice of Phaedra as if hunted beast (706ff.)—"high-spots" which focus theatrically major themes of both scene and play: the determinism of the past; spiritual struggle and its futility; delusion, impotence, man's ordained status as victim; the alleged "morality" of nature, reality's disquieting, cynical smile. Themes not distant from the lives of an audience.

In general it might be said that *Phaedra*'s status as emblem can be clearly seen in the moral and existential importance, and thus relevance, of the themes it explores, their evident centrality in human life. What needs adding, however, is that the play's ability to make that emblematic quality felt, its content lived through and possessed, depends upon such dramatic craftsmanship as has already been noted, and upon the emblematic and imagistic function of that craftsmanship, but depends too upon the presentation of the main figures of the drama, their psychology and behaviour, as humanly involving, as in important senses humanly intelligible. Depends in fact upon the play's status, in part at least, as in some sense psychological, behavioural image. The psychological intricacy and credibility of the presentation of Hippolytus were mentioned above, but in the dramatisation of Theseus too—the deluded, unthinking, self-confident and self-deceived man of action, psychological as well as biological father of Hippolytus, like Hippolytus himself incarcerated by his own self-image (see esp. 903ff.)—Seneca's concern with human psychology and intelligibility is evident. The dramatic focus in the final act (1199ff.) on Theseus' personal suffering (he demands "no easy end", 1208), on mental anguish, on the humanly involving and intelligible, exemplifies Senecan intent.

But it is in the dramatisation of Phaedra that Seneca's concern with the presentation of humanly intelligible psychology and action is especially revealed. Often unobserved, the subtlety and depth of her characterisation deserve close attention. Her opening speech (85-128) is both index and harbinger of Seneca's overall treatment of her. Its realistic chain of thought is noteworthy: Crete—the sea—Theseus —the shamelessness and faithlessness of this father of Hippolytus (*Hippolyti pater*, 98)—then (at mention of Hippolytus) her emotional chaos—suspension of normal domestic activities—withdrawal from chaste religious practices—the mysterious passion for the woods and the wild—her mother's "fateful" passion (*fatale malum*, 113)—the bull—Daedalus—the impossibility of a cure—the divine curse (*Venus uindex*). This is no series of debating points but the dramatisation of a psychology in operation. The speech is redolent with emotive, moral language ("shame", *pudor*, 97; "evil", *malum*, 101, 113; "chaste" *castis*, "pious", *pio*, 108; "sin", *peccare*, 114; "unspeakable evil", *infando malo*, 115; "guilt unspeakable", *probris nefandis*, 126f.; "sin", *nefas*, 128) used not as ingredient of a philosophical debate but as index of a human psychology, as Phaedra is presented—amid condemnation of husband and self— driven by shame (not simply reputation, for none as yet know) to absent herself from the Attic women's rites, finding herself fantasising about the hunt, caught up in an evil that bound her mother, moving headlong towards a love which repulses her, which seems to her unspeakable, *infandum*. What is dramatised is moral torment as experienced.

The psychological effectiveness of this opening speech continues into the scene as a whole, as the vacillating Phaedra becomes more confirmed in her sense of helplessness, starts to give in to the passion, rationalises rather than analyses (179-94), indulges in wish-fulfilment and fantasy (219-45), falling from fantasy to depressed talk of suicide (250-66), until the Nurse joins her in the fantasy world she has created. The movement into fantasy (esp. 233ff.) has particular psychological import; it seems a corollary of Phaedra's impotence. Victim of forces political (85-91), domestic (89-98), moral and emotional (99ff.), biological and historical (112-28), divine (124-28), Phaedra moves into a fantasy world of delusion—a fantasy world both fragile and, paradoxically, irresistible (250ff.)—to seize the control over her life so conspicuously absent in reality. The psychological focus continues into the next act both in the presentation of the deranged queen in her royal apartments and in the revelation scene itself, where Phaedra's actions and words (see esp. the soliloquy at 592-99) reveal psychological and moral discomfort. The revelation itself is handled in a masterly way—Hippolytus' observance of both courtesy and duty, his naivety and the words which seem to fall by accident from his lips drawing from the increasingly committed Phaedra the disclosure of her love. The grand machine of the universe, fate, fortune, *natura*, is shown moving through and by means of human psychologies and behaviour in ironic (and tragic) interaction. Observe, for example, how Hippolytus' address to Phaedra as *mater* at 608 proves starting point for Phaedra's self-revelation, while his blithe promise of filling his father's place (633) and reference to love of Theseus (645) enable Phaedra to carry through the declaration of her love, to exhibit her sensuous and physical passion for Hippolytus, and endeavour to make fantasy and reality one. On Hippolytus' violent and contemptuous rejection (671-97) Phaedra's fantasy world once more— and this time irrevocably—shatters, returning her to the realism of her opening speech in the play, awareness of the monstrosity of her passion (699), its irresistibility (698f.), its mindlessness (702), its futility (703). The prospect of dying by Hippolytus' hand—madness cured, honour saved, sexual desire vicariously satisfied—seems a consummation devoutly to be wished (710-12). It is little wonder that Hippolytus fails to cope.

In the act which follows the complexities of Phaedra's psychology are again evident in the dialogue with Theseus, as Phaedra, desperate to preserve her honour, her reputation, even to save Hippolytus, hides her true feelings behind a barrage of cryptic replies and *sententiae* in response to Theseus' questions. Even when driven by Theseus' assault on the Nurse to carry out the original plan, the accusation of Hippolytus, she delivers no open accusation of rape, but a series of ambiguities, ironies and innuendoes (891-93):

> temptata precibus restiti; ferro ac minis
> non cessit animus; uim tamen corpus tulit.
> labem hanc pudoris eluet noster cruor.

> Attacked by prayers, I resisted; steel and threats
> My mind repelled; my body suffered violence.
> This stain on honour shall my blood wash out.

Phaedra was indeed "attacked by prayers", "threatened by sword", and her body did indeed "suffer violence". And beneath the public sense of the last line, "suicide will wash away the stain of rape", lies for Phaedra a private sense, "suicide will wash away the stain of sin". Even the final accusation is left to the sword (896f.) and the slaves (901ff.). It is all as if, in the midst of the accusation itself, Phaedra is trying to preserve a sense of honesty, integrity, self-respect. For, despite all, Phaedra remains an intensely moral creature.

As her behaviour in Act Six (1159-98) makes clear. Echoing the opening words of her first speech in the opening words of her last (cf. 85 and 1159), Phaedra turns verbal echo into psychological cycle and manifests the moral consciousness displayed at her first appearance. Rebuking Theseus (1164-67) but acknowledging too her own guilt (1168f.), even placing herself in the company of death-dealing monsters slain in turn by Theseus (1169-73), Phaedra in language and deed enacts a suicide of atonement. Unrestrained by either shame or fear she addresses the mangled pieces of Hippolytus' body in words that would make the winds weep (1173-75):

> heu me, quo tuus fugit decor
> oculique nostrum sidus? exanimis iaces?
> ades parumper, uerbaque exaudi mea.

> O, where has your beauty fled
> And eyes that were my stars? Do you lie dead?
> Come back a little while and hear my words.

Her aim—a suicide of atonement for monstrous deeds, freeing her from both life (*anima*, 1178) and sin (*scelere*, 1178). After a momentary movement into fantasy (1179f.), the ritual of placation and offerings to the dead asserts control, enabling Phaedra to wrest from failure, suffering and sin a momentary triumph—union with Hippolytus in death (1183f.). Variations of a moral fugue follow (1184-87), as Phaedra's concern with shame, integrity, honour, reputation plays itself out and culminates (1188-90) in a prayer to death—balm of *malus amor* and ornament of blighted shame—to spread wide his merciful arms. Phaedra is now in full control and with careful, balanced diction (1191-98) confesses her guilt to the citizens of Athens, restores Hippolytus' reputation and character and puts meaning into her death which she had been unable to put into her life. Her supreme and only moment of control over her life resides in the ending of it.

Thus Seneca's presentation of Phaedra. A presentation which—like that of Hippolytus and Theseus—reveals Seneca's concern with the intricacies of human psychology and behaviour and their intelligible dramatisation, a concern with making his tragic world not simply symbol or emblem of a world outside itself but an image of that world—an involving, intelligible image. The commonplace that the dramatisation of human figures in Senecan tragedy is essentially ideological, emblematic, directed primarily or even entirely to the exemplification of abstract ideas or philosophical (especially Stoic) concepts, founders—like the "rhetorical display" thesis and other formalist approaches—on *Phaedra*'s psychological intricacy, the human logic, the imaging power of its constructed world. In *Phaedra* the dramatic mode is not simply representation but presentation, the dramatic focus not theme, idea, issue, but theme, idea, issue as experienced. Signification and likeness, symbol and picture, emblem and image: mimesis.

Quod Viuo: That I Live

Mimesis redolent with compassion. No impartial emblem, no indifferent image, *Phaedra* enshrines at its centre the unstoic virtue of compassion (see 623n). "Pity a widow", *miserere uiduae* (623), cries Phaedra; "Pity me", *miserere* (636); "Pity a lover", *miserere amantis* (671). To Phaedra's appeal Hippolytus reacts with frenzied self-righteousness, scornful horror, unmodified vilification (671-97). Though his response could not have been otherwise, the chasm between Phaedra's pitiable and pitiably presented torment and Hippolytus' manic response, sensitive only to the invasion of his self-constructed univeise and to Phaedra as paradigmatic female obscenity, marks Hippolytus' behaviour as humanly, as morally deficient.

Not that the play's evidenced compassion is limited to the Phaedra-Hippolytus confrontation scene. Permeating the play is a controlled manipulation of sympathy, a directing and redirecting of audience alienation and pity. The sympathetic-empathetic presentation of Phaedra in the second act, for example, the following chorus' focus on love's irresistibility and power, the third act's initial exhibition of Phaedra as distressed, even deranged victim, seem obviously designed among other things to prime the audience's emotions for Phaedra's confrontation with Hippolytus, from whom in addition—by the time the two meet—the audience has become alienated by the pathological self-righteousness and misogyny of his sermon to the Nurse. What needs to be observed, however, is that immediately after the confrontation scene Seneca begins to redirect the audience's sympathies, begins to move them in fact in the direction of Hippolytus. Hence the second chorus at 736ff. draws attention to his cosmic beauty, star-like splendour, his physical strength, skill and glory, while Phaedra (824ff.) is all *furor* ("passion") and *fraus feminea* ("female trickery"). This movement towards Hippolytus is accelerated in the fourth act by Phaedra's accusation (888ff.) and Theseus' damning outburst (903ff.), accelerated too by the *natura* chorus which follows (959ff.), in which Hippolytus is exhibited as test-case for the universe's moral structure. Effective climax is reached in the Messenger's overtly emotive and compassionate delineation of Hippolytus' courage, death and dismemberment, at the conclusion of which—as if to round off this section of sympathy—the second chorus' praise of Hippolytus' beauty and starry splendour is explicitly recalled (1110-14):

> Hocine est formae decus?
> qui modo paterni clarus imperii comes
> et certus heres siderum fulsit modo,
> passim ad supremos ille colligitur rogos
> et funeri confertur.

> Is this beauty's glory?
> Resplendent companion to his father's throne,
> Assured heir, who shone just now like the stars,
> Gathered from everywhere for the last fires,
> Assembled for his grave.

And then once more—at the precise moment of maximum sympathy for one figure—Seneca begins to move the audience's feeling towards another. This time towards Theseus (1114-17):

> O nimium potens,
> quanto parentes sanguinis uinclo tenes,
> natura, quam te colimus inuiti quoque.
> occidere uolui noxium, amissum fleo.

> O too potent
> Nature, with what bond of blood you tether
> Parents; we serve you even against our will.
> Guilty I wished him dead, lost I mourn him.

And again Seneca augments this redirection of sympathy through his deployment of the chorus, who draw poignant attention to Theseus' own tragic reversal (1143-48). The movement towards Theseus is suspended by Phaedra's eruption onto the scene, confession of guilt and suicide of atonement (1154-98), and then continues in the presentation of Theseus' suffering, the torture of his guilt, the pathos, horror, futility of his macabre attempt to piece together the shattered fragments of a shattered world, his son's dismembered body. Audience sympathy, however, is not allowed to stay unambiguously with Theseus. In the very last lines of the play—again at the moment of maximum sympathy—Seneca redirects (1275-80):

> patefacite acerbam caede funesta domum.
> Mopsopia claris tota lamentis sonet.
> uos apparate regii flammam rogi;
> at uos per agros corporis partes uagas
> inquirite.
>   Istam terra defossam premat
> grauisque tellus impio capiti incubet.

> Open the dismal palace sour with death.
> All Attica resound with loud lament.
> You prepare the flames of the royal pyre;
> You search the fields for parts of the body
> Astray.
>   This one—earth press deep upon her,
> And soil lie heavy on her impious head.

Emphasis on Theseus' guilt and acknowledgement of guilt in the final scene (esp. 1201ff., 1249ff.) makes the final comment on Phaedra and its simplistic moral judgement abhorrent. The audience's increasing sympathy for Theseus reaches here its maximum point only to be switched suddenly by this brilliant ending back to Phaedra. Like Jason in the final lines of *Medea*, Theseus reveals that he has understood little.

Oscillation of sympathy is a major Senecan dramatic mode. Especially evident in *Phaedra*, it has a signal role to play in the generation of the tone of the drama, in exhibiting its world as compassionate emblem and image. There are no villains in *Phaedra*. Each character, even the Nurse (e.g. 138f.), receives at various moments in the play sympathetic presentation. Human life, impotence, delusion are viewed not with the refined disdain of an Eliot or the affected indignation of a Juvenal, but with empathy and pathos reminiscent of Rome's greatest poet, Virgil, of whom Seneca, not Lucan, is the great Neronian successor. Like Virgil's epic world, the tragic world of Seneca contains no simple moral answers. Presentment, empathy, contemplation, pathos: both the structure of things, *res*, *natura*, and the tears, the *lacrimae*, for and of that structure.

As witness: the dramatisation of Phaedra immediately prior to her most unsympathetic moment, the accusation of Hippolytus (879f.):

THESEVS	Quod sit luendum morte delictum indica.
PHAEDRA	Quod uiuo.
THESEUS	Tell me what sin is to be purged by death.
PHAEDRA	That I live.

Theseus, of course, ignores Phaedra's reply, construing it, if at all, along the lines of the aristocratic tradition of death before dishonour. For the audience "that I live", *quod uiuo*, has other meanings. To Phaedra, who has lost both Hippolytus and honour, life is intolerable, valueless. More importantly, to Phaedra, for whom nature's ordinances and nature's inversion, life and monstrous love, existence and guilt, moral consciousness and the violation of integrity, of honour, of "shame", *pudor*, are inextricably interwoven, living is itself a sin, an obscenity, a *delictum*.

> fatale miserae matris agnosco malum.
> I recognise poor mother's fateful evil. (113)

> et ipsa nostrae fata cognosco domus:
> fugienda petimus.
> I too recognise the fate of our house:
> What we should shun, we seek. (698f.)

> Quod sit luendum morte delictum indica.
> Quod uiuo.
> Tell me what sin is to be purged by death.
> That I live. (879f.)

The timing of *quod uiuo* is dramatically important. Just before Phaedra is forced to accuse Hippolytus, the dramatic focus falls on the profoundly tragic nature of Phaedra's life, and simplistic moral judgments are averted. Compassion is integral to both presentation and elicited response.

Quod uiuo is emblem too of the Senecan *Weltanschauung*. Reflected sixteen centuries later in the perverse, even malicious world of Racine's finest tragedy, the sense of the inherent detestability of life, articulated by and through *Phaedra*'s heroine, pervades Seneca's tragic *opus*. Exaltation of "death's freedom", *mors libera*, and condemnation of the "love of life", *uitae amor*, are conspicuous motifs in *Hercules Furens* (426), *Troades* (397ff., 574ff., 952ff.), *Agamemnon* (589ff.) and *Thyestes* (e.g. 882ff.), while the perversity of things, their apparent cruelty, immorality, horror, godlessness, are inveighed against throughout the tragic corpus (e.g. *Med.* 1026f., *Pha.* 1242f., *Thy.* 1020f.). Like the world of Tacitus' *Annales*, that of Seneca's tragedies seems one in which to be human is to suffer, to be alive is to be entrapped in evil, to exist is to be located in the midst of a universe conspicuous for its apparent perversity, for its disregard of the human spirit, even for its malice—a universe in which it is Petronius' withered Sibyl who articulates the appropriate response (*Sat.* 48): *apothanein thelō*, "I want to die". So Phaedra in this play (710ff., 868ff., 879f., 1188ff.); so Theseus (1238-42). Inevitable corollary of Seneca's presentment of life as sin, as obscenity, as *delictum* and *monstrum*, as unbreakable circle of suffering, as entrapment in catastrophic revolutions and reversals (1123ff.), the death-wish is integral to *Phaedra*'s tragic world. It is also mirror of an age.

And yet the formal perfection of *Phaedra*, of its world, remains: the circle of fate, fortune, nature, the circle of action, events, history, language, the circle of situation, theme, sympathy, diction, imagery— the eternal revolutions of the planets, the stars, the seasons, standing *not* as/the third chorus proclaims (975ff.) far from the affairs of men, but acting as both metaphor for, and illustration of, the cyclicity and inexorability of *natura*. There is an order in human life— *natura*. It brings no comfort. Responsive to man's inadequacies, beyond his control, outside the moral categories that the human species throws upon the world, its inexorable logic ploughs through man's attempts to create his own separate universe, his attempts to control, to transform his condition from impotence to power. Temporary assaults on nature's order, albeit themselves part of nature's order, are repaid a hundredfold without regard for justice or desert, and the legacy of this is unendurable guilt and the shattering of the illusion of power. There is however room for towering humanity and it comes at the moment of death. Hippolytus' thunderous challenge and fearless skill when confronted with the bull from the sea, Phaedra's acceptance of guilt, resumption of integrity, enactment of love and atonement in death, present the spectacular paradox of the greatness of impotent humanity. It may be the case, as Seneca elsewhere writes (*Ep.* 107.11), that those whom the fates do not lead willingly they drag against their will, but much in Seneca's universe resides in the manner of the going. And in that, as the portrayal of Seneca's own death reveals (*Ann.* 15.60-64), the dramatist of *Phaedra* and the poetic historian of the *Annales* are at one.

[A more extensive analysis of the play may be found in my study of *Phaedra* in *ANRW* 32.2 (1985) 1284ff., on which the above section of the Introduction is based.]

5. THE TRANSLATION

The translation of *Phaedra* which follows aims to convey to the Latinless reader as much as it is possible to convey in English and without violation of English idiom about the form and meaning of the Senecan play. It is with few exceptions line-by-line, and employs as its standard dialogue verse-form the ten syllable iambic line of English blank verse. For the translator of Seneca, whose iambic trimeter had such a formative impact on the development of English blank verse, there is no real alternative. I have, however, not hesitated to use an eleven syllable line (allowing myself metrical substitutions and feminine endings) where appropriate. The result, I hope, is a dramatic verse-form which reproduces something of the subtlety and tautness of Seneca's own verse.

For the lyric metres I have used lines of fixed syllabic length where Seneca's line is similarly fixed, and lines of variable syllabic length where the Senecan line is also variable. For Seneca's asclepiads (twelve syllables) I have used a line of nine syllables, for his sapphics (eleven syllables) a line of eight syllables, and for his anapaests (eight to eleven syllables) a line of six to eight syllables. The goal was to produce a system of lyric metres whose syllabic relationship to my dialogue line is similar to that of Seneca's own lyric metres to his iambic trimeter. Occasional metres such as the trochaic or dactylic tetrameter have been represented in accordance with the same principle. For analysis of Seneca's dialogue and lyric metres in *Phaedra* see Appendix II.

TEXT

TRANSLATION

PHAEDRA

DRAMATIS PERSONAE

Hippolytus

Phaedra

Nutrix

Chorus

Theseus

Nuntius

Scaena Athenis ante regiam

PHAEDRA

DRAMATIS PERSONAE

Hippolytus, son of Theseus and Antiope, an Amazon.

Phaedra, wife of Theseus, princess of the house of Crete.

Theseus, king of Athens.

Nurse of Phaedra.

Messenger.

Companions of Hippolytus.

Slaves, Attendants and Guards.

Chorus of Cretan Women.

SCENE

Before the royal palace at Athens. In front of the palace stand a statue and altar of Diana.

TIME

The play begins at dawn.

ACTVS PRIMVS

HIPPOLYTVS

Ite, umbrosas cingite siluas
summaque montis iuga Cecropii.
celeri planta lustrate uagi
quae saxoso loca Parnetho
subiecta iacent, quae Thriasiis   5
uallibus amnis rapida currens
uerberat unda; scandite colles
semper canos niue Riphaea.

Hac, hac alii qua nemus alta
texitur alno, qua prata iacent,   10
qua rorifera mulcens aura
Zephyrus uernas euocat herbas,
ubi per graciles breuis Ilisos   13(14)
labitur agros piger et steriles   15
amne maligno radit harenas.

Vos qua Marathon tramite laeuo
saltus aperit, qua comitatae
gregibus paruis nocturna petunt
pabula fetae; uos qua tepidis   20
subditus austris frigora mollit
    durus Acharneus.

Alius rupem dulcis Hymetti,
paruas alius calcet Aphidnas.
pars illa diu uacat immunis,   25
qua curuati litora ponti
Sunion urget. si quem tangit
gloria siluae, uocat hunc Phyle:
hic uersatur, metus agricolis,
uulnere multo iam notus aper.   30

At uos laxas canibus tacitis
mittite habenas; teneant acres

ACT ONE

(Enter Hippolytus and Companions)

HIPPOLYTUS

Go, surround the gloomy woods
And Cecrops' mountain's highest ridge.
Range quickly on your feet, combing
The coverts topped by Parnes'
Craggy height, those too in Thria's
Vale which the racing stream lashes
With swift waters. Climb the hills
Always white with Riphaean snow.

There, there, go some, where tall alders
Weave a grove, where meadows lie,
Where soothing Zephyrus' dewy
Breath awakens springtime's grass;
Where meagre Ilissos idles
His way through parched fields and scratches
Barren sands with niggard stream.

You, by the left-hand path to
Marathon's open pass, where trailed
By their young at night suckling dams
Seek pasture; you, to where rugged
Acharneus tempers frosts beneath
    The warm south-wind.

Let someone mount sweet Hymettus'
Cliff, someone little Aphidnae.
That spot has long remained immune
Where Sunion thrusts its beaches
In the sea's arc. If someone's lured
By woodland glory, Phyle calls:
There lurks the farmer's terror
Famed for many wounds, the boar.

Now you, cast the leashes loose
From the silent hounds; hold the fierce

43

lora Molossos et pugnaces
tendant Cretes fortia trito
    uincula collo.   34b
at Spartanos—genus est audax   35
auidumque ferae—nodo cautus
propiore liga: ueniet tempus,
cum latratu caua saxa sonent.
nunc demissi nare sagaci
captent auras lustraque presso   40
quaerant rostro, dum lux dubia est,
dum signa pedum roscida tellus
    impressa tenet.

Alius raras ceruice graui
portare plagas, alius teretes   45
properet laqueos. picta rubenti
linea pinna uano cludat
    terrore feras.   47b
tibi uibretur missile telum;
tu graue dextra laeuaque simul
robur lato derige ferro.   50
tu praecipites clamore feras
subsessor ages; tu iam uictor
curuo solues uiscera cultro.

Ades en comiti, diua uirago,
cuius regno pars terrarum   55
secreta uacat, cuius certis
petitur telis fera quae gelidum
potat Araxen et quae stanti
ludit in Histro. tua Gaetulos
dextra leones, tua Cretaeas   60
sequitur ceruas; nunc ueloces
figis dammas leuiore manu.
tibi dant uariae pectora tigres,
tibi uillosi terga bisontes
latisque feri cornibus uri.   65
quicquid solis pascitur aruis,
siue illud Arabs diuite silua
siue illud inops nouit Garamans   68

Molossians with thongs; let the wild
Cretans strain at strong ropes
    On bruised necks.
And the Spartans (that breed is bold,
Avid for prey) tie carefully
With tighter knot. Time will come
When the hollows sound with their bark.
Now, heads lowered and nostrils keen,
Let them sniff the air and, muzzles
Down, search the haunts while light is dim,
While tracks of beasts imprint
    The dewy earth.

Someone carry on aching neck
The wide-meshed nets, someone quickly
The fine snares. Let the painted line's
Crimson feathers imprison beasts
    With idle terror.
You brandish the throwing spear;
You, both hands beneath its weight,
Hurl the oakshaft with iron head.
You, beater, will send beasts
Scurrying with shouts; you, victor,
With curved knife will loose their innards.

(Prays to Diana)
Come to your comrade, man goddess,
For whose kingdom earth's secret parts
Lie open, whose shafts seek out
Unerringly the beast that drinks
The cold Araxes' stream or plays
On frozen Hister. Yours the hand
That hunts Gaetulian lions,
Yours the Cretan hind; now you prick
With lighter touch the quick gazelle.
You receive the striped tiger's
Breast, the shaggy bison's back,
The spine of spreading-horned wild ox.
No creature feeds in lonely fields,
In rich Arabia's groves,
Or in poor Garamantia

uacuisque uagus Sarmata campis,	71
siue ferocis iuga Pyrenes	69
siue Hyrcani celant saltus,	70
arcus metuit, Diana, tuos.	72

Tua si gratus numina cultor
tulit in saltus, retia uinctas
tenuere feras, nulli laqueum   75
rupere pedes; fertur plaustro
praeda gementi; tum rostra canes
sanguine multo rubicunda gerunt
repetitque casas rustica longo
     turba triumpho.   80

En, diua, faues: signum arguti
misere canes. uocor in siluas.
hac, hac pergam qua uia longum
     compensat iter.

ACTVS SECVNDVS

PHAEDRA—NVTRIX

PHAEDRA

O magna uasti Creta dominatrix freti,   85
cuius per omne litus innumerae rates
tenuere pontum, quicquid Assyria tenus
tellure Nereus peruium rostris secat,
cur me in penates obsidem inuisos datam
hostique nuptam degere aetatem in malis   90
lacrimisque cogis? profugus en coniux abest
praestatque nuptae quam solet Theseus fidem.
fortis per altas inuii retro lacus
uadit tenebras miles audacis proci,
solio ut reuulsam regis inferni abstrahat.   95

And Sarmatian nomad's desert,
Hidden on wild Pyrene's
Ridge or in Hyrcanian ravines,
But fears, Diana, your bow.

If the worshipper favoured takes
Your power into the glades, nets
Grip fast entangled beasts, no feet
Break the snares; spoils are carried
On groaning cart; the hounds
Sport muzzles red with blood,
And a rustic band heads home
    Long-lined in triumph.

O goddess, you hear; the baying
Dogs gave sign. I'm called to the woods.
There, there I'll go, where the path cuts
    The long journey.

(Exeunt)

ACT TWO

(Enter Phaedra and the Nurse)

PHAEDRA—NURSE

PHAEDRA

O mighty Crete, mistress of endless sea,
Whose countless ships along every coast
Grip the deep, where even to Assyria's
Land Nereus cuts a passageway for prows,
Why compel me, hostage to a hated house,
Married to my foe, to consume a life
In pain and tears? My fugitive lord is gone;
Theseus shows his wife his usual faith:
Brave he walks the dense darkness of the lake
That none recross, a bold suitor's henchman,
To drag torn from hell's royal throne a bride.

pergit furoris socius, haud illum timor
pudorque tenuit: stupra et illicitos toros
Acheronte in imo quaerit Hippolyti pater.
  Sed maior alius incubat maestae dolor.
non me quies nocturna, non altus sopor   100
soluere curis: alitur et crescit malum
et ardet intus qualis Aetnaeo uapor
exundat antro. Palladis telae uacant
et inter ipsas pensa labuntur manus.
non colere donis templa uotiuis libet,   105
non inter aras, Atthidum mixtam choris,
iactare tacitis conscias sacris faces,
nec adire castis precibus aut ritu pio
adiudicatae praesidem terrae deam.
iuuat excitatas consequi cursu feras   110
et rigida molli gaesa iaculari manu.
  Quo tendis, anime? quid furens saltus amas?
fatale miserae matris agnosco malum:
peccare noster nouit in siluis amor.
genetrix, tui me miseret: infando malo   115
correpta pecoris efferum saeui ducem
audax amasti; toruus, impatiens iugi
adulter ille, ductor indomiti gregis—
sed amabat aliquid. quis meas miserae deus
aut quis iuuare Daedalus flammas queat?   120
non si ille remeet, arte Mopsopia potens,
qui nostra caeca monstra conclusit domo,
promittet ullam casibus nostris opem.
stirpem perosa Solis inuisi Venus
per nos catenas uindicat Martis sui   125
suasque, probris omne Phoebeum genus
onerat nefandis. nulla Minois leui
defuncta amore est: iungitur semper nefas.

NVTRIX

Thesea coniunx, clara progenies Iouis,
nefanda casto pectore exturba ocius,   130
extingue flammas neue te dirae spei
praebe obsequentem. quisquis in primo obstitit
pepulitque amorem, tutus ac uictor fuit;

Proceeds this soldier of passion. No fear
Or shame gripped him. Debauch and illicit beds
Deep in Acheron Hippolytus' father seeks.
   Yet other, greater pain broods in my distress.
Not the night's tranquillity, not deep sleep
Release me from care. Evil feeds and grows
And burns within like the billowing heat
In Etna's cave. Pallas' loom stands idle
And the day's wool even slips from my hands.
I have no heart to deck shrines with votive gifts,
Or to join Attic women at the altars
Torch-bearing in witness of the silent rites,
Or to approach with chaste prayer and pious vow
The guardian goddess granted this land.
My joy's to follow startled beasts in the chase
And to hurl stiff javelins with tender hand.
   Where to, my soul? Why this raging love for glades?
I recognise poor mother's fateful evil:
Her love and mine are skilled in forest sin.
Mother, I pity you. Unspeakable evil
Seized you when bold you loved that savage herd's
Wild leader; fierce, intolerant of the yoke,
Adulterous leader of an untamed herd—
Yet at least he loved. For my wretchedness
What god or Daedalus could ease the flames?
Not if that master of Attic arts returned,
Who immured our monster in his blind house,
Could he offer help to our misfortune.
Hating the despised Sun's offspring, Venus
Through us claims redress for her Mars' fetters
And her own, loads all Phoebus' stock with guilt
Unspeakable. No daughter of Minos
Has found love light; it is always joined to sin.

NURSE

Wife of Theseus, glorious child of Jove,
Banish this sin at once from your chaste heart.
Extinguish the flames and give no countenance
To dreadful hopes. Who from the first baulks love
And repels it, is safe and victorious;

qui blandiendo dulce nutriuit malum,
sero recusat ferre quod subiit iugum.   135
   Nec me fugit, quam durus et ueri insolens
ad recta flecti regius nolit tumor.
quemcumque dederit exitum casus feram:
fortem facit uicina libertas senem.
   Honesta primum est uelle nec labi uia,   140
pudor est secundus nosse peccandi modum.
quo, misera, pergis? quid domum infamem aggrauas
superasque matrem? maius est monstro nefas:
nam monstra fato, moribus scelera imputes.
si, quod maritus supera non cernit loca,   145
tutum esse facinus credis et uacuum metu,
erras. teneri crede Lethaeo abditum
Thesea profundo et ferre perpetuam Styga:
quid ille, lato maria qui regno premit
populisque reddit iura centenis, pater?   150
latere tantum facinus occultum sinet?
sagax parentum est cura. credamus tamen
astu doloque tegere nos tantum nefas:
quid ille rebus lumen infundens suum,
matris parens? quid ille, qui mundum quatit   155
uibrans corusca fulmen Aetnaeum manu,
sator deorum? credis hoc posse effici,
inter uidentes omnia ut lateas auos?
sed ut secundus numinum abscondat fauor
coitus nefandos utque contingat stupro   160
negata magnis sceleribus semper fides:
quid poena praesens, conscius mentis pauor
animusque culpa plenus et semet timens?
scelus aliqua tutum, nulla securum tulit.
compesce amoris impii flammas, precor,   165
nefasque quod non ulla tellus barbara
commisit umquam, non uagi campis Getae
nec inhospitalis Taurus aut sparsus Scythes;
expelle facinus mente castifica horridum
memorque matris metue concubitus nouos.   170
miscere thalamos patris et gnati apparas
uteroque prolem capere confusam impio?
perge et nefandis uerte naturam ignibus.
cur monstra cessant? aula cur fratris uacat?

Who flatters and nourishes the sweet bane,
Too late refuses the accepted yoke.
(Aside)   It hasn't escaped me how royal pride, stiff
And truth-averse, will not bend to virtue.
Whatever outcome fortune brings, I'll bear;
Imminent freedom makes the aged brave.
     To want the good is best and not to falter;
Shame comes next—to acknowledge wrong's limits.
What do you seek, wretch? To crush your ill-famed house,
Surpass your mother? Sin transcends the monstrous:
The monstrous comes from fate, sin from character.
If, because your husband doesn't see this world,
You suppose the crime safe and free from fear,
You are wrong. Suppose Theseus is held fast
In Lethe's depths and suffers eternal hell,
What of him whose wide realm presses the seas,
Who gives a hundred nations law, your father?
Will he allow such crime to lie concealed?
Parental care is shrewd. But let's suppose
Through cunning and craft we hide the great sin,
What of him who floods the universe with light,
Your mother's father? Or he who shakes the world
Brandishing Etna's bolts in gleaming hand,
Progenitor of gods? Do you suppose
You can evade all-seeing ancestors?
But grant that heaven's benign favour hides
This sinful coupling and debauchery
Earns the trust always denied to great crime,
What of punishment within, the mind's conscious
Dread, a soul filled with guilt and self-afraid?
Some have sinned without danger, none without fear.
Repress the fires of impious love, I beg,
And a sin which yet no barbaric land
Committed, no plain-wandering Getan,
Inhospitable Taur or scattered Scyth.
Expel this dreadful crime from your chaste mind;
Remember your mother and fear novel mates.
Will you confound beds of father and son,
In impious womb take mongrel progeny?
Go, convulse nature with your sinful fires.
No monsters yet? Your brother's palace empty?

prodigia totiens orbis insueta audiet,   175
natura totiens legibus cedet suis,
quotiens amabit Cressa?

PHAEDRA

              Quae memoras scio
uera esse, nutrix, sed furor cogit sequi
peiora. uadit animus in praeceps sciens
remeatque frustra sana consilia appetens.   180
sic, cum grauatam nauita aduersa ratem
propellit unda, cedit in uanum labor
et uicta prono puppis aufertur uado.
quid ratio possit? uicit ac regnat furor,
potensque tota mente dominatur deus.   185
hic uolucer omni pollet in terra impotens
laesumque flammis torret indomitis Iouem;
Gradiuus istas belliger sensit faces,
opifex trisulci fulminis sensit deus,
et qui furentes semper Aetnaeis iugis   190
uersat caminos igne tam paruo calet;
ipsumque Phoebum, tela qui neruo regit,
figit sagitta certior missa puer
uolitatque caelo pariter et terris grauis.

NVTRIX

Deum esse amorem turpis et uitio fauens   195
finxit libido, quoque liberior foret
titulum furori numinis falsi addidit.
natum per omnes scilicet terras uagum
Erycina mittit, ille per caelum uolans
proterua tenera tela molitur manu   200
regnumque tantum minimus e superis habet.
uana ista demens animus asciuit sibi
Venerisque numen finxit atque arcus dei.
quisquis secundis rebus exultat nimis
fluitque luxu, semper insolita appetit.   205
tunc illa magnae dira fortunae comes
subit libido: non placent suetae dapes,
non tecta sani moris aut uilis cibus.
cur in penates rarius tenues subit

Shall the world always hear of strange prodigies,
Shall nature always abandon its laws,
When a Cretan woman loves?

PHAEDRA

                              What you say
I know to be true, nurse, but passion compels
The worst. The mind moves to the brink knowingly
And retreats in vain to seek safe counsel.
So when a sailor drives his laden ship
Against opposing waves, toil proves pointless
And the vanquished craft hurtles down the stream.
What can reason do? Passion's conquered and reigns,
And a potent god commands my whole heart.
This winged one has power on earth uncontrolled
And with untempered flames strikes and scorches Jove.
Warmonger Gradivus has felt his torch,
The triple bolt's craftsman god has felt it—
Yes, he who stokes the ever-raging forge
On Etna's slopes grows hot with this small fire.
Even Phoebus, whose shafts fly straight from the bow,
This boy pricks with more unerring arrow,
As noxious to heaven in flight as to earth.

NURSE

That love is god is a fiction of vile
And sinful lust, which for greater freedom
Assigned a false deity's name to passion.
Erycina, I think, sends her son roaming
Through every land; he, flying through heaven,
Works wanton weapons with delicate hands
And tiniest of gods holds sovereign sway.
Demented minds adopted these conceits,
Invented Venus' power and the god's bow.
Whoever enjoys too much prosperity,
Bathed in luxury, always seeks the new.
Then that fatal companion of high estate
Enters, lust. Dislike sets in for normal fare,
For homes of sober fashion and cheap food.
Why does this pestilence seldom enter

haec delicatas eligens pestis domos?   210
cur sancta paruis habitat in tectis Venus
mediumque sanos uulgus affectus tenet
et se coercent modica? contra diuites
regnoque fulti plura quam fas est petunt?
quod non potest uult posse qui nimium potest.   215
quid deceat alto praeditam solio uides:
metue ac uerere sceptra remeantis uiri.

PHAEDRA

Amoris in me maximum regnum fero,
reditusque nullos metuo: non umquam amplius
conuexa tetigit supera qui mersus semel   220
adiit silentem nocte perpetua domum.

NVTRIX

Ne crede Diti. clauserit regnum licet
canisque diras Stygius obseruet fores,
solus negatas inuenit Theseus uias.

PHAEDRA

Veniam ille amori forsitan nostro dabit.   225

NVTRIX

Immitis etiam coniugi castae fuit:
experta saeuam est barbara Antiope manum.
sed posse flecti coniugem iratum puta:
quis huius animum flectet intractabilem?
exosus omne feminae nomen fugit,   230
immitis annos caelibi uitae dicat,
conubia uitat: genus Amazonium scias.

PHAEDRA

Hunc in niuosi collis haerentem iugis
et aspera agili saxa calcantem pede
sequi per alta nemora, per montes placet.   235

Poor homes, picking houses of affluence?
Why does pure love dwell under lowly roofs,
The common crowd have wholesome appetites,
Modest fortune self-control? While the rich
And empire-propped seek more than what is right?
Excess power desires power beyond its power.
You know what conduct fits a high-throned queen:
Fear and respect your returning lord's sceptre.

PHAEDRA

Love is the great sovereign I feel within
And I fear no one's return. Nobody
Has ever regained the vaulted skies, once
Descended to eternal night's mute house.

NURSE

Do not trust Dis. Though he bolt his kingdom
And the Stygian dog guard the gates of fear,
Theseus alone finds paths denied others.

PHAEDRA

Perhaps he'll give indulgence to my love.

NURSE

He was ungentle even to a chaste wife;
Foreign Antiope felt his savage hand.
But suppose a wrathful husband can be swayed:
Who'll bend the other's intractable will?
He detests and flees all name of woman,
Ungently gives his years to celibacy,
Shuns marriage. You know the Amazon breed.

PHAEDRA

Though he cling to ridges of snow-white hills
And tread jagged rocks with his speeding feet,
Through deep woods, across mountains I'll follow.

NVTRIX

Resistet ille seque mulcendum dabit
castosque ritus Venere non casta exuet?
tibi ponet odium, cuius odio forsitan
persequitur omnes? precibus haud uinci potest:
ferus est.

PHAEDRA

Amore didicimus uinci feros.   240

NVTRIX

Fugiet.

PHAEDRA

Per ipsa maria si fugiet, sequar.

NVTRIX

Patris memento.

PHAEDRA

Meminimus matris simul.

NVTRIX

Genus omne profugit.

PHAEDRA

Paelicis careo metu.

NVTRIX

Aderit maritus.

PHAEDRA

Nempe Pirithoi comes?

NVTRIX

Aderitque genitor.

NURSE

Will he stop and yield to your caresses
And strip off chaste rituals for unchaste love?
Will his hatred cease for you, for hate of whom
Perhaps he loathes all? Prayers can't conquer him.
He is wild.

PHAEDRA

Love, we've learnt, conquers the wild.

NURSE

He'll flee.

PHAEDRA

If he flees through ocean, I'll follow.

NURSE

Remember your father.

PHAEDRA

My mother too.

NURSE

He shuns the whole sex.

PHAEDRA

Then I fear no rival.

NURSE

Your husband will be here.

PHAEDRA

Pirithous' friend?

NURSE

And your sire.

PHAEDRA
Mitis Ariadnae pater?   245

NVTRIX
Per has senectae splendidas supplex comas
fessumque curis pectus et cara ubera
precor, furorem siste teque ipsa adiuua:
pars sanitatis uelle sanari fuit.

PHAEDRA
Non omnis animo cessit ingenuo pudor.   250
paremus, altrix. qui regi non uult amor,
uincatur. haud te, fama, maculari sinam.
haec sola ratio est, unicum effugium mali:
uirum sequamur, morte praeuertam nefas.

NVTRIX
Moderare, alumna, mentis effrenae impetus,   255
animos coerce. dignam ob hoc uita reor
quod esse temet autumas dignam nece.

PHAEDRA
Decreta mors est; quaeritur fati genus.
laqueone uitam finiam an ferro incubem?
an missa praeceps arce Palladia cadam?   260
proin castitatis uindicem armemus manum.

NVTRIX
Sic te senectus nostra praecipiti sinat
perire leto? siste furibundum impetum.
haud quisquam ad uitam facile reuocari potest.

PHAEDRA
Prohibere nulla ratio periturum potest,   265
ubi qui mori constituit et debet mori.

NVTRIX
Solamen annis unicum fessis, era,

58

PHAEDRA

Ariadne's gentle father?

NURSE

By these silvered hairs of age, I beg you,
By this care-worn heart and the breasts you sucked,
Please restrain this passion and save yourself.
Part of health is the desire to be healed.

PHAEDRA

All shame has not gone from this noble heart.
I yield, nurse. If love will not be governed
It must be vanquished. Honour will not be stained.
There's but one way, sole refuge from evil:
I'll follow my lord, by death avert sin.

NURSE

Check, child, your unbridled spirit's impulse.
Control your mind. Proof that you merit life
Is your assertion that you merit death.

PHAEDRA

Death is fixed; only its form lies open.
Suicide with the noose's snare or thrust of steel?
Or headlong leap from Pallas' citadel?
Let me arm my hand to save my honour.

NURSE

Is my old age to let you go headlong
To your death? Resist this raging impulse.
No one is easily recalled to life.

PHAEDRA

No reasoning has power to prevent death
When death is decided and death is due.

NURSE

Mistress, sole comfort of my weary years,

si tam proteruus incubat menti furor,
contemne famam. fama uix uero fauet,
peius merenti melior et peior bono.   270
temptemus animum tristem et intractabilem.
meus iste labor est aggredi iuuenem ferum
mentemque saeuam flectere immitis uiri.

CHORVS (CRESSAE)

Diua non miti generata ponto,
quam uocat matrem geminus Cupido,   275
impotens flammis simul et sagittis,
iste lasciuus puer et renidens
tela quam certo moderatur arcu.
labitur totas furor in medullas
igne furtiuo populante uenas.   280
non habet latam data plaga frontem,
sed uorat tectas penitus medullas.
nulla pax isti puero; per orbem
spargit effusas agilis sagittas:
quaeque nascentem uidet ora solem,   285
quaeque ad Hesperias iacet ora metas,
si qua feruenti subiecta cancro est,
si qua Parrhasiae glacialis ursae
semper errantes patitur colonos,
nouit hos aestus. iuuenum feroces   290
concitat flammas senibusque fessis
rursus extinctos reuocat calores,
uirginum ignoto ferit igne pectus
et iubet caelo superos relicto
uultibus falsis habitare terras.   295
Thessali Phoebus pecoris magister
egit armentum positoque plectro
impari tauros calamo uocauit.
induit formas quotiens minores
ipse qui caelum nebulasque ducit: 300
candidas ales modo mouit alas,
dulcior uocem moriente cygno;
fronte nunc torua petulans iuuencus

If this reckless passion broods in your soul,
Scorn reputation. Fame rarely favours truth,
Kind to the less worthy, cruel to the good.
Let's test that grim, intractable spirit.
I undertake to approach the wild youth
And to bend his savage, ungentle will.

(Exeunt into the palace)

(Enter a Chorus of Cretan Women)

CHORUS

Goddess born of ungentle sea
Called mother by dual Cupid
Flame violent and in arrows,
How your lascivious, smiling boy
Aims his shafts from unerring bow.
Passion steals to inmost marrow
As hidden fire ravages veins.
The wound received makes little show
But eats the marrow deep concealed.
No peace with your boy; world over
Active he scatters flying darts.
The land which sees the newborn sun,
The land beside Hesperia's goal,
The land beneath the burning Crab,
The Parrhasian bear's cold shore
Tilled by eternal wanderers
Know his heat. He arouses youth's
Ferocious flames, in tired age
Rekindles the extinguished blaze,
Strikes virgins' hearts with unknown fire,
And bids the High Ones, heaven left,
To dwell on earth in untrue forms.
Thessalia's herdsman Phoebus
Drove cattle, placed lyre aside
And summoned bullocks with scaled reeds.
How often *he* took lesser shapes
Who controls the sky and the clouds.
A bird, he fluttered gleaming wings
Voice sweeter than a dying swan's.
Ferocious-browed lusting bull,

61

uirginum strauit sua terga ludo,
perque fraternos noua regna fluctus 305
ungula lentos imitante remos
pectore aduerso domuit profundum,
pro sua uector timidus rapina.
arsit obscuri dea clara mundi
nocte deserta nitidosque fratri 310
tradidit currus aliter regendos:
ille nocturnas agitare bigas
discit et gyro breuiore flecti;
nec suum tempus tenuere noctes
et dies tardo remeauit ortu, 315
dum tremunt axes grauiore curru.
natus Alcmena posuit pharetras
et minax uasti spolium leonis,
passus aptari digitis smaragdos
et dari legem rudibus capillis; 320
crura distincto religauit auro,
luteo plantas cohibente socco;
et manu, clauam modo qua gerebat,
fila deduxit properante fuso.

Vidit Persis ditique ferax 325
Lydia regno deiecta feri
terga leonis, umerisque, quibus
sederat alti regia caeli,
tenuem Tyrio stamine pallam.
sacer est ignis—credite laesis— 330
nimiumque potens. qua terra salo
cingitur alto, quaque aetherio
candida mundo sidera currunt,
hac regna tenet puer immitis,
spicula cuius sentit in imis 335
caerulus undis grex Nereidum,
flammamque nequit releuare mari.
ignes sentit genus aligerum;
Venere instinctus suscipit audax
grege pro toto bella iuuencus; 340
si coniugio timuere suo,
poscunt timidi proelia cerui,
et mugitu dant concepti

He spread his back for virgins' play
And through strange realms, his brother's waves,
His hoofs employed like pliant oars,
He breasted the deep and tamed it,
Fearful for the cargo he'd raped.
The darkened world's bright goddess burned
And abandoned night, gave brother
Her shining chariot to rule.
He learns to drive nocturnal teams
And to turn in shorter orbit;
No night kept its accustomed length,
Day returned late-dawned, as axles
Tremble beneath chariot's weight.
Alcmena's son put quiver down
And huge lion's menacing spoil,
Had fingers set with emeralds
And untrained hair carefully dressed.
He bound his legs with ornate gold,
Cased his feet with yellow slippers,
And with the hand which bore the club
Spun out thread with whirling spindle.

Persia and fertile Lydia's
Rich realm saw the fierce lion's
Hide cast off and on shoulders
Once prop of high heaven's court
A gauzy cloak of Tyrian thread.
Cursed is the fire (believe the burnt),
Its power too great. Where land's skirted
By the salty sea, where bright
Stars rush in the firmament,
The ungentle boy is sovereign,
His darts felt in ocean deep
By the blue-green Nereid throng,
And his flame no sea can quench.
Winged creatures too feel his fires.
Pricked by Venus the daring bull
Takes on wars for all the herd;
Terrified for their mates
Timid stags demand battle
Bellowing signs of passion

signa furoris. tunc uirgatas
India tigres decolor horret,   345
tunc uulnificos acuit dentes
aper et toto est spumeus ore;
Poeni quatiunt colla leones
cum mouit amor. tum silua gemit
murmure saeuo. amat insani   350
belua ponti Lucaeque boues.

Vindicat omnes natura sibi.
nihil immune est, odiumque perit
cum iussit amor; ueteres cedunt
ignibus irae. quid plura canam?   355
uincit saeuas cura nouercas.   356/57

ACTVS TERTIVS

CHORVS

Altrix, profare quid feras; quonam in loco est
regina? saeuis ecquis est flammis modus?

NVTRIX—PHAEDRA—CHORVS

NVTRIX

Spes nulla tantum posse leniri malum,   360
finisque flammis nullus insanis erit.
torretur aestu tacito et inclusus quoque,
quamuis tegatur, proditur uultu furor;
erumpit oculis ignis et lassae genae
lucem recusant; nil idem dubiae placet,   365
artusque uarie iactat incertus dolor.
nunc ut soluto labitur moriens gradu
et uix labante sustinet collo caput;
nunc se quieti reddit, et, somni immemor,
noctem querelis ducit. attolli iubet   370
iterumque poni corpus et solui comas
rursusque fingi; semper impatiens sui

64

Conceived. Time it is when swarthy
India dreads the striped tigress,
When the boar sharpens fatal
Tusks and foams in all his mouth.
Punic lions toss their manes
When love stirs. Then the forest groans
With savage roar. Raging ocean's
Beast and Luca-bulls love.

Nature for itself claims all.
Nothing's immune; hatred dies
When love commands, old angers
Yield to fire. What more to tell?
Love conquers savage stepmothers.

ACT THREE

(Enter the Nurse from the palace)

CHORUS-LEADER

Nurse, tell us what news you have. How is it
With the queen? Have her savage fires abated?

NURSE—PHAEDRA—CHORUS

NURSE

No hope exists such suffering can be eased,
Those maddening fires will never finish.
She burns with silent heat; her cabined rage,
Although concealed, is traitored by her face.
Flame bursts from her eyes and her jaded cheeks
Shun the light; restless, nothing pleases long,
And limbs jerk fitfully with shifting pain.
Sometimes her steps fail, she sinks as if dying,
And her neck, wavering, scarce holds her head.
Or she takes her rest and careless of sleep
Wastes the night with sobs. She bids them lift her
And to put her down; to untie her hair,
Again to bind it. Ever discontent

65

mutatur habitus. nulla iam Cereris subit
cura aut salutis; uadit incerto pede,
iam uiribus defecta: non idem uigor,   375
non ora tinguens nitida purpureus rubor;
populatur artus cura, iam gressus tremunt,
tenerque nitidi corporis cecidit decor.
et qui ferebant signa Phoebeae facis
oculi nihil gentile nec patrium micant.   380
lacrimae cadunt per ora et assiduo genae
rore irrigantur, qualiter Tauri iugis
tepido madescunt imbre percussae niues.

   Sed en, patescunt regiae fastigia:
reclinis ipsa sedis auratae toro   385
solitos amictus mente non sana abnuit.

PHAEDRA

Remouete, famulae, purpura atque auro inlitas
uestes, procul sit muricis Tyrii rubor,
quae fila ramis ultimi Seres legunt.
breuis expeditos zona constringat sinus,   390
ceruix monili uacua, nec niueus lapis
deducat aures, Indici donum maris;
odore crinis sparsus Assyrio uacet.
sic temere iactae colla perfundant comae
umerosque summos, cursibus motae citis   395
uentos sequantur. laeua se pharetrae dabit,
hastile uibret dextra Thessalicum manus:
talis seueri mater Hippolyti fuit.
qualis relictis frigidi Ponti plagis
egit cateruas Atticum pulsans solum   400
Tanaitis aut Maeotis et nodo comas
coegit emisitque, lunata latus
protecta pelta, talis in siluas ferar.

CHORVS

Sepone questus: non leuat miseros dolor.
agreste placa uirginis numen deae.   405

She changes moods. There's no care at present
For food or health; she wanders aimlessly
Her strength now gone: no old vitality,
No roseate glow painting her bright cheeks.
Care ravages her limbs, her steps tremble,
That radiant body's sweet beauty set.
And eyes which bore the gleam of Phoebus' torch
No longer shine with their ancestral light.
Tears fall down her face and cheeks are moistened
With incessant dew, just as on Taurus' heights
Pierced by warming rain the snows turn to water.

> *(The upper storey of the palace opens to
> reveal Phaedra surrounded by attendants)*

But look, the top of the palace opens.
Lying on the couch of her golden throne,
Mind sick, she spurns her usual clothing.

PHAEDRA

Remove, slaves, this purple and dresses smeared
With gold, away the murex-scarlet of Tyre
And silk plucked from trees by distant Serics.
A narrow sash should tie these hanging folds,
My throat lack its chain; and let no snow-pearl,
Gift of India's sea, burden my ears.
Let my hair float—free of Assyrian nard.
Let it toss at random, pour over neck
And tops of shoulders, and streaming as I race
Trail the wind. The left hand will take the quiver,
The right will brandish Thessalia's spear:
Just such was stern Hippolytus' mother.
Like a woman of Tanais or Maeotis
Driving her hordes from frozen Pontus' shores
Thundering onto Attic soil, her hair
Knotted and streaming, her side protected
By crescent shield, so I will to the woods.

> *(The palace closes)*

CHORUS-LEADER

No more tears; grief doesn't help the afflicted.
Placate the virgin goddess' rural power.

> *(Exit Chorus)*

NVTRIX—HIPPOLYTVS

NVTRIX

Regina nemorum, sola quae montes colis,
et una solis montibus coleris dea,
conuerte tristes ominum in melius minas.
o magna siluas inter et lucos dea,
clarumque caeli sidus et noctis decus,   410
cuius relucet mundus alterna uice,
Hecate triformis, en ades coeptis fauens.
animum rigentem tristis Hippolyti doma:
det facilis aures; mitiga pectus ferum;
amare discat, mutuos ignes ferat.   415
innecte mentem. toruus auersus ferox
in iura Veneris redeat. huc uires tuas
intende: sic te lucidi uultus ferant
et nube rupta cornibus puris eas,
sic te regentem frena nocturni aetheris   420
detrahere numquam Thessali cantus queant
nullusque de te gloriam pastor ferat.
ades inuocata, iam faue uotis, dea.

Ipsum intuor sollemne uenerantem sacrum
nullo latus comitante—quid dubitas? dedit   425
tempus locumque casus: utendum artibus.
trepidamus? haud est facile mandatum scelus
audere, uerum iussa qui regis timet,
deponat omne et pellat ex animo decus:
malus est minister regii imperii pudor.   430

HIPPOLYTVS

Quid huc seniles fessa moliris gradus,
o fida nutrix, turbidam frontem gerens
et maesta uultu? sospes est certe parens
sospesque Phaedra stirpis et geminae iugum?

NVTRIX

Metus remitte. prospero regnum in statu est   435
domusque florens sorte felici uiget.

NURSE—HIPPOLYTUS

NURSE

(Prays to Diana)
Queen of the forests, sole lover of hills,
And on the lonely hills sole goddess loved,
Change these grim, menacing omens into good.
O mighty goddess of forest and grove,
Bright star of heaven and splendour of night,
Whose recurrent beams illumine the world,
Hecate triformed, come and bless my task.
Tame grim Hippolytus' unbending heart.
Make his ears docile; soften his wild soul;
Let him learn to love and feel flames in turn.
Snare his mind. Make this fierce, hostile, ferocious
Man return to Venus' law. Turn your powers
To this; so may you travel with features clear,
Pass through rifted clouds with your crescent pure;
So as you manage the heaven's night reins
May Thessaly's chants never pull you down
Or shepherd achieve glory over you.
Come, goddess, invoked; favour now this prayer.

(Enter Hippolytus)

(Aside)   I see him come to perform his due rites.
No one's at his side. Why delay then? Chance
Has given the time and place. Use your skill.
Afraid? It's not easy to dare an ordered
Crime, but one who fears royalty's commands
Must spurn and drive all honour from the heart.
For shame is a poor servant of a crown.

HIPPOLYTUS

Why drag your old steps this way wearily,
Faithful nurse, with disquiet in your brow
And sad-faced? Surely my father is safe,
And Phaedra safe and both their two children?

NURSE

Fear not. The realm's in a prosperous state,
The house blossoms and thrives with good fortune.

sed tu beatis mitior rebus ueni;
namque anxiam me cura sollicitat tui,
quod te ipse poenis grauibus infestus domas.
quem fata cogunt, ille cum uenia est miser; 440
at si quis ultro se malis offert uolens
seque ipse torquet, perdere est dignus bona
quis nescit uti. potius annorum memor
mentem relaxa: noctibus festis facem
attolle, curas Bacchus exoneret graues. 445
aetate fruere; mobili cursu fugit.
nunc facile pectus, grata nunc iuueni Venus:
exultet animus. cur toro uiduo iaces?
tristem iuuentam solue; nunc cursus rape,
effunde habenas, optimos uitae dies 450
effluere prohibe. propria descripsit deus
officia et aeuum per suos duxit gradus:
laetitia iuuenem, frons decet tristis senem.
quid te coerces et necas rectam indolem?
seges illa magnum fenus agricolae dabit 455
quaecumque laetis tenera luxuriat satis,
arborque celso uertice euincet nemus
quam non maligna caedit aut resecat manus.
ingenia melius recta se in laudes ferunt,
si nobilem animum uegeta libertas alit. 460
truculentus et siluester ac uitae inscius
tristem iuuentam Venere deserta coles?
hoc esse munus credis indictum uiris,
ut dura tolerent, cursibus domitent equos
et saeua bella Marte sanguineo gerant? 465
prouidit ille maximus mundi parens,
cum tam rapaces cerneret fati manus,
ut damna semper subole repararet noua.
excedat agedum rebus humanis Venus,
quae supplet ac restituit exhaustum genus: 470
orbis iacebit squalido turpis situ,
uacuum sine ullis classibus stabit mare,
alesque caelo derit et siluis fera,
solis et aer peruius uentis erit.
quam uaria leti genera mortalem trahunt 475
carpuntque turbam, pontus et ferrum et doli.
sed ista credas desse: sic atram Styga

But you should treat your blessings more gently.
Your harsh self-discipline and cruel torment
Harry my love for you to anxiety.
Misery is pardoned when fate compels;
But suffer willingly of your accord
And rack yourself, then you deserve to forfeit
Gifts you cannot use. Remember your years
And relax your spirit: on feast nights raise
The torch, let Bacchus lift your heavy cares.
Enjoy the time; with rapid speed it flies.
Now the heart's free, now Venus pleasures youth;
Let spirits soar. Why lie on an empty bed?
Untie your joyless youth, now seize the track,
Loosen the reins, prevent life's finest days
Escaping. God prescribed appropriate
Duties and gave life its inherent steps:
Joy befits youth, a gloomy brow old age.
Why curb yourself and kill your true nature?
That crop will give the farmer great return
Which riots early with exultant shoots;
That tree will top the grove with towering height
Which no envious hand cuts down or prunes back.
The finest natures achieve greater praise
If active freedom feeds a noble mind.
Like some harsh woodsman ignorant of life
Will you desert Venus for joyless youth?
Do you suppose it man's appointed task
To bear hardship, break horses on the track,
And conduct savage wars with bloody Mars?
The great father of the universe took care,
When he saw the rapacious hands of fate,
To repair all loss with new creation.
If Venus in fact abandoned mankind,
Who supplies and restores our depleted race,
The earth will lie ugly in vile neglect,
The ocean stand empty deprived of ships,
The heaven will lack birds, the forest beasts,
And winds alone will penetrate the air.
How various the forms of death which pull
And pluck our mortal throng, sea, steel, treachery.
Suppose them lacking: we seek murky Styx

iam petimus ultro. caelibem uitam probet
sterilis iuuentus: hoc erit, quicquid uides,
unius aeui turba et in semet ruet.   480
proinde uitae sequere naturam ducem:
urbem frequenta, ciuium coetus cole.

HIPPOLYTVS

Non alia magis est libera et uitio carens
ritusque melius uita quae priscos colat,
quam quae relictis moenibus siluas amat.   485
non illum auarae mentis inflammat furor
qui se dicauit montium insontem iugis,
non aura populi et uulgus infidum bonis,
non pestilens inuidia, non fragilis fauor.
non ille regno seruit aut regno imminens   490
uanos honores sequitur aut fluxas opes,
spei metusque liber; haud illum niger
edaxque liuor dente degeneri petit.
nec scelera populos inter atque urbes sata
nouit nec omnes conscius strepitus pauet   495
aut uerba fingit; mille non quaerit tegi
diues columnis nec trabes multo insolens
suffigit auro; non cruor largus pias
inundat aras, fruge nec sparsi sacra
centena niuei colla summittunt boues: 500
sed rure uacuo potitur et aperto aethere
innocuus errat. callidas tantum feris
struxisse fraudes nouit et fessus graui
labore niueo corpus Iliso fouet;
nunc ille ripam celeris Alphei legit,   505
nunc nemoris alti densa metatur loca,
ubi Lerna puro gelida perlucet uado,
sedesque mutat: hinc aues querulae fremunt
ramique uentis lene percussi tremunt
ueteresque fagi. iuuat aut amnis uagi   510
pressisse ripas, caespite aut nudo leues
duxisse somnos, siue fons largus citas
defundit undas siue per flores nouos
fugiente dulcis murmurat riuo sonus.
excussa siluis poma compescunt famem   515

Still without help. Let sterile youth approve
The single life and all you see will be
One generation's throng doomed to perish.
Therefore follow nature as your life's guide:
Frequent the city; cultivate its people.

HIPPOLYTUS

There is no life so free and virtuous
And which so cultivates our ancient ways
As far from city walls to love the woods.
No rage of avarice inflames the man
Self-vowed to innocence on mountain heights;
No people's breath, no base, disloyal mob,
No poisonous spite or fickle favour.
He serves no kingdom nor threatens kingship
Pursuing vain honours and fleeting wealth,
Liberated from hope and fear; no black,
Gnawing envy bites him with base-born tooth.
He knows nothing of crime spawned in teeming
Cities: no dreading every noise in guilt,
No lies told. He seeks no rich man's palace
Propped on a thousand pillars, nor rafters
Proud-encrusted with gold. No streaming blood
Soaks pious altars, no white bulls sprinkled
With sacred meal submit a hundred necks.
No, he's lord of empty fields and wanders
Blameless in open air. He knows only
To lay subtle traps for beasts and soothes toil-
Exhausted limbs in snowy Ilissos.
Now he skirts swift-flowing Alpheus' bank,
Now passes through the deep grove's dense demesne
Where cool Lerna's lucid waters shine pure,
And changes his abode. Here plaintive birds
Prattle and wind-struck branches gently quiver
And ancient beeches. His the joy to lie
By a vagrant stream or to drink soft sleep
On bare turf where a bounteous spring drops
Swirling waters or through the fresh-sprung flowers
There sounds an escaping brook's sweet murmur.
Fruit shaken from trees arrest his hunger,

et fraga paruis uulsa dumetis cibos
faciles ministrant. regios luxus procul
est impetus fugisse: sollicito bibunt
auro superbi; quam iuuat nuda manu
captasse fontem! certior somnus premit   520
secura duro membra uersantem toro.
non in recessu furta et obscuro improbus
quaerit cubili seque multiplici timens
domo recondit: aethera ac lucem petit
et teste caelo uiuit.

                Hoc equidem reor   525
uixisse ritu prima quos mixtos deis
profudit aetas. nullus his auri fuit
caecus cupido, nullus in campo sacer
diuisit agros arbiter populis lapis.
nondum secabant credulae pontum rates: 530
sua quisque norat maria; non uasto aggere
crebraque turre cinxerant urbes latus.
non arma saeua miles aptabat manu
nec torta clausas fregerat saxo graui
ballista portas, iussa nec dominum pati   535
iuncto ferebat terra seruitium boue:
sed arua per se feta poscentes nihil
pauere gentes; silua natiuas opes
et opaca dederant antra natiuas domos.
rupere foedus impius lucri furor   540
et ira praeceps quaeque succensas agit
libido mentes; uenit imperii sitis
cruenta, factus praeda maiori minor:
pro iure uires esse. tum primum manu
bellare nuda saxaque et ramos rudes   545
uertere in arma. non erat gracili leuis
armata ferro cornus aut longo latus
mucrone cingens ensis aut crista procul
galeae comantes: tela faciebat dolor.
inuenit artes bellicus Mauors nouas   550
et mille formas mortis. hinc terras cruor
infecit omnes fusus et rubuit mare.
tum scelera dempto fine per cunctas domos
iere, nullum caruit exemplo nefas:
a fratre frater, dextera gnati parens   555

And berries torn from tiny shrubs give food
Without effort. His instinct is to flee
Royal luxury. The arrogant drink
From anxious gold; he rejoices to catch
A spring with bare hands. Surer sleep grips him
On his hard bed tossing his carefree limbs.
He seeks no wanton, stolen joy in secret
Or on darkened couch nor hides terrified
In maze-like house; he courts the air and light
And lives beneath heaven's eye.
                                        Such a life
I think lived those the primal age produced
To mingle with the gods. No blind desire
For gold obsessed them, no sacred judgment-
Stone parted on the plains the people's fields.
No credulous vessels yet cut the sea,
Each knew his own waters; no massive wall
Or tower block enclosed a city's side.
No weapons filled the soldier's savage hand;
No hurling catapult's heavy stone shattered
Close-barred gates. The earth bore no master's rule
And endured the slavery of no ox's yoke.
Rather, self-productive fields nourished man
Without demand; the woods gave natural
Riches, shaded grottoes natural homes.
Impious rage for gain broke this covenant,
Precipitate wrath and mind-inflaming
Lust; then came the bloody thirst for power,
The weaker became spoils for the stronger,
Might in place of justice. At first men fought
Bare-handed and turned rocks and rough branches
Into weapons. There was no light cornel
Armed with tapered iron or long-edged sword
Gripping the side or high-crested helmets
Nodding from afar: grievance furnished arms.
War-loving Mavors invented new arts
And a thousand forms of death. Then streaming
Blood dyed each land and made the ocean red.
Crime—its limits now removed—invaded
Every home, no sin lacked example:
Brother slain by brother, father by the hand

cecidit, maritus coniugis ferro iacet
perimuntque fetus impiae matres suos.
taceo nouercas: mitius nil est feris.
sed dux malorum femina: haec scelerum artifex
obsedit animos, huius incestae stupris   560
fumant tot urbes, bella tot gentes gerunt
et uersa ab imo regna tot populos premunt.
sileantur aliae: sola coniux Aegei,
Medea, reddet feminas dirum genus.

NVTRIX

Cur omnium fit culpa paucarum scelus?   565

HIPPOLYTVS

Detestor omnes, horreo fugio execror.
sit ratio, sit natura, sit durus furor:
odisse placuit. ignibus iunges aquas
et amica ratibus ante promittet uada
incerta Syrtis, ante ab extremo sinu   570
Hesperia Tethys lucidum attollet diem
et ora dammis blanda praebebunt lupi,
quam uictus animum feminae mitem geram.

NVTRIX

Saepe obstinatis induit frenos amor
et odia mutat. regna materna aspice: 575
illae feroces sentiunt Veneris iugum.
testaris istud unicus gentis puer.

HIPPOLYTVS

Solamen unum matris amissae fero,
odisse quod iam feminas omnes licet.

NVTRIX

Vt dura cautes undique intractabilis   580
resistit undis et lacessentes aquas
longe remittit, uerba sic spernit mea.
    Sed Phaedra praeceps graditur, impatiens morae.

Of son, husband lay dead beneath wife's sword,
And impious mothers destroyed their offspring.
Stepmothers—I'm silent: beasts are more gentle.
But evil's prince is woman. Mistress of crime,
She besieges minds; for her sinful lusts
So many cities burn, so many states war,
So many peoples crushed by fallen kingdoms.
Others pass unnamed; alone, Aegeus' wife,
Medea, will prove woman a damned race.

NURSE

Why blame all women for the crimes of few?

HIPPOLYTUS

I loathe them all, I dread, I shun, I curse them.
Be it reason, nature or insensate rage,
I choose to hate them. Fire will sooner mix
With water and shifting Syrtis give friendly
Waves to ships, sooner from her distant lap
Hesperian Tethys will bring bright day
And wolves look tenderly on does, before I
Defeated show gentleness to woman.

NURSE

Often love puts bridles on stubborn hearts
And transforms hate. Look at your mother's realm:
Even those savage women feel Venus' yoke.
You are proof of this, the tribe's only son.

HIPPOLYTUS

I've one consolation for my mother's loss:
That I may now detest all womankind.

NURSE

(Aside) Like some hard and impenetrable rock
        Which resists the waves and flings far away
        The assailing waters, he spurns my words.   *(Enter Phaedra)*
    But Phaedra comes in haste, brooks no delay.

77

quo se dabit fortuna? quo uerget furor?
terrae repente corpus exanimum accidit 585
et ora morti similis obduxit color.
   Attolle uultus, dimoue uocis moras:
tuus en, alumna, temet Hippolytus tenet.

PHAEDRA—HIPPOLYTVS—NVTRIX

PHAEDRA

Quis me dolori reddit atque aestus graues
reponit animo? quam bene excideram mihi. 590

HIPPOLYTVS

Cur dulce munus redditae lucis fugis?

PHAEDRA

Aude, anime, tempta, perage mandatum tuum.
intrepida constent uerba: qui timide rogat
docet negare. magna pars sceleris mei
olim peracta est; serus est nobis pudor: 595
amauimus nefanda. si coepta exequor,
forsan iugali crimen abscondam face:
honesta quaedam scelera successus facit.
en, incipe, anime.
             Commodes paulum, precor,
secretus aures. si quis est abeat comes. 600

HIPPOLYTVS

En locus ab omni liber arbitrio uacat.

PHAEDRA

Sed ora coeptis transitum uerbis negant;
uis magna uocem mittit et maior tenet.
uos testor omnes, caelites, hoc quod uolo—
me nolle. 605

HIPPOLYTVS

Animusne cupiens aliquid effari nequit?

What will happen? Where will her passion end?
Her lifeless frame drops suddenly to the ground.
A death-pallor has enveloped her face.
(To Phaedra) Hold up your head and try to speak, my child;
Your Hippolytus is here and holds you.

PHAEDRA—HIPPOLYTUS—NURSE

PHAEDRA

Who brings back the pain and restores my mind's
Oppressive heat? Oblivion was bliss.

HIPPOLYTUS

Why shun the return of the light's sweet gift?

PHAEDRA

(Aside) Be brave, my soul, onwards, finish your task.
Speak firmly, unafraid. Who asks with fear
Invites denial. A great part of my crime
Was finished long ago; my shame comes late,
I've loved sinfully. If I follow it through,
I may perhaps hide the crime in marriage:
Success renders some sins honourable.
On, soul, begin.
(To Hippolytus)   Hear me for a moment, please,
In private. Let anyone with you leave.

HIPPOLYTUS

But look, the place is free of witnesses.

PHAEDRA

Yet my lips deny passage to my words.
A great force drives them, a greater restrains.
Witness, all heaven's gods, that what I wish—
I do not wish.

HIPPOLYTUS

Your heart desires something it cannot speak?

79

PHAEDRA

Curae leues loquuntur, ingentes stupent.

HIPPOLYTVS

Committe curas auribus, mater, meis.

PHAEDRA

Matris superbum est nomen et nimium potens;
nostros humilius nomen affectus decet.   610
me uel sororem, Hippolyte, uel famulam uoca,
famulamque potius; omne seruitium feram.
non me per altas ire si iubeas niues,
pigeat gelatis ingredi Pindi iugis;
non, si per ignes ire et infesta agmina,   615
cuncter paratis ensibus pectus dare.
mandata recipe sceptra, me famulam accipe:
te imperia regere, me decet iussa exequi.
muliebre non est regna tutari urbium;
tu qui iuuentae flore primaeuo uiges,   620
ciues paterno fortis imperio rege.
sinu receptam supplicem ac seruam tege:
miserere uiduae.

HIPPOLYTVS

       Summus hoc omen deus
auertat. aderit sospes actutum parens.

PHAEDRA

Regni tenacis dominus et tacitae Stygis   625
nullam relictos fecit ad superos uiam.
thalami remittet ille raptorem sui?
nisi forte amori placidus et Pluton sedet.

HIPPOLYTVS

Illum quidem aequi caelites reducem dabunt.
sed dum tenebit uota in incerto deus,   630
pietate caros debita fratres colam,

80

PHAEDRA

Light troubles speak, the heaviest lack voice.

HIPPOLYTUS

Commit your troubles to my ears, mother.

PHAEDRA

Mother is a proud name and much too great;
A humbler name better fits our feelings.
Call me sister, Hippolytus, or servant,
Better servant; I'll bear all servitude.
If you ordered me through the driven snow
I'd gladly stand on Pindus' frozen peaks;
And if through fire and bristling battle ranks,
I'd not hesitate to breast the drawn blades.
Take the regent's sceptre, accept my service:
You it befits to rule, me to obey.
It's no woman's task to guard a citied realm;
You in the first flower and vigour of youth,
Heir to your father's power, rule the state.
Shield in your arms this suppliant and slave.
Pity a widow.

HIPPOLYTUS

The highest god avert
This omen. Father will soon be here—safe.

PHAEDRA

Lord of mute Styx and the tenacious realm
Has built no way back to the upper world.
Will he release the ravisher of his bed?
Unless Pluto too sits and smiles at love.

HIPPOLYTUS

His return surely the just gods will grant.
But while a god still holds our prayers in doubt,
I'll care for my dear brothers with due love

et te merebor esse ne uiduam putes
ac tibi parentis ipse supplebo locum.

PHAEDRA

O spes amantum credula, o fallax amor!
satisne dixi? precibus admotis agam.   635
   Miserere, tacitae mentis exaudi preces—
libet loqui pigetque.

HIPPOLYTVS

        Quodnam istud malum est?

PHAEDRA

Quod in nouercam cadere uix credas malum.

HIPPOLYTVS

Ambigua uoce uerba perplexa iacis.
effare aperte.

PHAEDRA

      Pectus insanum uapor   640
amorque torret. intimas saeuus uorat
penitus medullas atque per uenas meat
uisceribus ignis mersus et uenis latens
ut agilis altas flamma percurrit trabes.

HIPPOLYTVS

Amore nempe Thesei casto furis?   645

PHAEDRA

Hippolyte, sic est: Thesei uultus amo
illos priores quos tulit quondam puer,
cum prima puras barba signaret genas
monstrique caecam Cnosii uidit domum
et longa curua fila collegit uia.   650
quis tum ille fulsit! presserant uittae comam
et ora flauus tenera tinguebat pudor.

And take from you all thought of widowhood.
I shall fulfil for you my father's place.

PHAEDRA

(Aside) Lovers' credulous hope, deceitful love!
Have I said enough? I'll approach with prayer.
(To Hippolytus) Pity me, hear the prayers of a silent heart.
I long and loathe to speak.

HIPPOLYTUS

What ill is this?

PHAEDRA

One you'd scarce think a stepmother would suffer.

HIPPOLYTUS

You talk in riddles, your words ambiguous.
Speak openly.

PHAEDRA

Smouldering love scorches
My frantic heart. A savage fire devours
Me deep inside; it courses through my veins,
Lodged within the body, hidden in the blood,
Like vibrant flame darting through vaulted beams.

HIPPOLYTUS

Surely chaste love of Theseus makes you rage?

PHAEDRA

Hippolytus, yes: Theseus' face I love,
Those looks he had long ago as a boy,
When his first beard set off unsullied cheeks
And he saw the Cnossian monster's blind house
And gathered long threads on the winding way.
Then how he shone! Head-band circling his hair,
Golden shame suffusing his gentle cheeks.

inerant lacertis mollibus fortes tori;
tuaeque Phoebes uultus aut Phoebi mei,
tuusue potius—talis, en talis fuit   655
cum placuit hosti, sic tulit celsum caput.
in te magis refulget incomptus decor.
est genitor in te totus et toruae tamen
pars aliqua matris miscet ex aequo decus:
in ore Graio Scythicus apparet rigor.   660
si cum parente Creticum intrasses fretum,
tibi fila potius nostra neuisset soror.
te te, soror, quacumque siderei poli
in parte fulges, inuoco ad causam parem:
domus sorores una corripuit duas,   665
te genitor, at me gnatus.
                            En supplex iacet
adlapsa genibus regiae proles domus.
respersa nulla labe et intacta, innocens
tibi mutor uni. certa descendi ad preces.
finem hic dolori faciet aut uitae dies: 670
miserere amantis.

HIPPOLYTVS

                    Magne regnator deum,
tam lentus audis scelera? tam lentus uides?
et quando saeua fulmen emittes manu,
si nunc serenum est? omnis impulsus ruat
aether et atris nubibus condat diem,   675
ac uersa retro sidera obliquos agant
retorta cursus. tuque, sidereum caput,
radiate Titan, tu nefas stirpis tuae
speculare? lucem merge et in tenebras fuge.
cur dextra, diuum rector atque hominum, uacat   680
tua, nec trisulca mundus ardescit face?
in me tona, me fige, me uelox cremet
transactus ignis. sum nocens, merui mori:
placui nouercae.
                    Dignus en stupris ego?
scelerique tanto uisus ego solus tibi   685
materia facilis? hoc meus meruit rigor?
o scelere uincens omne femineum genus,

Beneath delicate arms strong muscles moved;
His face—was your Phoebe's or my Phoebus',
Or rather yours; like you, like you he was
When he pleased his foe, so held his head high.
Your beauty shines more brightly unadorned.
All your sire is in you and yet something
Of your fierce mother blends with equal glory:
In your Greek face is austere Scythian strength.
If you'd entered Cretan waters with your sire,
My sister would have spun her thread for you.
You, sister, you, wherever in the spangled
Sky you shine, I call to a cause we share.
A single house has ravished two sisters:
The father you, me the son.
                  Look, the daughter
Of a king lies a suppliant at your knees:
Spotless, undefiled, innocent, untouched,
Changed for you alone. Resolved I kneel in prayer.
This day will end my misery or my life.
Pity a lover.

HIPPOLYTUS

           Great monarch of gods,
Hear these crimes and not act? See and not act?
When will your savage hand impel its bolts
If the sky is cloudless now? All heaven
Collapse in ruin, black clouds bury day,
Let stars run back and wrenched from course turn all
Into confusion. You too, lord of stars,
Titan radiate, see your daughter's sin?
Submerge your light and flee into the dark.
Ruler of gods and men, why is your right hand
Empty, the world not ablaze with triple flame?
Against me send your bolts, wound me, burn me
Pierced by darting fire. I'm guilty and should die:
I pleased a stepmother.
(To Phaedra)   Deserved I debauch?
Did I alone seem to you fit matter
For such crime? My austerity deserved this?
O first in sin out of all female kind,

o maius ausa matre monstrifera malum,
genetrice peior! illa se tantum stupro
contaminauit, et tamen tacitum diu 690
crimen biformi partus exhibuit nota,
scelusque matris arguit uultu truci
ambiguus infans—ille te uenter tulit.
o ter quaterque prospero fato dati
quos hausit et peremit et leto dedit 695
odium dolusque. genitor, inuideo tibi:
Colchide nouerca maius hoc, maius malum est.

PHAEDRA

Et ipsa nostrae fata cognosco domus:
fugienda petimus; sed mei non sum potens.
te uel per ignes, per mare insanum sequar 700
rupesque et amnes, unda quos torrens rapit;
quacumque gressus tuleris hac amens agar.
iterum, superbe, genibus aduoluor tuis.

HIPPOLYTVS

Procul impudicos corpore a casto amoue
tactus—quid hoc est? etiam in amplexus ruit? 705
stringatur ensis, merita supplicia exigat.
en impudicum crine contorto caput
laeua reflexi: iustior numquam focis
datus tuis est sanguis, arquitenens dea.

PHAEDRA

Hippolyte, nunc me compotem uoti facis: 710
sanas furentem. maius hoc uoto meo est,
saluo ut pudore manibus immoriar tuis.

HIPPOLYTVS

Abscede, uiue, ne quid exores, et hic
contactus ensis deserat castum latus.
quis eluet me Tanais aut quae barbaris 715
Maeotis undis Pontico incumbens mari?
non ipse toto magnus Oceano pater
tantum expiarit sceleris. o siluae, o ferae!

Daring greater evil than monster-pregnant
Mother, worse than your creator. She stained
But herself with lust and, though long concealed,
The crime appeared in her child's hybrid form,
And the mongrel infant's brutish face proved
It's mother's guilt; and that belly bore you.
O thrice and four times blessed by fate are those
Devoured, destroyed and delivered to death
By guile and hate. Father, I envy you:
Here's greater evil than Colchic stepmother.

PHAEDRA

I too recognise the fate of our house:
What we should shun, we seek. But I'm powerless.
Even through fire and frantic seas I'll follow,
Across crags and streams seized by roaring flood;
Where your steps go, my madness will drive me.
Once more, proud man, I grovel at your feet.

HIPPOLYTUS

Remove your vile touch from my chaste body.
Away! What? She thrusts herself into my arms?
Out, sword, exact the fitting penalty.
Behold her twisted hair in my left hand,
Her vile head bent back. Your altars never
Received juster blood, goddess of the bow.

PHAEDRA

Hippolytus, you now fulfil my prayer:
You heal my passion. This transcends my prayer:
At your hands to die with my honour safe.

HIPPOLYTUS

Begone, live, lest your prayer be granted; now
This polluted sword must leave my chaste side.
What Tanais or wild Maeotian lake
Beside the Pontic sea will wash me clean?
Not even the great father with all Ocean
Could expiate this crime. O woods! O beasts!   *(Exit Hippolytus)*

87

NVTRIX

Deprensa culpa est. anime, quid segnis stupes?
regeramus ipsi crimen atque ultro impiam   720
Venerem arguamus. scelere uelandum est scelus;
tutissimum est inferre, cum timeas, gradum.
ausae priores simus an passae nefas,
secreta cum sit culpa, quis testis sciet?
    Adeste, Athenae! fida famulorum manus,   725
fer opem! nefandi raptor Hippolytus stupri
instat premitque, mortis intentat metum,
ferro pudicam terret.
                   En praeceps abit
ensemque trepida liquit attonitus fuga.
pignus tenemus sceleris. hanc maestam prius   730
recreate. crinis tractus et lacerae comae
ut sunt remaneant, facinoris tanti notae.
perferte in urbem.
              Recipe iam sensus, era.
quid te ipsa lacerans omnium aspectus fugis?
mens impudicam facere, non casus, solet.   735

CHORVS

Fugit insanae similis procellae,
ocior nubes glomerante Coro,
ocior cursum rapiente flamma,
stella cum uentis agitata longos
    porrigit ignes.   740

Conferat tecum decus omne priscum
fama miratrix senioris aeui:
pulchrior tanto tua forma lucet,
clarior quanto micat orbe pleno
cum suos ignes coeunte cornu   745
iunxit et curru properante pernox
exerit uultus rubicunda Phoebe
nec tenent stellae faciem minores;
qualis est, primas referens tenebras,
nuntius noctis, modo lotus undis   750

NURSE

The crime is out. Soul, why inert and dumb?
Let's rebound the guilt on him, ourselves charge
Impious love. Crime must be veiled with crime;
In fear the safest tactic is attack.
Whether we first dared this sin or suffered it,
Since no one saw her guilt, who'll testify?
  Be quick, Athens! Loyal band of servants,
Help! Hippolytus, foul and sinful rapist,
Presses and attacks us, brandishes death,
Terrifies chastity with steel.   *(Enter slaves and attendants)*
                    Off he speeds
Leaving his sword in dazed and fearful flight.
We hold the proof of crime. But our poor queen—
First revive her. Her pulled hair and torn locks
Remain as they are, marks of this great crime.
Take the news to the city.   *(Exeunt some to the city)*
                Revive, mistress.
Why torture yourself and flee every look?
The mind makes one unchaste, not circumstance.
                 (Exeunt into the palace)

(Enter the Chorus)
CHORUS

Fled like a furious tempest,
Faster than cloud-rolling Corus,
Faster than darting paths of flame
When long fingers of fire shoot
    From stars on the wind.

With you let antique-loving fame
Now compare all earlier form.
Your body's brighter beauty shines
Like the moon's clearer light full-orbed
When her crescent closes and fires
Join and in speeding chariot
Red-blushing Phoebe shows her face
Nightlong and lesser stars are dimmed;
Like Hesperus, night's harbinger,
Bringing in the first darkness fresh

Hesperus, pulsis iterum tenebris
   Lucifer idem.

Et tu, thyrsigera Liber ab India,
intonsa iuuenis perpetuum coma,
tigres pampinea cuspide territans   755
ac mitra cohibens cornigerum caput,
non uinces rigidas Hippolyti comas.
ne uultus nimium suspicias tuos:
omnes per populos fabula distulit,
Phaedrae quem Bromio praetulerit soror.   760

Anceps forma bonum mortalibus,
exigui donum breue temporis,
ut uelox celeri pede laberis.

Non sic prata nouo uere decentia
aestatis calidae despoliat uapor,   765
saeuit solstitio cum medius dies
et noctes breuibus praecipitat rotis.
languescunt folio ut lilia pallido
et gratae capiti deficiunt rosae,
et fulgor teneris qui radiat genis   770
momento rapitur nullaque non dies
formonsi spolium corporis abstulit.

Res est forma fugax: quis sapiens bono
confidit fragili? dum licet, utere.
tempus te tacitum subruit, horaque   775
semper praeterita deterior subit.

Quid deserta petis? tutior auiis
non est forma locis: te nemore abdito,
cum Titan medium constituit diem,
cingent turba licens Naides improbae,   780
formonsos solitae claudere fontibus,
et somnis facient insidias tuis
    lasciuae nemorum deae
Panas quae Dryades montiuagos petunt.
aut te stellifero despiciens polo   785
sidus post ueteres Arcadas editum

Sea-bathed, or expelling the dark
   Become Lucifer.

And you, Liber from thyrsed India,
Youth perpetual tresses unshorn,
Terror of tigers with vine-clad spear,
Head of horns encircled by turban,
Can't surpass Hippolytus' stiff hair.
Do not gaze too fondly at your looks:
Word has spread to every nation
Whom Phaedra's sister chose to Bromius.

Beauty doubtful boon to men,
Little moment's briefest gift,
Flying fast quicksilver feet.

Not so swiftly young spring's fair meadows
Are despoiled by burning summer's heat
When at the solstice midday rages
And the nighttimes sweep their shortened course.
As the lily withers leafing pale
And the garlanding rose petals fade,
The radiant glow of tender cheeks
Is ravished in a moment; no day
Has not despoiled the body's beauty.

Fleeting thing is beauty: what sage trusts
A fragile gift? While you can, use it.
Mute time undermines you and the hour
Ever approaches worse than the last.

Why seek the wilds? Beauty's no safer
In pathless places. Hide in the wood
When Titan halts the noon, a lusty
Troop of wanton Naiads will surround
Who ensnare the beautiful in springs;
Traps too will be laid for your slumbers
   By lascivious woodland
Dryads who pursue the hillside Pans.
Or seeing you from the spangled sky
The star whose birth old Arcady saw

currus non poterit flectere candidos.
en nuper rubuit, nullaque lucidis
nubes sordidior uultibus obstitit;
at nos solliciti numine turbido,   790
tractam Thessalicis carminibus rati,
tinnitus dedimus. tu fueras labor
et tu causa morae, te dea noctium
dum spectat celeres sustinuit uias.

Vexent hanc faciem frigora parcius,   795
haec solem facies rarius appetat:
lucebit Pario marmore clarius.
quam grata est facies torua uiriliter
et pondus ueteris triste supercili.
Phoebo colla licet splendida compares: 800
illum caesaries nescia colligi
perfundens umeros ornat et integit;
te frons hirta decet, te breuior coma
nulla lege iacens. tu licet asperos
pugnacesque deos uiribus audeas   805
et uasti spatio uincere corporis:
aequas Herculeos nam iuuenis toros,
Martis belligeri pectore latior.
si dorso libeat cornipedis uehi,
frenis Castorea mobilior manu   810
Spartanum poteris flectere Cyllaron.
ammentum digitis tende prioribus
et totis iaculum derige uiribus:
tam longe, dociles spicula figere,
non mittent gracilem Cretes harundinem.   815
aut si tela modo spargere Parthico
in caelum placeat, nulla sine alite
descendent, tepido uiscere condita
praedam de mediis nubibus afferent.

Raris forma uiris (saecula perspice)   820
impunita fuit. te melior deus
tutum praetereat formaque nobilis
deformis senii monstret imaginem.

Will not control her chariot of light.
Indeed lately she blushed, and no dull
Cloud obscured her radiant visage.
And we, alarmed by the goddess' pain,
Thinking her drawn by Thessaly's chants,
Clashed the cymbals. You were her labour,
The cause of her delay; watching you
The goddess of night checked her swift course.

Let the frost more rarely blast your face
And that face more seldom seek the sun,
It'll shine purer than Paros marble.
What grace in that fierce and manly look
And that sombre brow's stern gravity.
With Phoebus your splendid neck compares.
His hair flows streaming over shoulders
Unconfined, ornaments and covers;
You the shaggy brow becomes, short hair
In disarray. With your strength you may
Challenge the fierce and violent gods
And vanquish them with vast body's bulk:
Young you match Hercules in muscles,
Chest wider than warmongering Mars.
Choose to ride on horseback and you would
Handle the reins better than Castor
In controlling Spartan Cyllaros.
Stretch the javelin thong with your fingers
And hurl the weapon with all your power,
It will fly further than well-tutored
Cretan archers shoot the slender reed;
Or if you scattered in Parthian style
The heavens with arrows, none will fall
Without its bird; buried in warm flesh
They'll carry spoils from a clouded sky.

Rare has man's beauty (scan the ages)
Been without cost. May a kinder god
Pass you safely and noble beauty
Show old age's hideous imprint.

ACTVS QVARTVS

CHORVS

Quid sinat inausum feminae praeceps furor?
nefanda iuueni crimina insonti apparat.   825
en scelera! quaerit crine lacerato fidem,
decus omne turbat capitis, umectat genas:
instruitur omni fraude feminea dolus.
    Sed iste quisnam est regium in uultu decus
gerens et alto uertice attollens caput?   830
ut ora iuueni paria Pirithoo gerit,
ni languido pallore canderent genae
staretque recta squalor incultus coma.
en ipse Theseus redditus terris adest.

THESEVS—NVTRIX

THESEVS

Tandem profugi noctis aeternae plagam   835
uastoque manes carcere umbrantem polum,
et uix cupitum sufferunt oculi diem.
iam quarta Eleusin dona Triptolemi secat
paremque totiens libra composuit diem,
ambiguus ut me sortis ignotae labor   840
detinuit inter mortis et uitae mala.
pars una uitae mansit extincto mihi:
sensus malorum. finis Alcides fuit,
qui cum reuulsum Tartaro abstraheret canem,
me quoque supernas pariter ad sedes tulit.   845
sed fessa uirtus robore antiquo caret
trepidantque gressus. heu, labor quantus fuit
Phlegethonte ab imo petere longinquum aethera
pariterque mortem fugere et Alciden sequi.
    Quis fremitus aures flebilis pepulit meas?   850
expromat aliquis. luctus et lacrimae et dolor,
in limine ipso maesta lamentatio?
hospitia digna prorsus inferno hospite.

94

ACT FOUR

CHORUS-LEADER

What would not frantic female passion dare?
She plans to charge this guiltless youth with sin.
What infamy! For proof she tears her hair,
Mars her head's full beauty and floods her cheeks.
The trap is set with every female trick.   *(Enter Theseus)*
   But who is this man who shows in his face
The grace of kings and carries his head high?
How he is like young Pirithous in looks,
Except ashen pallor whitens his cheeks
And his matted hair stiffens with raw filth.
Look, it's Theseus, restored to earth—now here.

THESEUS—NURSE

THESEUS

At last I have fled night's eternal world,
The dead's vast prisonhouse of glooming sky.
My eyes scarce endure the light they longed for.
Four times Eleusis cut Triptolemus'
Gifts, four times Libra brought the equinox,
While a doubtful lot's ambiguous task
Detained me among pains of death and life.
One part of life remained with me when dead:
The sense of pain. Alcides ended it
When he dragged the dog torn from Tartarus
And brought me with him to the upper world.
But my strength is spent, its old vigour gone;
My steps falter. What a labour it's been
From deep Phlegethon to seek the distant sky,
To flee death and to follow Alcides.
   What cry of lamentation struck my ears?
Someone tell me. Sorrow and tears and grief,
Doleful wailing even at my doorstep?
Fit welcome indeed for a guest from hell.
                    (Enter the Nurse from the palace)

NVTRIX

Tenet obstinatum Phaedra consilium necis
fletusque nostros spernit ac morti imminet.   855

THESEVS

Quae causa leti? reduce cur moritur uiro?

NVTRIX

Haec ipsa letum causa maturum attulit.

THESEVS

Perplexa magnum uerba nescio quid tegunt.
effare aperte quis grauet mentem dolor.

NVTRIX

Haut pandit ulli; maesta secretum occulit   860
statuitque secum ferre quo moritur malum.
iam perge, quaeso, perge: properato est opus.

THESEVS

Reserate clausos regii postes laris.

THESEVS—PHAEDRA—NVTRIX tacita

THESEVS

O socia thalami, sicine aduentum uiri
et expetiti coniugis uultum excipis?   865
quin ense uiduas dexteram atque animum mihi
restituis et te quicquid e uita fugat
expromis?

PHAEDRA

Eheu, per tui sceptrum imperi,
magnanime Theseu, perque natorum indolem

NURSE

Phaedra is determined to kill herself.
She rejects our tears and verges on death.

THESEUS

For what reason? Death—as her lord returns?

NURSE

That very reason has hastened her death.

THESEUS

Your riddling words conceal some great matter.
Speak openly. What sorrow loads her mind?

NURSE

She unfolds nothing, hides her secret in tears,
Resolved to take with her the fatal grief.
Now hurry, please, hurry; you must be quick.

THESEUS

Unbar the doors of the royal palace.
> *(The palace doors open to reveal Phaedra*
> *with Hippolytus' sword. Servants and*
> *Guards are present.)*

THESEUS—PHAEDRA—NURSE (silent)

THESEUS

Consort of my bed, is this how you greet
Your lord's return, your longed-for husband's face?
Come now, divorce sword and hand and restore
My spirit. Disclose what is driving you
From life.

PHAEDRA

      O, by your imperial sceptre,
Noble Theseus, and by your children's lives,

97

tuosque reditus perque iam cineres meos,   870
permitte mortem.

THESEVS

Causa quae cogit mori?

PHAEDRA

Si causa leti dicitur, fructus perit.

THESEVS

Nemo istud alius, me quidem excepto, audiet.

PHAEDRA

Aures pudica coniugis solas timet.

THESEVS

Effare: fido pectore arcana occulam.   875

PHAEDRA

Alium silere quod uoles, primus sile.

THESEVS

Leti facultas nulla continget tibi.

PHAEDRA

Mori uolenti desse mors numquam potest.

THESEVS

Quod sit luendum morte delictum indica.

PHAEDRA

Quod uiuo.

THESEVS

Lacrimae nonne te nostrae mouent?   880

By your return and my ashes soon to be,
Permit my death.

THESEUS

What reason impels your death?

PHAEDRA

If death's cause is spoken, its fruit is lost.

THESEUS

Nobody will hear it except for me.

PHAEDRA

Chaste women fear only their husband's ears.

THESEUS

Speak. I'll seal your secret in my faithful heart.

PHAEDRA

When you want silence kept, first silence keep.

THESEUS

No means of death will be given to you.

PHAEDRA

If death is wished, death can never dissent.

THESEUS

Tell me what sin is to be purged by death.

PHAEDRA

That I live.

THESEUS

But surely our tears move you?

PHAEDRA

Mors optima est perire lacrimandum suis.

THESEVS

Silere pergit. uerbere ac uinclis anus
altrixque prodet quicquid haec fari abnuit.
uincite ferro. uerberum uis extrahat
secreta mentis.

PHAEDRA

Ipsa iam fabor, mane.   885

THESEVS

Quidnam ora maesta auertis et lacrimas genis
subito coortas ueste praetenta optegis?

PHAEDRA

Te te, creator caelitum, testem inuoco,
et te, coruscum lucis aetheriae iubar,
ex cuius ortu nostra dependet domus: 890
temptata precibus restiti; ferro ac minis
non cessit animus; uim tamen corpus tulit.
labem hanc pudoris eluet noster cruor.

THESEVS

Quis, ede, nostri decoris euersor fuit?

PHAEDRA

Quem rere minime.

THESEVS

Quis sit audire expeto.   895

PHAEDRA

Hic dicet ensis quem tumultu territus
liquit stuprator ciuium accursum timens.

PHAEDRA

The finest death is to die mourned by kin.

THESEUS

She persists in silence. Chains and the lash
Will make the old nurse betray what this one won't.
(To the Guards) Bind her in irons. Let the whip force out
Her mind's secrets.

PHAEDRA

I'll tell you myself, stop!

THESEUS

Why do you turn your face in grief and hold
Your dress to veil sudden tears on your cheeks?

PHAEDRA

Creator of the gods, I call on you
To be my witness, and on you, bright flame
Of heaven's light from whom our house descends:
Attacked by prayers I resisted; steel and threats
My mind repelled; my body suffered violence.
This stain on honour shall my blood wash out.

THESEUS

Who was it, tell me, defiled our honour?

PHAEDRA

Whom least you'd think.

THESEUS

I want to hear his name.

PHAEDRA

This sword will say. Terrified by the tumult
The rapist left it, fearing the town's approach.

THESEVS

Quod facinus, heu me, cerno? quod monstrum intuor?
regale paruis asperum signis ebur
capulo refulget, gentis Actaeae decus.   900
sed ipse quonam euasit?

PHAEDRA

                    Hi trepidum fuga
uidere famuli concitum celeri pede.

THESEVS

Pro sancta pietas, pro gubernator poli
et qui secundum fluctibus regnum moues,
unde ista uenit generis infandi lues?   905
hunc Graia tellus aluit an Taurus Scythes
Colchusque Phasis? redit ad auctores genus
stirpemque primam degener sanguis refert.
est prorsus iste gentis armiferae furor,
odisse Veneris foedera et castum diu   910
uulgare populis corpus. o taetrum genus
nullaque uictum lege melioris soli.
ferae quoque ipsae Veneris euitant nefas,
generisque leges inscius seruat pudor.
ubi uultus ille et ficta maiestas uiri   915
atque habitus horrens, prisca et antiqua appetens,
morumque senium triste et affectus graues?
o uita fallax, abditos sensus geris
animisque pulchram turpibus faciem induis:
pudor impudentem celat, audacem quies,   920
pietas nefandum; uera fallaces probant
simulantque molles dura. siluarum incola
ille efferatus castus intactus rudis,
mihi te reseruas? a meo primum toro
et scelere tanto placuit ordiri uirum?   925
iam iam superno numini grates ago,
quod icta nostra cecidit Antiope manu,
quod non ad antra Stygia descendens tibi
matrem reliqui. profugus ignotas procul
percurre gentes. te licet terra ultimo   930

102

THESEUS

O, what crime do I see? What monstrous sight?
Royal ivory finely engraved gleams
On the hilt, glory of the Attic house.
But where did he go?

PHAEDRA

These servants saw him
Running quickly away in fearful flight.

THESEUS

O sacrosanct love, O firmament's lord,
And you whose billows shake the second realm,
Whence came this foul infection of our race?
Was he fed by Greek soil or Tauric Scyth
And Colchic Phasis? Race returns to source,
Degenerate blood repeats its primal stock.
This is the rage of that warrior tribe
To loathe Venus' covenants and prostitute
Long-chaste bodies to the crowd. O vile race
Subject to laws of no civilised land.
Even wild beasts shun sin against Venus;
Unconscious shame preserves the laws of birth.
Where is that look and his feigned majesty,
The rough dress that aped pristine, antique ways,
His stern moroseness, his sombre spirit?
O treacherous life, you keep true feelings dark
And clothe hideous minds with fair features:
Shame hides shamelessness; meekness, effrontery;
Piety, heinous sin. Liars praise truth,
Weaklings feign hardihood. Forest-dweller,
Renowned savage, chaste, innocent, untouched,
Do you keep yourself for me? Did you choose
To start manhood with my bed and this sin?
Now, now I give god in heaven my thanks
That Antiope was dead by my hand,
That when I descended to Stygian caves
I left you not your mother. Flee, run far
To unknown nations. Though a distant land

103

summota mundo dirimat Oceani plagis
orbemque nostris pedibus obuersum colas,
licet in recessu penitus extremo abditus
horrifera celsi regna transieris poli,
hiemesque supra positus et canas niues   935
gelidi frementes liqueris Boreae minas
post te furentes, sceleribus poenas dabis.
profugum per omnes pertinax latebras premam.
longinqua clausa abstrusa diuersa inuia
emetiemur, nullus obstabit locus: 940
scis unde redeam. tela quo mitti haud queunt,
huc uota mittam. genitor aequoreus dedit
ut uota prono terna concipiam deo,
et inuocata munus hoc sanxit Styge.
en perage donum triste, regnator freti.   945
non cernat ultra lucidum Hippolytus diem
adeatque manes iuuenis iratos patri.
fer abominandam nunc opem gnato, parens.
numquam supremum numinis munus tui
consumeremus, magna ni premerent mala.   950
inter profunda Tartara et Ditem horridum
et imminentes regis inferni minas,
uoto peperci: redde nunc pactam fidem.
    Genitor, moraris? cur adhuc undae silent?
nunc atra uentis nubila impellentibus   955
subtexe noctem, sidera et caelum eripe,
effunde pontum, uulgus aequoreum cie
fluctusque ab ipso tumidus Oceano uoca.

CHORVS

O magna parens, natura, deum,
tuque igniferi rector Olympi,   960
qui sparsa cito sidera mundo
cursusque uagos rapis astrorum
celerique polos cardine uersas,
cur tanta tibi cura perennes
agitare uias aetheris alti,   965
ut nunc canae frigora brumae

At earth's end keep you beyond Ocean's tracts
And you dwell in the world antipodean,
Though you hide deep in earth's furthest corner
Far across the high north's shuddering realms
And, placed beyond winter and gleaming snow,
Have left icy Boreas' howling threats
Raging behind you, you'll pay for these crimes.
Flee, through every covert I'll cling and press.
The remote, closed, hidden, private, trackless
I shall traverse, no place will impede me:
You know whence I come. Where spears can't be hurled
I'll hurl my curses. My father of the sea
Granted me three prayers with divine consent
And invoked the Styx to sanction this favour.
Now fulfil this grim gift, king of the sea.
Let young Hippolytus see the bright day
No more but meet the dead his father angered.
Render your son this dire service now, sire.
I should never use your divinity's
Last gift, unless grievous ills beset me.
In deep Tartarus and before dread Dis
And the infernal monarch's hounding threats
I forebore this prayer. Keep now your sworn pledge.
    No action, sire? The waters silent still?
Now veil the night with murky clouds impelled
By the winds, wrench stars and heaven from sight,
Disgorge the sea, rouse multitudes from the deep
And summon Ocean's floods to your tumescence.

>   *(Exeunt into the palace apart from the*
>   *Chorus. The doors close.)*

CHORUS

O nature, great mother of gods,
And you, fiery Olympus' lord,
Who through whirling sky pull scattered
Stars and wandering planet's course,
Turn the world on speeding axis,
Why such care to spin eternal
The pathways of the soaring sky,
That now grey winter's frosts denude

nudent siluas, nunc arbustis
redeant umbrae, nunc aestiui
   colla leonis
Cererem magno feruore coquant   970
uiresque suas temperet annus?
sed cur idem qui tanta regis,
sub quo uasti pondera mundi
librata suos ducunt orbes,
hominum nimium securus abes,   975
non sollicitus prodesse bonis,
   nocuisse malis?

Res humanas ordine nullo
fortuna regit sparsitque manu
munera caeca, peiora fouens.   980
uincit sanctos dira libido,
fraus sublimi regnat in aula;
tradere turpi fasces populus
gaudet, eosdem colit atque odit.
tristis uirtus peruersa tulit   985
praemia recti; castos sequitur
mala paupertas uitioque potens
regnat adulter. o uane pudor
   falsumque decus.   988b

ACTVS QVINTVS

CHORVS

Sed quid citato nuntius portat gradu
rigatque maestis lugubrem uultum genis?   990

NVNTIVS—THESEVS

NVNTIVS

O sors acerba et dura, famulatus grauis,
cur me ad nefandi nuntium casus uocas?

The woods, now the plantation's shade
Returns, now the summer lion's
   Neck with fervent
Heat ripens Ceres' grain
And the year tempers its strength?
Why do you who have such power,
Beneath whom the vast world's balanced
Mass drives its wheeling courses,
Stand so far from man indifferent,
Not anxious to reward the good,
   To harm the wicked?

Human life without order
Fortune rules and with blind hand
Scatters gifts, fostering the worst.
Vile lust defeats purity,
Crime reigns in towering courts,
Mobs love to hand authority
To villains, they serve whom they hate.
Grim virtue gains perverse rewards
For honesty; the chaste are dogged
By evil want and, strong in vice,
Adulterers rule. O worthless shame
   And honour false.

ACT FIVE

(Enter Theseus from the palace and a Messenger from the country)

CHORUS-LEADER

But what does that messenger bring in haste?
His grim face is rivered with mournful tears.

MESSENGER—THESEUS

MESSENGER

O bitter, harsh fate, grievous servitude,
Why call me to speak the unspeakable?

THESEVS

Ne metue clades fortiter fari asperas:
non imparatum pectus aerumnis gero.

NVNTIVS

Vocem dolori lingua luctificam negat.   995

THESEVS

Proloquere quae sors aggrauet quassam domum.

NVNTIVS

Hippolytus, heu me, flebili leto occubat.

THESEVS

Gnatum parens obisse iam pridem scio:
nunc raptor obiit. mortis effare ordinem.

NVNTIVS

Vt profugus urbem liquit infesto gradu   1000
celerem citatis passibus cursum explicans,
celso sonipedes ocius subigit iugo
et ora frenis domita substrictis ligat.
tum multa secum effatus et patrium solum
abominatus saepe genitorem ciet   1005
acerque habenis lora permissis quatit—
cum subito uastum tonuit ex alto mare
creuitque in astra. nullus inspirat salo
uentus, quieti nulla pars caeli strepit
placidumque pelagus propria tempestas agit.   1010
non tantus Auster Sicula disturbat freta
nec tam furenti pontus exsurgit sinu
regnante Coro, saxa cum fluctu tremunt
et cana summum spuma Leucaten ferit.
consurgit ingens pontus in uastum aggerem,   1015
tumidumque monstro pelagus in terras ruit.
nec ista ratibus tanta construitur lues:
terris minatur. fluctus haud cursu leui

THESEUS

Fear not. Speak painful disaster boldly.
I have a heart not unprepared for woe.

MESSENGER

My tongue denies the tragic sorrow speech.

THESEUS

Proclaim what fate presses this shattered house.

MESSENGER

Hippolytus —ah! lies in tearful death.

THESEUS

That his son was dead the father long knew;
Now the rapist is dead. Report how he died.

MESSENGER

When he left the city in hostile flight
Dashing swiftly away with speeding steps,
He quickly yokes his high-prancing horses
And bridles fast their heads with tightened reins.
Then talking much to himself and cursing
His native soil, calls often on his father,
Fiercely flings the reins loose and shakes the lash—
When suddenly far out the vast sea thundered
And grew to the stars. No wind blows the sea,
No region of the tranquil heavens roars.
The sea's calm is stirred by a storm from itself,
Wilder than Auster lashing Sicily's strait,
Swelling more furiously than the sea
When Corus reigns and cliffs tremble with waves
And the white spray strikes Leucate's summit.
The huge ocean rises to a vast wall;
Monster-bellied the sea rushes landward.
This towering holocaust is not for ships;
It threatens the land. Heavily the flood

prouoluitur; nescio quid onerato sinu
grauis unda portat. quae nouum tellus caput   1020
ostendit astris? Cyclas exoritur noua?
latuere rupes numine Epidauri dei
et scelere petrae nobiles Scironides
et quae duobus terra comprimitur fretis.
haec dum stupentes querimur, en totum mare   1025
immugit, omnes undique scopuli adstrepunt.
summum cacumen rorat expulso sale,
spumat uomitque uicibus alternis aquas
qualis per alta uehitur Oceani freta
fluctum refundens ore physeter capax.   1030
inhorruit concussus undarum globus
soluitque sese et litori inuexit malum
maius timore, pontus in terras ruit
suumque monstrum sequitur.
                       Os quassat tremor.
quis habitus ille corporis uasti fuit.   1035
caerulea taurus colla sublimis gerens
erexit altam fronte uiridanti iubam.
stant hispidae aures, orbibus uarius color,
et quem feri dominator habuisset gregis
et quem sub undis natus: hinc flammam uomunt 1040
oculi, hinc relucent caerula insignes nota.
opima ceruix arduos tollit toros
naresque hiulcis haustibus patulae fremunt;
musco tenaci pectus ac palear uiret,
longum rubenti spargitur fuco latus;   1045
tum pone tergus ultima in monstrum coit
facies et ingens belua immensam trahit
squamosa partem. talis extremo mari
pistrix citatas sorbet aut frangit rates.
tremuere terrae, fugit attonitum pecus   1050
passim per agros, nec suos pastor sequi
meminit iuuencos; omnis e saltu fera
diffugit, omnis frigido exsanguis metu
uenator horret. solus immunis metu
Hippolytus artis continet frenis equos   1055
pauidosque notae uocis hortatu ciet.
    Est alta ad agros collibus ruptis uia,
uicina tangens spatia supposoti maris:

Rolls forward, the wave carries some burden
In its swollen womb. What new land shows its head
To the stars? Is a new Cyclad now born?
It hid the cliff-haunts of Epidaurus'
God and the far-famed rocks of Sciron's crime,
The land too which the double strait hems in.
While cries stick in our mouths, the whole ocean
Bellows, all the surrounding cliffs roar back.
The wave's high summit drips with driven spray,
It foams and vomits the water by turns,
As a cavernous whale riding Ocean's
Deep waters spouts back the flood from its mouth.
The great ball of water shook, shivered, broke,
And carried shorewards a thing of evil
Worse than terror. The sea rushed to the land
Chasing its monster.
                    My lips still tremble:
The sight of it, that creature's vast body.
Towering there was a bull with dark blue neck
And a lofty mane soaring from green brow.
Its shaggy ears stand stiff, its eyes change hue,
Both that the leader of a wild herd might have,
And that of some sea-born creature—eyes now
Spewing flame, now flashing a wondrous blue.
Bulging muscles ripple on brawny neck
And gaping nostrils roar with draughts of air.
Breast and dewlap shine green with clinging moss
And the long flank is strewn with red lichen.
Then in the rear its final part becomes
A monstrous shape and the huge beast drags scaled
A massive tail. In remote seas just such
A beast swallows or breaks the fastest ships.
The land trembled, the herds fled everywhere
In terror through the fields, herdsmen forgot
To chase their cattle. Every wild beast fled
From its covert, every hunter shivered
Pale with chilling fear. Alone undaunted,
Hippolytus holds his team with tightened reins
And allays their fear with the voice they knew.
  A deep pass opens the hills to the fields,
Touching the land which skirts the sea below.

111

hic se illa moles acuit atque iras parat.
ut cepit animos seque praetemptans satis 1060
prolusit irae, praepeti cursu euolat,
summam citato uix gradu tangens humum,
et torua currus ante trepidantes stetit.
contra feroci gnatus insurgens minax
uultu nec ora mutat et magnum intonat: 1065
"haud frangit animum uanus hic terror meum:
nam mihi paternus uincere est tauros labor."
inobsequentes protinus frenis equi
rapuere currum iamque derrantes uia,
quacumque rabidos pauidus euexit furor, 1070
hac ire pergunt seque per scopulos agunt.
at ille, qualis turbido rector mari
ratem retentat, ne det obliquum latus,
et arte fluctum fallit, haud aliter citos
currus gubernat: ora nunc pressis trahit 1075
constricta frenis, terga nunc torto frequens
uerbere coercet. sequitur adsiduus comes,
nunc aequa carpens spatia, nunc contra obuius
oberrat, omni parte terrorem mouens.
    Non licuit ultra fugere: nam toto obuius 1080
incurrit ore corniger ponti horridus.
tum uero pauida sonipedes mente exciti
imperia soluunt seque luctantur iugo
eripere rectique in pedes iactant onus.
praeceps in ora fusus implicuit cadens 1085
laqueo tenaci corpus et quanto magis
pugnat, sequaces hoc magis nodos ligat.
sensere pecudes facinus, et curru leui,
dominante nullo, qua timor iussit ruunt.
talis per auras non suum agnoscens onus 1090
Solique falso creditum indignans diem
Phaethonta currus deuio excussit polo.
late cruentat arua et inlisum caput
scopulis resultat; auferunt dumi comas,
et ora durus pulchra populatur lapis 1095
peritque multo uulnere infelix decor.
moribunda celeres membra peruoluunt rotae:
tandemque raptum truncus ambusta sude
medium per inguen stipite erecto tenet,

Here that hulk sharpens and prepares its rage.
When it gained its strength, rehearsing fully
And practising its wrath, it flies off quickly
Scarce touching the ground with its rapid strides,
And fierce stood before the quivering team.
Your son responds with a ferocious glare
Rising with threats; gaze steadfast thunders loud:
"This idle terror does not break my spirit;
For to vanquish bulls is my father's trade."
Straightaway his horses defied the reins,
Seized the chariot, veering from the road
They rush wherever raging fear bore them
Frantic, and hurl themselves among the rocks.
But as a helmsman on a heaving sea
Holds fast his ship lest it dip to the waves
And skilfully dupes the deep, so he steers
His flying team. Now pulls their mouths with reins
Tight, now lashing their backs repeatedly
Keeps control. His relentless comrade follows,
Now keeping equal pace, now changing course
To face the team, from all sides bringing fear.
   Further flight was checked. For the ocean's horned
Creature charged full front upon them bristling.
Then the prancing horses crazed with terror
Break command, struggle to tear from the yoke,
Rear up and cast their burden at their feet.
He plunged headlong and entangled his falling
Body in the gripping snare; and the more
He fights, the more he binds the clinging knots.
The beasts felt the deed and, their chariot light
Without its master, rush where fear commands.
So Phaethon's team not knowing their burden,
Angry to see a false Sun with the day,
Hurled him through the air from his devious path.
Far and wide he bloodies the fields; his battered
Head rebounds from rocks; brambles tear his hair,
And the hard stones ravage his handsome face,
His ill-starred beauty destroyed by wound on wound.
The speeding wheels trundle his dying limbs.
At length a tree trunk's charred stake ravishes
And holds him mid-groin on its upright stump.

paulumque domino currus affixo stetit. 1100
haesere biiuges uulnere—et pariter moram
dominumque rumpunt. inde semanimem secant
uirgulta, acutis asperi uepres rubis
omnisque truncus corporis partem tulit.
errant per agros funebris famuli manus, 1105
per illa quae distractus Hippolytus loca
longum cruenta tramitem signat nota,
maestaeque domini membra uestigant canes.
necdum dolentum sedulus potuit labor
explere corpus.

            Hocine est formae decus? 1110
qui modo paterni clarus imperii comes
et certus heres siderum fulsit modo,
passim ad supremos ille colligitur rogos
et funeri confertur.

THESEVS

            O nimium potens,
quanto parentes sanguinis uinclo tenes, 1115
natura, quam te colimus inuiti quoque.
occidere uolui noxium, amissum fleo.

NVNTIVS

Haut flere honeste quisque quod uoluit potest.

THESEVS

Equidem malorum maximum hunc cumulum reor,
si abominanda casus optata efficit. 1120

NVNTIVS

Et si odia seruas, cur madent fletu genae?

THESEVS

Quod interemi non, quod amisi fleo.

The car stopped a moment, its master impaled;
His wound stayed the team. Then they break delay
And master. The thickets rend his half-dead
Body, sharp-pointed spines of thorn-bushes
And every tree trunk shared in his flesh.
A grieving band of servants roams the fields
Through places which the dragged Hippolytus
Marks out with a long trail of bloody signs.
Melancholy hounds track their master's limbs.
Nor has the mourners' careful toil sufficed
To make the body.

(Enter some of Hippolytus' Companions
with fragments of the body)

Is this beauty's glory?

Resplendent companion to his father's throne,
Assured heir, who shone just now like the stars,
Gathered from everywhere for the last fires,
Assembled for his grave.

THESEUS

O too potent

Nature, with what bond of blood you tether
Parents; we serve you even against our will.
Guilty I wished him dead, lost I mourn him.

MESSENGER

No one can rightly weep for what he wished.

THESEUS

I think this the summit of adversity
If fortune makes what should be loathed desired.

MESSENGER

If hate remains, why wet your cheeks with tears?

THESEUS

I weep not that I killed, but that I lost him.

(All remain on stage)

115

CHORVS

Quanti casus humana rotant.
minor in paruis fortuna furit
leuiusque ferit leuiora deus;   1125
seruat placidos obscura quies
praebetque senes casa securos.

Admota aetheriis culmina sedibus
Euros excipiunt, excipiunt Notos,
    insani Boreae minas   1130
    imbriferumque Corum.
raros patitur fulminis ictus
    umida uallis.
tremuit telo Iouis altisoni
Caucasus ingens Phrygiumque nemus   1135
matris Cybeles; metuens caelo
Iuppiter alto uicina petit.
non capit umquam magnos motus
humilis tecti plebeia domus;
    circa regna tonat.   1140

Volat ambiguis mobilis alis
hora, nec ulli praestat uelox
fortuna fidem. hic qui clari
    iterum uidet   1143b
sidera mundi nitidumque diem
morte relicta, luget maestos   1145
tristis reditus ipsoque magis
flebile Auerno sedis patriae
    uidet hospitium.

Pallas Actaeae ueneranda genti,
quod tuus caelum superosque Theseus   1150
spectat et fugit Stygias paludes,
casta nil debes patruo rapaci:
constat inferno numerus tyranno.

CHORUS

How man spins on chance's wheel.
Among the low fortune rages
Less, god lightly smites the little;
Dim peace protects quiet souls,
The cottage gives carefree age.

But the roofs assaulting heaven's heights
Receive Eurus' blasts, receive Notus,
    Boreas' mad threats
    And rain-filled Corus.
Thunder's stroke is seldom felt
    By dew-moist vale.
But high-roaring Jupiter's bolt
Shakes great Caucasus and mother
Cybele's Phrygian grove; in fear
Jove seeks high heaven's neighbours.
His mighty blasts are never felt
By low-roofed plebeian home;
    Around thrones he thunders.

On doubtful wings flies fickle
The hour, swift fortune holds faith
With no one. Here's a man who sees
    Once more the bright
World's stars and shining day,
Death behind him, but grimly mourns
His sad return, sees a welcome
In his father's house more doleful
    Than Avernus.

Pallas adored by Athens' race,
That your Theseus sees sky and earth
And fled the Stygian pit, you owe,
Pure one, your uncle's greed nothing.
For hell's king the numbers tally.

ACTVS SEXTVS

CHORVS

Quae uox ab altis flebilis tectis sonat
strictoque uecors Phaedra quid ferro parat? 1155

THESEVS—PHAEDRA—CHORVS

THESEVS

Quis te dolore percitam instigat furor?
quid ensis iste quidue uociferatio
planctusque supra corpus inuisum uolunt?

PHAEDRA

Me me, profundi saeue dominator freti,
inuade et in me monstra caerulei maris 1160
emitte, quicquid intimo Tethys sinu
extrema gestat, quicquid Oceanus uagis
complexus undis ultimo fluctu tegit.
o dure Theseu semper, o numquam tuis
tuto reuerse: gnatus et genitor nece 1165
reditus tuos luere; peruertis domum
amore semper coniugum aut odio nocens.
   Hippolyte, tales intuor uultus tuos
talesque feci? membra quis saeuus Sinis
aut quis Procrustes sparsit aut quis Cresius, 1170
Daedalea uasto claustra mugitu replens,
taurus biformis ore cornigero ferox
diuulsit? heu me, quo tuus fugit decor
oculique nostrum sidus? exanimis iaces?
ades parumper, uerbaque exaudi mea. 1175
nil turpe loquimur: hac manu poenas tibi
soluam et nefando pectori ferrum inseram,
animaque Phaedram pariter ac scelere exuam;
et te per undas perque Tartareos lacus,
per Styga, per amnes igneos amens sequar. 1180
   Placemus umbras: capitis exuuias cape

118

ACT SIX

CHORUS-LEADER

What howl of grief sounds from the high palace?
*(Enter Phaedra with the sword of
Hippolytus in her hand)*
And Phaedra—sword in hand, frantic. But why?

THESEUS—PHAEDRA—CHORUS

THESEUS

What demented passion stirs you to grief?
What do this sword and protestation mean
And this wailing over a hated corpse?

PHAEDRA

Me, me, savage master of unplumbed sea,
Enter me. Into me send the blue sea's
Monsters, all that distant Tethys bears deep
In her womb, all that Ocean's restless waves
Embrace and bury in his furthest flood.
Ever brutal Theseus, never returning
To kin without harm. Your son's and sire's death
Paid for your returns. You destroy your house
Through love of wife or hate, baneful always.
   Hippolytus, is this your face I see,
This what I made it? What cruel Sinis
Or Procrustes savaged you, what Cretan
Bull loud-bellowing in Daedalean
Jail, ferocious-faced horn-sprouting mongrel,
Ripped you apart? O, where has your beauty fled
And eyes that were my stars? Do you lie dead?
Come back a little while and hear my words.
I speak no baseness. With this hand I'll pay
My debt to you, thrust sword in sinful breast
And so strip Phaedra of both life and sin.
Then you through waters and Tartarean lakes,
Through Styx, through streams of fire—mad, I'll follow.
   Let us placate the dead. Take spoils from my head

119

laceraeque frontis accipe abscisam comam.
non licuit animos iungere, at certe licet
iunxisse fata.
                    Morere, si casta es, uiro;
si incesta, amori. coniugis thalamos petam   1185
tanto impiatos facinore? hoc derat nefas,
ut uindicato sancta fruereris toro.
o mors amoris una sedamen mali,
o mors pudoris maximum laesi decus,
confugimus ad te: pande placatos sinus.   1190
    Audite, Athenae, tuque, funesta pater
peior nouerca: falsa memoraui et nefas,
quod ipsa demens pectore insano hauseram,
mentita finxi. uana punisti pater,
iuuenisque castus crimine incesto iacet,   1195
pudicus, insons.
                    Recipe iam mores tuos.
mucrone pectus impium iusto patet
cruorque sancto soluit inferias uiro.

THESEVS

Quid facere rapto debeas gnato parens
disce a nouerca: condere Acherontis plagis.   1200

Pallidi fauces Auerni, uosque, Taenarii specus,
unda miseris grata Lethes, uosque, torpentes lacus,
impium rapite atque mersum premite perpetuis malis.
nunc adeste, saeua ponti monstra, nunc uastum mare,
ultimo quodcumque Proteus aequorum abscondit sinu,   1205
meque ouantem scelere tanto rapite in altos gurgites,
tuque, semper, genitor, irae facilis assensor meae.
morte facili dignus haud sum qui noua natum nece
segregem sparsi per agros quique, dum falsum nefas
exsequor uindex seuerus, incidi in uerum scelus.   1210
sidera et manes et undas scelere compleui meo.
amplius sors nulla restat: regna me norunt tria.

    In hoc redimus? patuit ad caelum uia,
bina ut uiderem funera et geminam necem,

And accept this wounded brow's severed lock.
We could not unite our hearts, we can at least
Unite our fates.
(To herself)   Die—for your lord, if chaste;
If unchaste, for your love. Seek a husband's couch
Defiled by such crime? This one sin I lacked:
To claim and enjoy the marriage-bed, pure.
O death, sole remedy of wicked love,
O death, great ornament of blighted shame,
We fly to you; spread your merciful arms.
    Hear me, O Athens, and you, father worse
Than murderous stepmother: I lied, and sin
Which I myself conceived in mad heart crazed
Falsely alleged. You punished vainly, father,
And this pure youth lies here impurely charged,
Chaste, innocent.
(To Hippolytus)   Now receive your honour back.
To the just sword my impious breast opens,
Blood pays the death-dues for a sinless man.

                                        (She stabs herself)

THESEUS

A father's duty to a ravaged son
Let his stepmother teach: tomb yourself in hell.

Jaws of pallid death and you, caverns of Taenarus,
Balm of the damned, Lethe's stream, and you, the stagnant pools,
Ravage this impious man, sink him in ceaseless pain.
Come, savage monsters of the deep, come, endless sea,
And all that Proteus hides in ocean's furthest womb,
For my evil triumph snatch me to your deep abyss,
And help them, father, ever compliant with my wrath.
I deserve no easy end, creator of new death
Scattering dismembered son afield, stern avenger
Who hunting fictitious sin committed the true crime.
Stars, shades and ocean I have sated with my sins.
No region now remains: all three kingdoms know me.

    Returned I for this? Was a path cleared skywards
To see two funerals and double death,

121

caelebs et orbus funebres una face   1215
ut concremarem prolis ac thalami rogos?
donator atrae lucis, Alcide, tuum
Diti remitte munus; ereptos mihi
restitue manes. impius frustra inuoco
mortem relictam. crudus et leti artifex,   1220
exitia machinatus insolita effera,
nunc tibimet ipse iusta supplicia irroga.
pinus coacto uertice attingens humum
caelo remissum findat in geminas trabes,
mittarue praeceps saxa per Scironia?   1225
grauiora uidi, quae pati clausos iubet
Phlegethon nocentes igneo cingens uado:
quae poena memet maneat et sedes, scio.
umbrae nocentes, cedite et ceruicibus
his, his repositum degrauet fessas manus   1230
saxum, seni perennis Aeolio labor.
me ludat amnis ora uicina alluens;
uultur relicto transuolet Tityo ferus
meumque poenae semper accrescat iecur.
et tu mei requiesce Pirithoi pater: 1235
haec incitatis membra turbinibus ferat
nusquam resistens orbe reuoluto rota.
dehisce tellus, recipe me dirum chaos,
recipe; haec ad umbras iustior nobis uia est:
gnatum sequor. ne metue qui manes regis: 1240
casti uenimus. recipe me aeterna domo
non exiturum.
               Non mouent diuos preces;
at, si rogarem scelera, quam proni forent.

CHORVS

Theseu, querelis tempus aeternum manet;
nunc iusta nato solue et absconde ocius   1245
dispersa foede membra laniatu effero.

THESEVS

Huc, huc reliquias uehite cari corporis
pondusque et artus temere congestos date.
Hippolytus hic est? crimen agnosco meum.

122

That bereaved and widowed with but one torch
I might light the death-pyres of son and wife?
Alcides, giver of black light, return
Your boon to Dis; restore me to the dead
I lost. Impious prayer and vain—to call
For the death I fled. Brutal craftsman of blood,
Creator of death savage and unknown,
Now inflict on yourself just punishment.
Should the top of a pine forced to the ground
Split me in two as it shoots to heaven,
Or should I drop headlong from Sciron's cliff?
Worse things I saw Phlegethon bid sinners
Suffer, enclosed in its circle of fire.
What penalty and place await me, I know.
Make way you sinful dead, and on my neck,
Mine, as burden for these wearied hands, place
The rock, the old Aeolian's constant toil.
Let elusive streams mock my nearby lips;
Let Tityos' fierce vulture fly to me
And my liver grow endlessly for pain.
And you, father of my Pirithous, rest:
Let mine be the body on the ever
Turning wheel as its swift revolutions whirl.
Gape earth, receive me awful emptiness,
Receive. My path to death is juster now:
I follow my son. Fear not, death's king, we come
Chaste. Receive me in your eternal house,
Never to escape.
        My prayers move no gods.
But if I prayed for sin, how prompt they'd be.

CHORUS-LEADER

Theseus, eternity awaits your complaints.
Now give your son his rites and quickly hide
His foul dismembered limbs savagely torn.

THESEUS

Bring here, here, that precious body's remains;
Give me the heavy, random mass of limbs.
Hippolytus...this? I recognise my guilt.

123

ego te peremi; neu nocens tantum semel   1250
solusue fierem, facinus ausurus parens
patrem aduocaui: munere en patrio fruor.
o triste fractis orbitas annis malum.
complectere artus, quodque de nato est super,
miserande, maesto pectore incumbens foue.   1255
disiecta, genitor, membra laceri corporis
in ordinem dispone et errantes loco
restitue partes. fortis hic dextrae locus,
hic laeua frenis docta moderandis manus
ponenda; laeui lateris agnosco notas.   1260
quam magna lacrimis pars adhuc nostris abest.
durate trepidae lugubri officio manus,
fletusque largos sistite, arentes genae,
dum membra nato genitor adnumerat suo
corpusque fingit. hoc quid est forma carens   1265
et turpe, multo uulnere abruptum undique?
quae pars tui sit dubito; sed pars est tui.
hic, hic repone, non suo, at uacuo loco.
haecne illa facies igne sidereo nitens,
inimica flectens lumina? huc cecidit decor?   1270
o dira fata, numinum o saeuus fauor.
sic ad parentem natus ex uoto redit.
    En haec suprema dona genitoris cape,
saepe efferendus; interim haec ignes ferant.
    Patefacite acerbam caede funesta domum.   1275
Mopsopia claris tota lamentis sonet.
uos apparate regii flammam rogi;
at uos per agros corporis partes uagas
inquirite.
           Istam terra defossam premat,
grauisque tellus impio capiti incubet.   1280

I killed you. And lest I sin alone or once,
Intending a father's crime, I invoked
A father's aid. This is my father's gift.
O bereavement, grim blight on broken years.
Embrace these limbs, and what's left of your son
Kneel, vile wretch, and clutch to sorrowing breast.
Set in order, father, the dispersed limbs
Of this torn body; return to their place
The scattered parts. His strong right hand goes here,
Here put his left hand which controlled the reins
With skill; I recognise signs of his left side.
But how great the part still lacking our tears.
Endure, my trembling hands, this sad service;
Be dry, cheeks, restrain these copious tears
While a father counts out his own son's limbs
And constructs his body. What's this ugly,
Misshapen thing, torn with wounds on all sides?
Which part I know not; but it's part of you.
Put it here, here—not in its place but a void.
Is this the face that shone with starry fire,
Turned hostile eyes aside? This that beauty set?
O perverse fate, O savage favour of gods.
See how a father's prayer brings back a son.
    Accept from your father these final gifts.
Many death-biers wait you. Meanwhile fire take this.
    Open the dismal palace sour with death.
All Attica resound with loud lament.
You prepare the flames of the royal pyre;
You search the fields for parts of the body
Astray.
(Points to Phaedra) This one—earth press deep upon her,
And soil lie heavy on her impious head.

        (Exeunt)

SELECTIVE CRITICAL APPARATUS

The text of Seneca's tragedies is preserved in two distinct branches: E and A. Neither is to be preferred in respect of authority. The main ms. of the E branch is the eleventh century "codex Etruscus" (E), housed in the Laurentian Library in Florence, from which all succeeding members of the E branch are derived. The A branch exists in two subdivisions: delta and beta. Its main mss. are: (delta) P (early thirteenth century) and T (early fifteenth century—recently reappraised by MacGregor, see Bibliog.), both to be found in the Bibliothèque Nationale in Paris; (beta) C (early thirteenth century), now in the library of Corpus Christi College Cambridge, and S (fourteenth century), now in the Biblioteca Real, Escorial. The text of *Phaedra* in this edition is based essentially on these five mss. I have consulted E and C both *in situ* and on photographs, and P, T and S on microfilm. For the readings of other mss. and the conjectures of scholars I have relied primarily on the apparatuses of Woesler, Giardina and Zwierlein. Since a full critical apparatus would be inappropriate to the format of this series, for simplicity's sake I have noted all places where I have adopted a reading other than E, indicating its source and the reading of E which it replaces, and elsewhere selective (important) EA disagreements. Where I have accepted the reading of a ms. other than EPTCS or the conjecture of a scholar, the readings of both E and A are given. Trivial spelling mistakes or variants have not been recorded. Appendix III lists the departures from Zwierlein's Oxford text of 1986.

SIGLA

E	Florence, Biblioteca Medicea-Laurenziana. Plut. Lat. 37.13 (*Codex Etruscus*). Late eleventh century.
P	Paris, Bibliothèque Nationale. Lat. 8260. Thirteenth century (first half).
C	Cambridge, Corpus Christi College 406. Early thirteenth century.
S	Escorial, Biblioteca Real. 108 T III 11. Fourteenth century (second half).
T	Paris, Bibliothèque Nationale. Lat. 8031. Fifteenth century.
A	Consensus of *PTCS*.
r	Rome (Vatican City), Biblioteca Apostolica Vaticana. Reg. Lat. 1500. Written 1389.
K	Cambrai, Bibliothèque Municipale 555. Early to middle fourteenth century.
Q	Monte Cassino, Biblioteca dell' Abbazia 392P. About 1350.
e	Eton, College Library 110. About 1350.
recc.	More recent mss.

E^2, E^3 etc. indicate a second or third hand. E^1 is E's original scribe. Where conjectures are given the name of the scholar believed to be the first to have made the conjecture follows. *Edd.* = editors.

4 saxa solo caparnetho *PTC* saxosa loca parnetho E **5** Thriasiis *Scoppa* tristis E thyasis A **11** qua ES^2 que A **13(14)** per graciles leuis Ilisos *Pontanus* breuis *Axelson* per glaciles leuis illissos E per...il *omitted A* meander super inequales C^2T^2 **17** qua marathon A quem arathon E **19** gregibus ET^2S^2 regibus A **22** Acharneus *Gronouius* acharnan E **24** aphidnas r^2 (*Auentius*) ep(h)idnas PT^1CS apidanas T^2 athytnas E **28** Phyle *Frenzel* flius E philippis A **39** demissi A dimissi E **40** captent A capient E **45** portare ET^2 rotare *PCS* **48** uibretur E libretur A **60** cret(h)eas A cresseas E **62** figis A figit E **65** uri E tauri A **67** *Before 68 in E after 68 in A* **71** *Placed after 68 by Leo after 70 in EA* **77** gementi E trementi A **81** faues *recc.* faue EA **88** peruium *TCS* peruius EP **102** aetneo E ethneus A **103** antro A andro E; telae E tela A **106** choris A choros E **112** anime A animae E **123** promittet E promittat A **124** perosa A perosam E; uenus A nemus *corrected to* uenus E^{2-3} **138-39** *Assigned to Nurse in recc., to Phaedra in EA* **140** honesta *Heinsius* non ista E obstare A **148** ferre perpetuam A ferri perpetuain E **155** quid ille A quid ille quid ille E **162** conscius E conscie A; mentis *EPT* noctis *CS* **171** gnati A gnata *changed to* gnato E^{2-3} **174** fratris A patris E **186** pollet E regnat A; impotens *Heinsius* potens EA **187** lesumque E ipsumque A **190** furentes A furentis E **195** fauens A (*Augustine contr. faust. 20.9*) furens E **198** omnes A omnis E **208** uilis A ullus E **213** coercent *most edd.* coernent E co(h)ercet A **216** preditam A perditam E **218** fero A puto E **227** est A *omitted E* **233-35** *Assigned to Phaedra in E, to Nurse in A* **236-37** *Assigned to Nurse in A, to Phaedra in E* **238-39** *Assigned to Nurse in EA* **239** haud ES^2 aut *PTC* **240** A *assigns* ferus est *to Nurse* amore...feros *to Phaedra* E *assigns whole line to Phaedra* **241b** fugiet E fugiat A **246** splendidas A splendida E **249** pars A par E **250** ingenuo A ingenio *corrected to* ingenuo E^1 **255** mentis E mortis A **256** uita A ultra E **262** sic ET^2 si A **264** *Omitted A* **Before 274** CHORVS.GRESSAE E Chorus A **274** generata EC (g)nata *PTS* **277** l.p. et renidens E p.l. et acre nitens P^2TCS **278** moderatur E spiculatur P iaculatur *TCS* **279-80** *Omitted A* **282** uorat E uocat A **285** ora E hora A **288** parrhasiae E maioris A **290** estus A hestus E **300** ducit A fecit E **302** uocem *recc.* uoce EA **305** noua E mala A **325** uidit A uidi E **326** deiecta A reiecta E **330** lesis A laesi E **331** salo E mari A **332** ethereo A per ipsum E **333** mundo A mundum E **334** hac *PT* h(a)ec *ECS* **336** cerulus A peruius E; grex A rex E **339** instinctus suscipit audax E instincti quam magna gerunt A **340** iuuencus E iuuenci A **355** quid plura canam A *omitted E* **359** *Here in EPT, after 340 in CS*; ecquis P et quis *ETC* **Before 360** NVTRIX. PHAEDRA.CHORVS E Nutrix.phedra A **360** leniri A lenire E **365** nil

A nichil *E*   383 imbre *TCS* ymbre *P* hymbrae *E*   379 ferebant *E* tenebant
A   382 irrigantur *E* nigrantur *A*   383 percussae *E* perfuse *A*   392 aures
A auris *E*   401 tanaitis *PTS* tanais alti *E*   404 *Assigned to Chorus in E, to
Nurse in A*   405 *Here in E, after 359 in PT, before 341 in CS*   **Before 406**
Nutrix.ypolitus *C* (H)yp(p)olitus.Nutrix *EPTS*   411 uice *E* face *A*   412 en
ades *TS* en adeis *P* aenades *E*   414 *Here in E, after 415 in A*   428 audere *E*
audire *A*;   iussa qui regis *Heinsius* iusta qui reges *EA*   429 omne et *Heinsius*
omne *EA*   438 anxiam *A* anxia *E*   439 domas *E* grauas *A*   440 ille cum
uenia est *E* hic quidem uiuat *A*   441 at si quis *TCS* aut si quis *E*$^{2-3}$ *from
antiquis E*   444 noctibus *E* montibus *PCS*   449 cursus *E* lusus *PCS*
454 coherces *A* cohercets *E*   464 domitent *E* doment *A*   467 manus *E*
minas *A*   470 restituit *A* restituet *E*; exhaustum *E* humanum *A*   475 leti *A*
loeti *E*   477 ista *Leo* fata *EA*;   desse *S* deesse *PTC* de esse *E*   482 coetus *A*
coetum *E*   492 haud *E* aut *A*   494 sata *Trevet, Heinsius* sita *EA*   496 non
E aut *A*   498 suffigit *A* sufficit *E*   504 iliso *P* yliso *T* eliso *E*   505 celeris
alphei *A* celerisale et *E*   516 uulsa *E* pulsa *A*   522 obscuro *A* obscura *E*
527 profudit *TCS* perfudit *EP*   537 feta *PTC* foeta *E*   541 preceps *A*
precesp *E*   543 cruenta factus *E* cruentum facinus *A*   552 omnes *A* omnis
E   558 mitius nil *CS* micius nichil *E*   559 haec *E* et *A*   560 huius *E* cuius
A;   inceste *A* incesti *E*   565 cur *A* cor *E*   566 omnes *A* omnis *E*   567
durus *EPCS* dirus *T*   **Before 574** Nutrix *CS omitted but added in the margin
by another hand in E*   579 omnes *A* omnis *E*   582 *A, whole line unreadable
in E*   584 uerget *A* uergit *E*   585 accidit *E* cadit *A*   588 alumna *E*
alumnus *A*   **Before 589** p(h)edra.hippolitus (ypo- *P* hypo- *S*).nutrix *PTS*
PHAEDRA ET IDEM *E*   591 *Assigned to Hippolytus in E, to Phaedra in A*
595 serus *ET*^{2} seruus *PCS*   598 honesta *A* non ista *E*   600 secretus *A*
secretas *E*   601 *Assigned to Hippolytus in E, to Phaedra in A*   604 omnes *A*
omnis *E*   607 curc *E* aure *A*   619 urbium *E* patris *A*   632 merebor *E*
tuebor *A*   641 amorque torret intimas seuus uorat *A* amore torret intimis
ferit ferus *E*^{1} amorque torret intima ferus uorat *E*^{2} 642 *Contained in A
omitted E*   651 uitte *TCS*^{2} uitae *EP*   652 pudor *E* rubor *A*   654 tuaeque
Bothe tu(a)eue *EA*   655 tuusue *Bothe* tuusque *EA*   658 est genitor *Heinsius*
et genitor *EA*;   totus *E* toruus *A*   662 neuisset *CST*^{2} neuidisset *E*
663 siderei *A* syderea *E*   669 mutor *E* mittor *A*;   descendi *A* discendi *E*
671b-97 *Assigned to Hippolytus in A, to Phaedra E*^{1} *(corrected in the margin E*^{3}*)*
673 emittes *TCS* emittis *EP*   674 si *E* sic *A*   676 uersa *A* uestra *E*
677 tuque sidereum *A* tuquae syderium *E*   678 titan tu *A* tantum ne *E*
691 biformi *edd.* biformis *A* triformi *E*   695 *Omitted A*   696 inuideo *ET*
inuidet *PCS*   702 agar *E* sequar *A*   707 en *A* et *E*   710 facis *A* facies *E*
711 sanas *E* sana *A*   712 saluo *A* soluo *E*   714 contactus *E* contractus *A*
719 anime *A* animae *E*   729 trepida *A* trepidam *E*   733 perferte *E* referte
A   734 quid *A* quit *E*;   lacerans *A* laceras *E*   740 porrigit *E* corripit *A*
747 exerit *A* exeret *E*   755 pampinea *PTS* panpinea *EC*   759 omnes *Ke*
omnis *EA*   768 ut lilia *E* lilia *A*   769 rose *A* comae *E*   770 et *Richter* ut

EA; genis *A* genus *changed to* genis *E*   **775** te *E* sed *A*; subruit *KQ recc.*
subruet *EA*   **780-81** *Arranged as three lines EA*: c.t.l./ N.i.f.s./ c.f.
780 cingent *Richter* cinget *A* cingnet *E*   **784** panas quae driades montiuagos
petunt *E* montiuagiue panes *A*   **788** en *KQ¹e¹* et *EA*   **790** numine *E*
lumine *A*   **805** audeas *E* arceas *A*   **807** iuuenis *A* iuuenes *E*   **809** libeat *E*
liceat *A*   **810** mobilior *A* nobilior *E*   **817-18** *Arranged as here E, as three
lines A*: i.c.p./ n.s.a.d.t./ u.c.   **817** alite *A* aue *E*   **820** perspice *E* prospice *A*
823 senii *A* seni *E¹*; monstret imaginem *E* limina transeat *A*   **825** insonti *A*
insomti *E*   **828** omni *E* omnis *A*   **829** quisnam *A* quidnam *E*   **837** et *E* ut
A   **838** triptolemi *PTS* treptolemi *E*   **844** reuulsum *A* reuulso *E*
860 haut *A* aut *E*   **863** *Assigned to Theseus in A, to the Nurse in E*   **Before**
864 THESEVS.PHAEDRA.NVTRIX TACITA *E* Theseus.phedra *A*   **867**
quicquid e *E* quod quidem *PCS*   **868** imperi *edd.* imperii *EA*   **873-75**
Assigned as here in E, all three lines to Theseus in A   **877** continget *A*
contingnet *E*   **878** desse *P* deesse *ETCS*   **880** *Assigned as here in E, whole
line to Phaedra in A*   **881-85a** *Assigned as here in E, to Theseus in A*
883 prodet *PTC* prodest *E*   **887** coortas *E* obortas *PTS*   **893** eluet *E* elauet
A   **897** liquit *A* liquid *E*   **900** gentis *A* generis *E*   **901** *Assigned as here in
E, whole line assigned to Phaedra in TCS (corrected T²)*   **904** fluctibus...
moues *E* in fluctibus...tenes *A*   **907** colchusque phasis *A* cholchusque phisis
E   **908** stirpemque *A* strirpemque *E*   **909** armifere *E* armigere *A*
912 nullaque *E* nulla *P* non ulla *TCS*; uictum *ET* uinctum *PCS*   **919**
turpibus *E* turbidus *A*   **926** *Omitted A*   **937** post te *A* poste *E*   **938**
omnes *A* omnis *E*   **939** longinqua *A* longinquam *E*   **941-42** *As here in E,*
scis unde redeam *and* huc uota mittam *transposed in A*   **947** iratos patri *E*
irato patre *A*   **949** supremum *KQ²*...suppremum *EA*   **958** ipso *A* ipsos *E*;
tumidus *CS* tumidos *E*   **964** perennes *C* perhennes *EPS*   **965** alti *ET²* acti
PCS   **966-78** *Here in A, after 990 in E (corrected E¹)*   **966** ut *A* et *E*
967-70 *Arranged E*: n.s.n.a./ r.u.n.ae./ c.l.C./ m.f.c. *arranged A*: n.s./ n.a.r.u./
n.ae.c.l./ C.m.f.c.   **975** abes *E* ades *A*   **979** manu *A* manum *E*
983 fasces *A* fasce *E*   **988-88b** *Arranged as here E arranged A*: r.a./ o.v.p.f.d.
988 uane *A* uani *E*   **990** rigatque maestis...genis *E* restatque mestus...
gerens *A*   **991** grauis *A* graues *E*   **992** nefandi *A* nefandum *E*; uocas *A*
uocat *E*   **993** clades *A* cladis *E*   **994** gero *A* fero *E*   **995** luctificam
Gronouius luctifica *EA*   **996** quassam *A* luctificam *E*   **996** sors *CS* fors
EPT   **997** l(o)eto occubat *ET²* uoto accubat *PCS*   **999** nunc *EP* non *TCS*
1000 liquit *A* liquid *E*   **1002** celso *Heinsius* celsos *EA*   **1008** salo *A* solo *E*
1013 coro *P* choro *ETCS*   **1020** caput *CST²* capud *E*   **1022** rupes *E* nube
A; numine *Leo* numen *EA*   **1025** querimur *A* quaerimus *E*   **1026**
adstrepunt *PT* astrepunt *ECS*   **1027** rorat *PCS* rotat *E*   **1033** maius *A*
maius malum *E*   **1034** os *recc.* hos *A* ossa *E*   **1035** *Assigned to Theseus in*
A   **1036** cerulea *E* herculea *A*   **1038** aures *A* auris *E*; orbibus *E* cornibus
A   **1041** insignes *Gronouius* insignis *EA*   **1044** *Omitted E¹(added in*
margin by later hand)   **1045** rubenti *A* rubente *E*; fuco *E* su(c)co *A*

1049 frangit *E* reddit *PTC*   **1053** diffugit *E* discessit *A*; omnis *E omitted A*
1057 agros *E* argos *A*   **1058** uicina *A* uicini *E*   **1070** quacumque *A*
quaquumque *E*; rabidos pauidus *E* pauidos rapidus *A*   **1075** trahit *PC*
thrahit *E*   **1079-80** *Omitted A*   **1081** *Omitted but added in margin E*[1]
1085 fusus *E* gnatus *A*   **1099** erecto *Trevet* eiecto *A* iecto *E*   **1102**
semianimē *A* semianimen *E*   **1105** funebris *A* funebres *E*   **1115** quanto
ET[2] natura *PCS*   **1118** haut flere honeste *PC* h a odere non est *E*; potest *A*
potens *E*   **1120** optata *A* optanda *E*   **1129** euros...notos *E* duros excipiunt
not(h)os *A*   **1131** Corum *edd.* chorum *EA*   **1135** nemus *A* noemus *E*
1143-44 *Lacuna assumed in E by Leo between 1143 and 1144 for which edd.*
suggest iterum uidet *or* laetus uidet *as possible supplements* fortuna fidem./
qui clara uidet sidera mundi *A* *Zwierlein places the lacuna after 1144*
Before **1156** Theseus.phedra.chorus *A* THESEVS PHAEDRA ET IDEM *E*
1161 Tethys *edd.* thethis *E* t(h)etis *A*   **1164** tuis *A* ad tuos *E*   **1169** quis *A*
qui *E*; Sinis *Gronouius* cinis *ECS* citus *PT*   **1176** hac *A* hoc *E*   **1178**
Phaedram *E* memet *A*   **1184** casta es *A* castes *E*   **1186** impiatos *A*
impletos *E*   **1188-89** una...pudoris *omitted A*   **1194** uana *E* falsa *A*
1195 incesto *E* incerto *PCS*   **1199-1200** *Assigned to Theseus in E, to Phaedra*
in A   **1201** tenarei *A* tenerai *E*   **1205** sinu *A* sinum *E*   **1207** assensor *A*
ascensor *E*   **1208** facili dignus haud *E* dignum (dignus *P*) facinus ausus *A*
1210 seuerus...scelus *E* scelestus...nefas *TCS*   **1211** scelere *A* sceleri *E*
1215 face *A* face *changed from* fioce *or* uoce *E*[1]   **1221** effera *E* efferar *A*
1222 irroga *ET*[2] irrogo *A*   **1227** cingens *A* cingnens *E*   **1234** accrescat
TCS accressat *changed to* accrescat *E*[1]   **1249** crimen agnosco *E* facinus
cognosco *A*   **1251** fierem *A* flerem *E*   **1256-80** *Assigned to Theseus in A, to*
the Chorus in E   **1258** dextr(a)e *ET*[2] humeri *PT*[1]*CS*   **1259** leua *ET*[2] dextra
PCS   **1265** quid *E* quidem *A*   **1266** abruptum *E* ambesum *A*   **1271** fauor
E furor *A*   **1273** en *A* een *E*; dona *E* uota *A*

131

NOTES

The following notes are exegetic and analytic. Their primary aim is to provide the reader with literary, historical, geographical, mytho-logical and (especially for the Latin student) linguistic information relevant to an understanding of the play. Literary interpretation as such has generally been excluded (for which see the Introduction), but related incidents in the play and the thematic repetition of words and phrases have often been noted. That Seneca's particular dramatisation (rewriting) of the myth and relationship to the poetic and dramatic tradition may be apparent, especial attention has been given to the treatment of the story in Euripides, Ovid and Racine, and to the play's allusions to Virgil. Attention has also been given to *Phaedra*'s relationship to other Senecan dramatic texts not only for their bearing on *Phaedra*, but that this edition may function in part as an introduction to Seneca *tragicus*. Lemmata in bold are from the translation, in bold italics from the Latin text.

Abbreviations

The following abbreviations have been used for Seneca's works.
Tragedies:

Ag.	*Agamemnon*
HF	*Hercules Furens*
Med.	*Medea*
Oed.	*Oedipus*
Pha.	*Phaedra*
Pho.	*Phoenissae*
Thy.	*Thyestes*
Tro.	*Troades*

(also *HO* = [Sen.] *Hercules Oetaeus*, *Oct.* = [Sen.] *Octauia*)

Prose works:

Apoc.	*Apocolocyntosis*
Ben.	*De Beneficiis* ("On Benefits")
Brev.	*De Breuitate Vitae* ("On the Shortness of Life")
Clem.	*De Clementia* ("On Clemency")
Const.	*De Constantia* ("On Firmness")
Ep.	*Epistulae Morales Ad Lucilium* ("Moral Epistles")
Helv.	*Ad Heluiam De Consolatione* ("To Helvia on Consolation")
Ira	*De Ira* ("On Anger")
Marc.	*Ad Marciam De Consolatione* ("To Marcia on Conso-lation")
NQ	*Naturales Quaestiones* ("Natural Questions")

Ot.	*De Otio* ("On Leisure")
Pol.	*Ad Polybium De Consolatione* ("To Polybius on Consolation")
Prov.	*De Prouidentia* ("On Providence")
Tran.	*De Tranquillitate Animi* ("On Tranquillity of Mind")
Vit.	*De Vita Beata* ("On the Happy Life").

Other frequent abbreviations are:

Cic. *Ac.*	Cicero *Academica*
Clu.	*Pro Cluentio*
De Orat. ·	*De Oratore*
Div.	*De Diuinatione*
Fam.	*Epistulae ad Familiares* ("Letters to Friends")
Inv.	*De Inuentione*
ND	*De Natura Deorum* ("On the Nature of the Gods")
Off.	*De Officiis* ("On Duties")
Op. Gen.	*De Optimo Genere Oratorum* ("On the Best Kind of Orators")
Orat.	*Orator*
Phil.	*Philippicae*
Pis.	*In Pisonem*
Q.Fr.	*Epistulae ad Quintum Fratrem* ("Letters to his Brother Quintus")
Rep.	*De Republica*
Sest.	*Pro Sestio*
Tusc.	*Tusculanae Disputationes*
Ver.	*In Verrem*
Eur. *Hipp.*	Euripides *Hippolytus*
Ovid *Am.*	Ovid *Amores*
Ars	*Ars Amatoria* ("Art of Love")
Her.	*Heroides*
Met.	*Metamorphoses*
Rem.	*Remedia Amoris* ("Remedies of Love")
Petron. *Sat.*	Petronius *Satyricon*
Pliny *NH*	Pliny *Natural History*
Quint. *Inst.*	Quintilian *Institutio Oratoria*
Rac. *Phd.*	Racine *Phèdre*
Sen. Rhet. *Con.*	Seneca the Elder *Controuersiae*
Suas.	*Suasoriae*
Tac. *Ann.*	Tacitus *Annales*
Dial.	*Dialogus de Oratoribus* ("Dialogue on Orators")
Ger.	*Germania*
Hist.	*Historiae*
Virg. *Ecl.*	Virgil *Eclogues*
Geo.	*Georgics*
Aen.	*Aeneid*

Act Division

Lines 1-273 may be regarded either as a unique (in Seneca) first act with two distinct scenes, one of them in lyric form, or as two separate acts (1-84, 85-273). For the latter point of view see K. Heldmann, *Untersuchungen zu den Tragödien Senecas* (Wiesbaden 1974), 71, who points out that the two prologues of this play—one by Hipp. (1-84), one by Ph. (85-128)—correspond to first and second act prologues (one "external", one "internal") in *Ag.*, *HF* and *Thy.*, and suggests that the absence of a choral ode division has been compensated for by the lyric form given to Hipp.'s monologue. In this edition lines 1-273 have been divided into two acts and accordingly a six act division has been adopted, which seems to suit the play as a whole (e.g. 358-735 seem more appropriately classified as a Senecan third act rather than a second—see preliminary note on Act Three). Of the other six "complete" (and genuine) Senecan tragedies only *Oed.* has a six act division.

Stage-Directions

The Latin mss. of Seneca's tragedies contain no stage-directions as such, but do contain scene-headings (apparently not original) indicating the speakers in a particular scene. These have been reproduced.Since it is regular Senecan practice to make stage-directions implicit in the dialogue (see, e.g., 583ff., 705ff., 1154f.), few explicit stage-directions seem required. The ones in the present translation are the editor's own and are mainly restricted to the entry and exit of characters, asides and changes of addressee. Where a stage-direction is controversial it is discussed in the notes.

Stage-Setting

The scene is set before the royal palace at Athens. The exit to the country is (from the audience's viewpoint) stage-left, the exit to the city stage-right. Before the palace stand a statue and altar of Diana (see 54ff., 406ff., 707ff., but esp. 424 and 708f.). Palace and altar form the stage-setting of four other plays: *HF.*, *Med.*, *Oed.* and *Ag.*

Time

As line 41 indicates, the play begins at dawn. The dawn opening is the most frequent one in Seneca (see *HF*, *Oed.*, *Ag.*, *Thy.*), who obviously saw it as particularly appropriate to the commencement of tragic action.

ACT ONE (1-84)

The form of Sen.'s opening act varies. The monologue is favoured in *HF*, *Tro.*, *Med.*, *Pha.* and *Ag.*; in *Oed.* and *Thy.* a monologue leads to dialogue; in *Pho.* dialogue-form is employed throughout. The opening speech is delivered by a major character in *Tro.*, *Pho.*, *Med.*,*Pha.*, and *Oed.*; by a ghost in *Ag.* and *Thy.*; by a deity in *HF*. *Pha.* is unique in three ways. It is the only genuine play of Sen. to open in the lyric mode (*Oct.* also begins in anapaests), i.e. its monologue is a monody; the monologue is in no sense an expository prologue but plunges us *in medias res*; the opening act is not followed by a choral ode (this lack being compensated for by the lyric form of the act itself). Differences between *Pha.* and Eur.'s *Hipp.*, which opens with an expository prologue delivered by a goddess (Aphrodite) in non-lyric form, are marked. For other monodies in Sen. see *Tro.* 705ff. (Andromache), *Med.* 740ff. (Medea), *Ag.* 759ff. (Cassandra), *Thy.* 920ff. (Thyestes).

The evidence for the delivery of Roman tragic verse is sparse, but it seems clear that the lyric sections (monodies and choral odes, etc.) were delivered to the accompaniment of music provided by a flute-player or piper (*tibicen*)—see, e.g., Cic. *De Orat.* 1.254, *Orat.* 183f., *Ac.* 2.20.

Metre: anapaestic. See Appendix II.

2 Cecrops: the first king of Athens, according to legend half man and half serpent. For "Cecropian" as an elevated word for "Athenian" see *Med.* 76, *Thy.* 1049. Take *Cecropii* as genitive with *montis*. *Cecropius* seems to be used only as an adjective in Sen.

4 Parnes: a mountain range north of Athens on the border of Attica and Boeotia.

quae saxoso loca: hyperbaton of *loca*. Trans.: *loca quae saxoso*.

5 Thria: the Thriasian plain is in Attica north-west of Athens.

8 Riphaean: the Riphaean or Rhipaean mountains were a quasi-mythical range situated in the extreme north, sometimes associated with actual mountains in Scythia (modern southern Russia).

**9 *hac, hac alii: ite* is understood from line 1. So too at 17 and 20 below.

11 Zephyrus: the west wind.

13(14) Ilissos: a river that flows past Athens into the Bay of Phaleron.

Ilisos: Greek nominative.

17 You...: Hipp. addresses a particular group of his companions. Similarly at 20 and 31. With these instructions compare Th.'s instructions to the same huntsmen at 1277ff.

tramite laeuo: perhaps best taken as ablative of route (an instrumental ablative) with *ite* understood. See Woodcock §43.

18 Marathon: a township on the north-east coast of Attica, famous for Th.'s slaying of the Marathonian bull and for the Athenian defeat of the Persians there in 490 B.C.

19 suckling dams: *fetae* (20). Presumably deer, whose practice of night pasture at times of vulnerability or fear was well known: see Pliny *NH* 8.117. Others interpret as ewes put out to pasture before dawn to benefit from the early dew, but the context militates against this.

21 Acharneus: a mountain to the north of Athens near the village of Acharnae.

23 Hymettus: a mountain in Attica south-east of Athens. It was famous for its bees and honey. Hence "sweet".

24 Aphidnae: a place in Attica north-east of Athens, not far from Marathon.

calcet: jussive subjunctive, as at 32 (*teneant*), 34 (*tendant*), 40 (*captent*), 41 (*quaerant*), 46 (*properet*), 47 (*cludat*) and 48 (*uibretur*). See Woodcock §109.

25 immune: the Latin *immunis* has the specific implication "exempt from taxes or tribute".

diu uacat: the present indicative with *diu* often has the force of a perfect (= lit. "has long been idle..."). Cf. *Tro.* 308f.

26 Sunion: a promontory in south-east Attica.

28 Phyle: a place in Attica in the mountains north of Athens.

30 Famed for many wounds: as Hipp. at 1096, 1266.

uulnere multo: ablative of cause as at Lucan 2.591, *noti erepto uellere Colchi*, "Colchians famed for the stolen fleece". See Woodcock §45.

31-53 Detailed instructions for the hunt. With 31-43 cf. Lucan 4.437-44. See also 1277f. and n., and Virg. *Aen.* 4.130-32.

31 *laxas:* proleptic use of the adjective, "so that they are loose". So too *praecipites* (51).

32 **silent hounds:** tracker dogs or blood-hounds. Cf. *Thy.*497ff. Also Grattius *Cynegetica* 223ff., esp. 231, Lucan 4.441ff., Oppian *Cynegetica* 1.449f.

33-35 **Molossians...Cretans...Spartans:** breeds of hunting-dog. The same three breeds are mentioned at Lucan 4.440f.

36 *cautus:* the adverbial use of adjectives is very common in Latin, in which adverbs seem to have evolved rather late.

39 *demissi:* sc. *caput* perhaps as internal accusative of respect, although it is not strictly necessary (see Sen. *NQ* 7.1.1).

40 **sniff the air:** *captent auras.* The expression is Virgilian (*Geo.* 1.376).

41 *dubia:* lit. "uncertain"; cf. *dubius dies, Tro.* 1142 (of dusk), *Titan dubius, Oed.* 1 (of dawn).

45f. **wide-meshed nets:** used to surround a cover.

fine snares: "trap-nets", made of very fine material (Pliny *NH.* 19.11) set in the track of the game. One of Diana's cult-names was Dictynna , "Lady of the Nets" (cf. *Med.* 795 and Eur. *Hipp.* 146).

46f. **The painted line's/ Crimson feathers:** a rope adorned with feathers of various colours, esp. red, used to frighten game into the nets. It was called a *formido.* See *Oed.* 758, *Ira* 2.11.5, *Clem.* 1.12.5; also Virg. *Geo.* 3.372, *Aen.* 12.750, Grattius *Cynegetica* 75ff., Lucan 4.437f. and (for the fullest description) Nemesianus *Cynegetica* 303ff.

47b **idle terror:** *uano terrore.* The phrase is echoed in Hipp.'s reported words at 1066.

48-53 **You...you...you...you...:** Hipp. assigns individual roles to the huntsmen. The pronouns are singular.

48 *tibi:* the dative of agent occurs more often with the gerundive or perfect passive participle. It does however occur in verse, as here, with other passive forms.

50 **oakshaft with iron head:** *robur lato...ferro.* This is the heavy hunting-spear (*uenabulum*) requiring two hands for its use. Cf. Virg. *Aen.* 4.131: *lato uenabula ferro,* "hunting-spears with iron heads". See also 546f. *Lato ferro* is an ablative of quality or description, a type of sociative ablative. See Woodcock §§43 and 83, and cf. *latis... cornibus* at 65 below.

51 **beater:** *subsessor* (52), a technical term from hunting. There would of course be several "beaters" involved.

52f. **victor:** see 80n.

ages...solues: the use of the future indicative instead of the imperative often signals a polite command/request, as in the so-called "future of invitation" (e.g. Plautus *Curculio* 728, Horace *Ep.* 1.7.71, Martial 11.52.1). Here, however, the change to the future suggests control and self-confidence.

curved knife: the *culter uenatorius* or hunting-knife.

54-80 Hipp. prays to Diana, goddess of the wilderness and the hunt. It is the first of several prayers in this play: see 406ff., 671ff., 945ff., 1159ff., 1201ff., 1223ff. The prayer-motif is one used extensively by Sen. and with potent dramatic effect: see, e.g., *HF* 516ff., 592ff., 900ff., 926ff., 1063ff., 1202ff.; *Tro.* 500ff.; *Med.* 1ff., 595ff., 740ff.; *Oed.* 248ff., 868ff.; *Ag.* 310ff., 802ff.; *Thy.* 122ff., 1006ff., 1068ff. With the prayer here cf. also Hipp.'s prayer to Artemis at Eur. *Hipp.* 73-87.

54 Come: *ades* is the standard term in invocations. Cf. 412, 423 below, and *Med.* 703, *Oed.* 405, *Ag.* 348.

comrade: to Eur.'s Hipp. Artemis is the "mistress" (*despoina, Hipp.* 74, 82), he the "servant" (*hypēretēs, Hipp.* 1397), seeking unshared communion with his goddess (*Hipp.* 84ff.).

man goddess: *diua* ("divine") *uirago. Virago* connotes a woman with the qualities of a man (cf. Virg. *Aen.* 12.468, Ovid *Met.* 2.765, 6.130). In this context especially the word suggests—and the audience would have expected—*uirgo* ("virgin"), Diana's traditional title (see *Tro.* 827, *Med.* 87), and one applied to the goddess by the chorus-leader at 405 but absent both from this prayer and Hipp.'s invocation of Diana at 708f. Contrast Hipp.'s prayer in Eur. *Hipp.*, where the focus is on Artemis' chastity (*Hipp.* 66) and inviolate nature (*Hipp.* 73ff.), on Artemis as *uirgo*, not *uirago. Virago* is used twice elsewhere in the tragedies at *Tro.* 1151 of Polyxena (in whose case the *uirago/uirgo* verbal play is explicit: see *Tro.* 1167), and at *Ag.* 668 of Cassandra.

55ff. On the sexual imagery see Intro. p. 19, 21 and 23.

56 *certis:* "unerring" as at 193 and 278 below. Cf. also Catullus 68.113, Virg. *Aen.* 11.767, Ovid *Am.* 1.1.25.

58 Araxes: the river Aras in Armenia. It suggests the eastern extremity of the Roman world. For "the cold Araxes' stream" see also *Med.* 372f. *Araxen* is a Greek accusative.

59-72 Yours...Yours...you...you...your: *tua...tua...tibi...tibi...tuos.* Note the anaphora characteristic of the formal prayer or hymn. Cf. the following: Lucretius 1.6ff. (to Venus), Catullus 34.13ff. (to Diana), Horace *Odes* 2.19.17ff. (to Bacchus), Virg. *Aen.* 8.293ff. (to Hercules).

59 Hister: the lower Danube in the north.

60 Gaetulian: the Gaetulians were a people of north-west Africa. The phrase "Gaetulian lion" is a standard formula of Roman poetry: see Horace *Odes* 1.23.10, 3.20.2; Virg. *Aen.* 5.351.

61 Cretan hind: cf. Virg. *Aen.* 4.69ff., where the love-sick Dido is compared to a Cretan hind "pricked (*fixit*) by a huntsman".

64f. bison...wild ox: creatures of the north-west (Germany, see Caesar *De Bello Gallico* 6.28, Pliny *NH.* 8.38), complementing those from the south, east and north.

66-72 For the significance of this catalogue of places on the fringes of the Roman empire see Intro. p. 19. Cf. Cupid's "dominion" at 285-90. For the "global" catalogue elsewhere in Sen., see, e.g., *HF* 1323ff., *Med.* 707ff., *Thy.* 369ff. Most such catalogues have a recognisably Roman colouring.

66 lonely fields: cf. 407 ("lonely hills") for a similar focus on the solitary wilderness which is Diana's kingdom.

67ff. *siue illud...*: lit. "whether the Arabian in his rich forest or the poor Garamantian knows it...". *diuite silua* is probably local ablative; so too *uacuis campis* (71). See Woodcock §§51ff.

67 rich Arabia's groves: cf. *Oed.* 117f. Arabia provided perfumes and aromatic substances for the luxury market at Rome, among which were frankincense and myrrh (Pliny *NH.* 12.51ff., 82ff.).

68 Garamantia: the Garamantians lived in the eastern Sahara.

71 Sarmatian nomad: the Sarmatians (also at *HF* 539, *Thy.* 375) were a nomadic people who lived in the area between the Vistula and the Don.

69f. Pyrene's Ridge: the Pyrenees, named on one account (see Silius Italicus 3.415ff.) after Pyrene, daughter of king Bebryx, who, raped by Hercules, gave birth to a serpent. She fled to the mountains (now called the Pyrenees), where she was consumed by wild beasts. The epithet "wild" fits both woman and mountain range. For another account of the origin of the name (connecting it with the Greek for "fire", *pyr*), see Diodorus Siculus 5.35. *Pyrenes* is a Greek genitive.

70 Hyrcanian ravines: Hyrcania was a country on the south-east side of the Caspian sea.

72 Diana: the only occurrence of the goddess' name in the play.

arcus: plural for singular as often in verse, although influenced here perhaps by the Greek plural form, *toxa*, which was used for the singular even in prose. Cf. another bow at 192, 203, 278.

75f. *tenuere...rupere* (= *tenuerunt...ruperunt*): these perfects are what is called "gnomic" in function, i.e. they state what has been true in the past and can be taken as a general rule. "Gnomic" perfects are used instead of the present to articulate a general truth and are common in proverbs (*gnōmai*) and *sententiae*. The "gnomic" past is sometimes found in English: "A May flood never did good"; "A wild goose never laid a tame egg".

76 spoils: *praeda.* Cf. 543, 819, and see 80n.

80 long-lined in triumph: *longo triumpho.* A specifically military image suggesting the triumphal procession of a victorious Roman general. Cf. "victor", 52, "spoils" (*praeda*), 76. *longo triumpho* is ablative of accompaniment, lit. "with a long triumph(al procession)".

See Woodcock §§43 and 46.

81 The baying of dogs can be heard. With the apparent "signs" here of Diana's immediate answering of Hipp.'s prayer cf. the similar situation at 423-25 below. See Intro. p. 26.

84 *compensat:* lit. "avoids by a short-cut" as at Lucan 8.249. *Compendia* (neut. plural) frequently means "short-cut" (Pliny *NH.* 6.101).

ACT TWO (85-273)

In three other Senecan plays (*Ag.* 108ff., *Med.* 116ff., *Thy.* 176ff.) the second act begins, as here, with a speech by a protagonist revealing his/her emotional state, followed by a dialogue with a subordinate character who advises restraint. The subordinate character is ignored during this opening speech, which is thus in essence a soliloquy. In *Ag.* and *Med.* the subordinate character, as in *Pha.*, is a nurse; in *Thy.* it is a *satelles* or attendant. This use of a subordinate figure— especially a nurse—to draw out a character probably derives from Euripides. It was taken up enthusiastically by French and English tragedians, who employ the nurse as both foil and confidante to the heroine (e.g. Oenone in Rac. *Phd.*, Juliet's nurse in Shakespeare's *Romeo and Juliet*).

Metre: iambic trimeter (senarius). See Appendix II.

85 *O:* vocatives in Latin are not normally accompanied by *o*, as in Greek. *O* with the vocative in Latin indicates a formal (as, e.g., in prayers or hymns—see 409), impassioned (687f., 1164f.) or pathetic address. Its frequent use in tragedy and epic is to be attributed among other things to their "elevated" literary style.

magna uasti Creta...freti: note the parallel arrangement of adjectives and nouns (abAB) as often in Sen. See, e.g., 318, 500, 650, 858, 961, *Tro.* 240, *Pho.* 95. Cf. the chiastic arrangement of 113 etc. In the notations employed in these notes—abAB, abBA, etc.—AB represent nouns, ab their corresponding adjectives.

Crete: Ph.'s original home. She is the daughter of Minos, king of Crete, and his wife, Pasiphae. With 85 cf. 274, 1159.

mistress: *dominatrix* occurs only here in Sen. and is extremely rare in classical Latin. Its masculine equivalent *dominator* is also rare but occurs five times in the tragedies (*HF* 1181, *Med.* 4, *Pha.* 1039, 1159, *Thy.* 1078) and once in the prose-works (*Ep.* 107.11). The portentous quality of the words obviously appealed to Sen. Note that *dominatrix freti* in Pha.'s opening speech is echoed by *dominator freti* (1159) in her final one.

86 *cuius:* modifies *rates.*

87 **Assyria:** Assyria is part of Mesopotamia. By "Assyria" Sen. here probably means Syria.

tenuere (= *tenuerunt*): "gnomic" perfect (see 75f.n.).

quicquid: sc. *ponti* (partitive genitive), lit. "whatever of the deep".

88 **Nereus:** a sea-god, husband of Doris and father of the Nereids. The metrical pattern of this line (spondees alternating with iambs: __ ◡_ __ ◡_ __ ◡_) is the most common in Sen. tragedy: so, e.g., 89, 90, 92, 93, etc.

89 **hostage to a hated house:** Ph.'s marriage to Th. seems part of a political settlement between Crete and Athens. Ovid details Ph.'s grounds for hate (the murder of her brother and desertion of her sister) at *Her.* 4.111-16.

penates means lit. "household gods" but it often functions metonymically for "house" or "home". According to Cicero (*ND* 2.68) the name of the *penates* was derived either from *penus* (= "store") or from the fact they resided *penitus* (in the recesses of the house). Hence they are also called *penetrales.*

91ff. Cf. Ovid *Her.* 4.109ff.

91 **fugitive lord:** *profugus coniux.* Echoed in Th.'s first words in the play at 835. See also 1000n.

92 Hyperbaton again. The normal order would be: *Theseus fidem quam solet.*

usual faith: Th. was a notorious womaniser. Previous wives/women include Ariadne, Ph.'s sister, whom Th. abandoned on the island of Naxos, and Antiope, Hipp.'s mother, whom he killed. See also 226ff., 245, 578f., 662ff., 761, 926ff. Cf. Rac. *Phd.* 20ff.

93 **Brave:** *fortis.* Sen. seems fond of the ironic use of this word; see, e.g., *HF* 1283, *Tro.* 755.

inuii retro: the latter word modifies the former, "having no way back". Cf. *inuii sinus,* "folds allowing no way out", *Ag.* 889.

94 **bold suitor's henchman:** the suitor is Pirithous, king of the Lapithae in Thessaly. Th. is assisting him in his attempt to rape Proserpina, queen of the underworld. In Sophocles' lost *Phaedra* (frr. 624N and 625N) Th. may have been away in Hades and believed dead. Contrast Eur., whose Th. is absent visiting an oracle (*Hipp.* 790ff.) and Rac., who has his Th. help Pirithous abduct the wife of the king of Epirus (*Phd.* 957-59). In Ovid *Her.* 4.109f. Th. is away in Thessaly with Pir. For other "bold" (Latin *audax*) breaches of natural law see 116 and *Med.* 301ff.

95 *ut:* the postponement of *ut* is not uncommon in verse.

reuulsam: substantival use of the participle, much rarer in Latin on the whole than in Greek due to the former's lack of a definite article. See Woodcock §101. The use however (together with the substantival use of adjectives generally) is more widespread in Roman writers of the first century A.D. (with their love of brevity and point) than in the works of their predecessors, and Sen. is quite free with it even in his prose-works. In Sen., as in Petronius, it is almost a habit of style. *Reuulsam* refers to Proserpina.

96 **Proceeds:** *pergit* suggests unremitting persistence.

passion: *furoris. Furor* is an important thematic term in Senecan tragedy (see, e.g., the last line of *Ag.*). It connotes a violent brainstorm or frenzied emotional state, and is used referentially of a wide range of such states, including passionate desire, hostile rage and prophetic frenzy. In *Pha.* it is used primarily of Ph.'s "passion" for Hipp. (e.g. 178ff.) and of various forms of "rage" (e.g. 567, 1124), and has been translated accordingly.

97 *pudorque:* "or shame". The use of *-que* to indicate disjunction in Latin, where we might have expected *-ue*, is common. It is found in poetry from Lucretius (e.g. 2.825) and Catullus (e.g. 45.6) onwards.

98f. With this use of Hipp.'s name as the starting-point of Ph.'s self-revelation, cf. Eur. *Hipp.* 310ff. and Rac. *Phd.* 205ff.

98 **Acheron:** a river of the underworld, for which it often functions, as here, as a metonym.

99 *incubat:* in this context especially the sense "broods" seems appropriate. See also below 268. There is perhaps an echo here of Virg. *Aen.* 4.82f.

maestae: sc. *mihi.*

100f. **Not the night's tranquillity**: a traditional motif in the presentation of sexual love; cf., e.g., the description of Dido at Virg. *Aen.* 4.5. See also Propertius 1.1.33f.

101f. **Evil feeds...and burns within:** cf. Dido again at Virg. *Aen.* 4.2: "She feeds the wound within her veins and is wasted by blind fire", *uulnus alit uenis et caeco carpitur igni.*

102 **burns within:** *ardet intus.* Cf. Ovid *Her.* 4.19f.

103 **Etna's cave:** the mouth of Mt. Etna, a volcano in Sicily still active today and of considerable interest to Sen. (see *Ep.* 79.2). For the comparison of love's fire to that of Etna see Catullus 68.53, Ovid *Her.* 15.12, *Met.* 13.868. See also 190 below. Elsewhere in Senecan tragedy Etna's flames image not sexual desire as such but the fire of anger (*ira*) and rage (*furor*): *HF* 106, *Med.* 410. Cf. *HO* 284ff.

Pallas: Athena = (Roman) Minerva, patron goddess of Athens and the loom. She is addressed by the chorus at 1149ff.

106 *mixtam:* sc. *me.*

107 **silent rites:** the mysteries celebrated in honour of Ceres (Demeter) and Proserpina (Persephone) at Eleusis north-west of Athens. In Eur. *Hipp.* 24ff. and Ovid *Her.* 4.67ff. it was at the Eleusinian mysteries that Pha. fell in love with Hipp.

  tacitis...sacris: dative after *conscias.* Cf. *Med.* 6 and Tibullus 1.7.48.

108f. An allusion to the Panathenaic procession held yearly in honour of Athena by the people of Athens. A famous representation of this is to be found on the frieze of the Parthenon.

109 **guardian goddess:** Pallas Athena (Minerva), to whom the gods awarded Athens after a contest between her and Neptune.

110f. Cf. Eur. *Hipp.* 215ff., Ovid *Her.* 4.37ff., esp. 38: "I'm impelled to go among savage beasts" (*est mihi per saeuas impetus ire feras*). See also Rac. *Phd.* 176ff.

111 *gaesa:* a word of Gallic origin (= Gallic javelins), first found in Caesar *De Bello Gallico* (3.4.1).

112 **Where to, my soul:** *quo tendis, anime.* This kind of self-address and self-questioning is common in Senecan tragedy. See, e.g., *Med.* 895, 937, 988; *Oed.* 933, 952, 1024; *Ag.* 108, 228, 915; *Thy.* 283, 423; *HO* 842, 1828. And cf. *Pha.* 592, 599, 719. The use of *anime* to signal a soliloquy occurs also in republican tragedy (e.g. Pacuvius 284R^2 and possibly Accius 489R^2, although the latter is based on Ribbeck's emendation). For the use of the *anime* formula in Roman declamation see Sen. Rhet. *Con.* 2.3.6. With Pha.'s thoughts here cf. Eur. *Hipp.* 239f.

113 **I recognise:** *agnosco.* So Virgil's Dido: "I recognise the traces of that old flame" (*agnosco ueteris uestigia flammae, Aen.* 4.23). For this important "recognition" motif see 698, 1249, and in other plays: *HF* 624, 1016, 1196, *Med.* 1021, *Thy.* 1005f. See also *HO* 1946 and Ovid *Her.* 4.53ff.

  poor mother: Pha.'s mother, Pasiphae, the Cretan queen. She fell in love with a great bull sent by Neptune to her husband Minos and consummated this love with the assistance of a contraption made by Daedalus. As a result she bore a monstrous offspring, half-bull, half-man, the Minotaur. It was slain by Theseus. References both to Pasiph.'s "monstrous" union and to the Minotaur pervade the play: see, e.g., 122, 174ff., 242, 649, 688ff., 1067, 1170ff. Contrast Eur. *Hipp.*, where no reference is made to the Minotaur and only one to Pasiph.'s love for the bull (*Hipp.* 337f.). See also Ovid *Her.* 4.57f.

  fateful: *fatale.* Cf. Ovid *Her.* 4.53f., 63. *Fatale* here fuses the notions of "fated" and "fatal", "bringing destruction". Cf. the "fateful spear", *telum fatale,* which Aeneas hurls at Turnus at Virg. *Aen.* 12.919, and the description of Paris at *Ag.* 730f. as the "fateful judge", *fatalis arbiter.* See also *Ag.* 628: *fatale munus*, "fateful/fatal gift". For the family curse see 124ff. and n. See also 698. Both "fateful" and "recognise" were taken up by Rac., *Phd.* 277f.: *Je reconnus Venus et ses feux redoutables,/ D'un sang qu'elle poursuit tourments inévitables* ("I recognised Venus and her dreaded fires,/ Fated torments of a race she pursues"). Cf. also *Phd.* 249f., 257f., 306, 679f., 1289.

Sen.'s dramatic verse is highly alliterative. This line is one of his most brilliant in that respect.

114 Analogies with the past are a pervasive feature of Senecan drama (apart from *Pha.* see esp. *Tro.*, *Med.*, *Ag.* and *Thy.*). They seem part of Sen.'s tragic concept of "fate" (see 698n.). For other references to the past, esp. to Pasiph., the bull and the Minotaur, see 113n. See further Introd. p. 27.

115 So Cassandra in Ennius' *Alexander* 60V²: "My mother, I pity you" (*mea mater, tui me miseret*).

117 *amasti:* syncopated form of *amauisti.*

118 leader of an untamed herd: cf. 1039.

119-23 Cf. the similar remarks made by Iphis at Ovid *Met.* 9.738ff.

119f. *aliquid:* either internal accusative ("felt some love") or adverbial accusative of extent ("loved to some degree"). See Woodcock §3, and cf. Propertius' lament that he was "always in love to some degree/ felt some love" (*aliquid semper amare*, 2.22.18).

quis...deus aut quis...Daedalus: the adjectival use of *quis* is common in verse. *Qui* is more usual in prose.

120 Daedalus: the great craftsman who constructed the Cretan labyrinth (see Ovid *Met.* 8.155ff.) and also made an artificial "cow" in which Pasiph. could be placed to mate with the bull.

queat: potential subjunctive. See Woodcock §118.

121 Attic arts: Latin *arte Mopsopia.* Mopsopia was an old name for Attica, the district in central Greece which had Athens as its capital. See Tibullus 1.7.54, Callimachus fr. 709, and 1276 below.

returned: Daedalus, imprisoned for helping Theseus kill the Minotaur, escaped from Crete by making himself wings and flying north to Cumae. He was accompanied by his son Icarus, who fell into the sea and drowned. The flight is the subject of the fourth choral ode of *Oed.* (esp. 892ff.). See also Virg. *Aen.* 6.14ff., Ovid *Met.* 8.183ff., and *HO* 683ff.

122 Our monster: the Minotaur (see 113n.), to house which Daedalus built the labyrinth, "blind house", at Cnossos in Crete. Cf. Ovid *Met.* 8.158.

123 *promittet:* future indicative instead of present subjunctive to express greater certainty. See 815, 818f. Cf. Horace *Odes* 3.3.7f.

124ff. The sun-god, Phoebus Apollo, disclosed Venus' affair with Mars to her husband, Vulcan, who trapped the couple *in flagrante delicto* with fine chains ("fetters", 125) which he had forged (Homer *Odyssey* 8.266ff.). Hence Venus' hatred of the sun-god and his descendants. Pasiph. is a daughter of the sun, Pha. a granddaughter. In Eur. *Hipp.* Aphrodite bears no ill will towards Pha., whose death she describes as an unfortunate by-product of the retribution she exacts from Hipp. (*Hipp.* 47ff.). Ovid however (*Her.* 4.53ff.) presents Pha.'s love, as here, as part of the "tribute" (*tributa*) exacted by Venus from Pha.'s family. Venus' hatred of Pha.'s family is pointed up in Racine (see 113n.). For inherited evil/guilt elsewhere in Sen. tragedy see, e.g., *Pho.* 338, *Ag.* 233, *Thy.* 23ff., 314.

124 *perosa:* perfect participles of deponent verbs are often used in a present sense (e.g. 230, 1163 below). See Woodcock §103.

125 **claims redress:** *uindicat.* Cf. 352 and n.

127f. Cf. Ovid *Her.* 4.61f.

129 **Glorious child of Jove:** *clara progenies Iouis.* Cf. *magna progenies Iouis,* "great child of Jove", Catullus 34.6 (of Diana). Jove is king of the gods and father of Minos, of whom Pha. is daughter.

130 *ocius:* comparative for positive as often in verse.

131f. *neue...praebe: ne* plus the imperative is used frequently in verse for prohibitions, as at Virg. *Aen.* 7.202. So too at 222, 993 and 1240 below, *Med.* 1016, *Ag.* 976. Sen. uses the construction often in the tragedies, but never *noli* or *nolite* with the infinitive (common in the prose works). The construction is even found at *Const.* 19.4: *ne repugnate.* See Woodcock §128. The *-ue* in *neue* implies no disjunction here (= "and...not").

132-35 An amatory and (extended to emotion, *affectus*, or passion) philosophical, even Stoic, commonplace. Cf. Ovid *Rem.* 91, Sen. *Ep.* 85.9, 116.3, *Ira* 1.7.2ff.

133 *fuit:* gnomic perfect again. See 75f.n.

134 *blandiendo:* instrumental ablative of the gerund. In poetry and post-Augustan prose the ablative of the gerund came to be used like the present participle simply to express attendant circumstances. Here the instrumental force is still apparent.

136-39 Asides are common in Sen. tragedy (see, e.g., below 424ff., 580ff., 592ff., 634f.). No aside of pure form however (i.e. involving suspension or freezing of dramatic time) occurs in extant fifth-century Attic tragedy. The earliest instances attested are in Aristophanes, and the convention becomes a common and accepted one in later comedy (and probably in Hellenistic drama as a whole). It was perhaps a standard feature of Augustan tragedy.

136f. Cf. *Med.* 203-06.

quam...nolit: indirect exclamation. The verb is in the subjunctive as in an indirect question.

139   imminent freedom: death. For death (*mors*) as freedom (*libertas*) see *Tro.* 145, 791, *Ag.* 591 (*libera mors*), 796, *Prov.* 2.10, *Ira* 3.15, *Ep.* 12.10, 26.10, 70.14, 91.21. Cf. Lucan 7.818, Statius *Thebaid* 3.216f.

140   honesta (neut. plural) is object of *uelle*.

141   wrong's limits: this runs counter to Stoic thought which allowed no gradation of sin. To the Stoic all sins were equally bad. The absence or rejection of "limit" (*modus, finis*) is a frequent motif in Sen. tragedy: see, e.g., 553, *Med.* 397, *Thy.* 1051ff.

143   monstro: ablative of comparison, an off-shoot of the "true" ablative (the ablative of source and separation). See Woodcock §§78-79.

144   imputes: potential subjunctive. See 120n.

148   Lethe: the river of forgetfulness in the underworld, for which as here it often functions as a metonym.

149-58   The Nurse uses against Pha.'s passion the triple ancestry which Ovid's Pha. cites at *Her.* 4.157-60. See also 671ff. and 888-90.

149   Hyperbaton of *qui*. Postponement of the relative is not uncommon in verse.

150   A hundred nations: "Crete of the hundred cities" (*Krētē hekatompolis*) is the standard Homeric description (e.g. *Iliad* 2.649). Cf. *HF* 230, *Tro.* 820, *HO* 27.

   your father: Minos.

   centenis: distributive for cardinal numeral, as often in verse. Cf. 500, 1214 below, Virg. *Aen.* 10.207, 329, 566.

151   occultum: an adverbial or predicative use of the participle. See Woodcock §88.

152   credamus: concessive use of the jussive subjunctive. See Woodcock §112.

155   mother's father: Phoebus Apollo, the sun-god.

   He who shakes the world: perhaps another Homeric allusion (*Iliad* 1.530). Cf. *Oed.* 1028.

156   Etna's bolts: the thunderbolts of Jupiter, "progenitor of gods" (157), were forged by the Cyclopes and Vulcan on Mount Etna in Sicily (see 190f. and Virg. *Aen.* 8.424-32).

157   Progenitor of gods: *sator deorum*. An "epic", Virgilian expression (*Aen.* 1.254, 11.725), derived perhaps from the early epic poet and tragedian, Ennius. It is the opening phrase of *HO*. Cf. also

Oed. 1028: *diuum sator*; Statius *Thebaid* 3.218: *sator astrorum*, "progenitor of stars", also of Jupiter; and 959 below.

158 Hyperbaton. Translate: *ut lateas inter auos omnia uidentes.*

159f. *ut...ut:* note the concessive use of *ut*, "even though", "even supposing".

163 *semet:* emphatic form of *se*; *-met* forms are used frequently in *Pha.*

164 Cf. *Ep.* 97.13: "Sin can be without danger (*tuta*), not without fear (*secura*)." See also *Ep.* 105.8 and Pha.'s remarks at Eur. *Hipp.* 415ff.

167 Getan: the Getae were a Thracian tribe on the lower Danube and an epitome of the "barbaric". At Virg. *Geo.* 3.462f. they are associated with the drinking of milk curdled with horse-blood.

168 Inhospitable Taur: *inhospitalis Taurus*. An inhabitant of the Tauric Chersonese (modern Crimea). *Inhospitalis* translates the Greek *axenos*, the original name (Strabo 7.3.6) for the Black Sea, in which the Tauric Chersonese—itself called *axenos* by Eur. *Iphigenia in Tauris* 94—was situated. The Tauri were renowned for sacrificing strangers to their goddess (see Eur. *Iph. Taur.* 37ff.).

Scyth: the Scyths were a nomadic tribe in southern Russia (Scythia). They are a paradigm of barbarity not only in ancient literature (see Shakespeare *King Lear* i.1.116).

170 novel: *nouos*. Cf. the similar ironic use of *nouus* at *Tro.* 900, *Med.* 894.

173 Nature: this is the first occurrence in the play of the Latin word *natura*. There are six other occurrences of it in *Pha.* (176, 352, 481, 567, 959, 1116), but only ten in the remaining seven plays. For the meaning of this term in Sen. see Appendix I. For *natura uersa* ("nature convulsed") see also *Pho.* 84f., *Oed.* 371, *Ag.* 34.

174 brother's palace: the Cretan labyrinth in which the Minotaur was imprisoned. See 1171f.

176 Cf. *Pho.* 478, *Oed.* 942f., *HO* 46.

legibus suis: ablative of separation, one of the functions of the "true ablative" (see Woodcock §§38ff.), as at 250 below. See also Virg. *Aen.* 9.620 (*cedite ferro*) and Tac. *Hist.* 2.3 (*scientia cessere*).

177-83 Sen. frames the opening sentences of Pha.'s reply so as to allude to two famous passages in earlier Roman poetry:

1. Ovid *Met.* 7.19ff., where Medea describes the battle within her soul between desire (*cupido*) and reason (*mens*): "I see and approve the better course,/ I follow the worse" (*uideo meliora proboque,/ deteriora sequor, Met.* 7.20f.—cf. esp. *Pha.* 178f., *cogit sequi/ peiora*, lit. "compels [me] to follow the worse"). Ovid is of course following

147

the unplatonic (even antiplatonic) tradition of the impotence of knowledge/reason against the constraints of desire/passion/pleasure (cf. Eur. *Med.* 1078f., *Hipp.* 380ff., Aristotle *Nicomachean Ethics* 1139a35). The thesis is brilliantly dramatised in Act Three of *Thy.* Cf. also *Med.* 953, *Thy.* 100, where emotion or a Fury leads and the subject "follows" (*sequor*).

2. Virg. *Geo.* 1.199-203:

> sic omnia fatis
> in peius ruere ac retro sublapsa referri,
> non aliter quam qui aduerso uix flumine lembum
> remigiis subigit, sic bracchia forte remisit,
> atque illum in praeceps prono rapit alueus amni.

> So all things by law of fate
> Speed towards the worst, slip back, are swept away;
> Just as an oarsman struggling to drive his skiff
> Against the opposing stream needs but chance to drop his arms
> And the current whirls him away headlong down the river.

Cf. *Ag.* 138ff., *Thy.* 438f., and *Ep.* 122.19 where the oarsman metaphor is employed in a context which has obvious ramifications for the interpretation of Pha.'s mental conflict: "If we fight against nature our life is no different than that of men rowing against the current" (*contra illam* [sc. *naturam*] *nitentibus non alia uita est quam contra aquam remigantibus*).

180   seek safe counsel: cf. Clytemnestra's opening words at *Ag.* 108: "Why, sluggish soul, do you seek safe counsel (*tuta consilia expetis*)?"

181-83   The use of so-called "epic" similes is a common feature of Sen. dialogue: see 382f., 399-403, 580-82, and cf. *Tro.* 572ff., 672ff., 794ff., 1093ff., 1140ff., *Med.* 382ff., 940ff., *Ag.* 138ff., *Thy.* 497ff., 707ff., 732ff. On the simile here see also 177-83n.

181f.   aduersa...unda: ablative of attendant circumstances, one of the sociative functions of the case. See Woodcock §43. The phrase is modelled on *aduerso flumine*, Virg. *Geo.* 1.201 (quoted in 177-83n.).

184ff.   Similarly Pha. at Ovid *Her.* 4.12: "Love reigns and has power over our lords, the gods" ([*Amor*] *regnat et in dominos ius habet ille deos*). On the power of love see also Eur. *Hipp.* 443ff., fr. 431 Nauck (from the first *Hipp.*), and *Oct.* 806-19. Cf. 274ff. below. The impotence of reason was taken up by Rac., *Phd.* 760.

184   possit: potential subjunctive. See 120n.

185   tota mente: probably a local ablative, lit. "in all my heart", as at *Tro.* 1f.: *magna potens/ dominatur aula*, lit. "lords it supreme in a great court". Cf. also Lucretius 3.281: *anima...dominatur toto corpore*. "the soul commands (lit. lords it in) the whole body".

186 **winged one:** Cupid.

188 **Gradivus:** Mars.

189 **craftsman god:** Vulcan, who forges the triple-pointed thunder-bolts of Jupiter. See 156 above.

trisulci fulminis: lit. "triple-forked thunderbolt." The phrase is first attested in Varro *Menippean Satires* 54. Cf. *trisulcis ignibus*, Ovid *Am.* 2.5.52, *Met.* 2.848, *trisulca face*, *Pha.* 681, *trisulco telo*, *Thy.* 1089.

190 **et:** "even".

191 **Etna's slopes:** see 103n.

igne...paruo: instrumental or causal ablative. See Woodcock §45.

192 **Phoebus:** Apollo, the sun-god, but also god of music, prophecy and archery. Cf. Ovid *Met.* 1.519f., where the conceit of the archer-god wounded by love's "more unerring arrow" (*sagitta certior*) is used by Apollo himself in his attempt to seduce Daphne.

193 Cupid's "unerring arrows" are proverbial. Cf. Ovid *Am.* 1.1.25: "That boy had unerring arrows" (*certas habuit puer ille sagittas*). See 278 below and cf. 56f.

195-217 The Nurse's speech is a dramatic *suasoria* (see Introd. p. 13). So too is that of the Nurse at *Ag.* 203ff.

195-97 Cf. Hecuba's retort to Helen at Eur. *Tro.* 988f. and the remarks of the dramatised Sen. to "Nero" at *Oct.* 557ff. See also *Brev.* 16.5

196 *foret:* = *esset.* The subjunctive is final.

197 *numinis falsi:* probably genitive of definition (appositional genitive)—see Woodcock §72 and 230 below— with *falsi* qualifying both the whole expression, *titulum numinis*, and the noun to which it is attached, *numinis*. With the Nurse's comments here cf. Thyestes' attack on the "false titles", *falsa nomina*, given to the life of wealth and power at *Thy.* 446ff.

198 **Erycina:** Venus, who had a famous temple on the top of Mount Eryx in the north-west corner of Sicily, restored in A.D. 25 by Tiberius (Tac. *Ann.* 4.43.6).

scilicet: this ironic use is common. Cf. *Ag.* 290f.

203 *arcus:* see 72n.

204f. Cf. Sen.'s attack on the luxury that attends prosperity (*felicitas*) at *Ep.* 114.9ff.

206f. At Eur. fr. 437 Nauck (from the first *Hipp.*) prosperity (*eupraxia*) is said to produce not "lust" but *hybris* ("insolence").

208 *sani moris:* genitive of quality or description. See Woodcock §§84-85.

209-15 Moral contrasts between poor and rich, obscure and famous, impotent and powerful, etc., are common in Senecan tragedy. See, e.g., *HF* 159ff., *Thy.* 339ff., 446ff. Related to this is the contrast between the "natural"(rural) and "artificial" (urban) life: see *Pha.* 483ff.; also *Ep.* 95.18ff., 114.9ff.

209 *penates:* see 89n.

212 *medium...uulgus:* "common crowd", as at Ovid *Met.* 7.432. Cf. *media turba* at *Ag.* 103, *Thy.* 533f.

213 *contra:* adverbial, "on the other hand".

215 This kind of terse, trenchantly expressed, epigrammatic maxim is called a *sententia*. *Sententiae*, esp. climactic *sententiae*, are a major feature of first century A.D. rhetorical practice and one of the defining features of the declamatory style. See Quint. *Inst.* 8.25ff. and Intro. p. 13.

216 Cf. Eur. *Hipp.* 411f., where it is Pha. who puts the argument of *noblesse oblige*. In Sen. the appeal to "what is fitting (*decet*)" occurs often: see, e.g., *Tro.* 332, 336, 1002, *Med.* 49f., 175, 281, *Ag.* 52, 124, and 453, 610, 618, 803 below.

deceat: subjunctive of indirect question.

praeditam: substantival use of participle. Cf. 95n.

217 *sceptre:* for this important symbol of kingship, law, patriarchal authority and political power (esp. "male" power) see 617, 868 below, and *Pho.* 40f., 275, *Med.* 982, *Oed.* 240, 513, 642f.

219-24 Cf. the similar exchange between Pha. and Hipp. at 625-29 below. See also Rac. *Phd.* 623-26.

220 **vaulted skies:** the Latin expression, *conuexa supera*, is Virgilian. See *Aen.* 6.241, 750, 10.251. Cf. also Statius *Thebaid* 10.916f.

221 *nocte perpetua:* a sociative-instrumental ablative, almost an ablative of description. Cf. *HF* 620: *tristi silentem nubilo...domum* ("the silent house of mournful gloom"). See Woodcock §§43 and 85.

222 **Dis:** Pluto, king of the underworld. The name is a contraction of *diues* ("the rich one"), a translation of the Greek *Ploutōn*.

ne crede: see 131f.n.

clauserit: subjunctive in a concessive clause with *licet* (= "although"). The subject of *clauserit* is Dis.

223 **the Stygian dog:** Cerberus, who guards the entrance to the underworld. He is called "Stygian" after the main river of the underworld, the Styx.

225 Cf. the argument used by the Nurse in Eur. *Hipp.* 462ff.

forsitan dabit: forsitan used adverbially with the indicative is attested as early as Lucretius (see Lucr. 5. 104f.). The more frequent construction is with the subjunctive.

227 **Antiope:** Th.'s Amazon wife, whom he killed (cf. Ovid *Her.*

4.117-22). According to some accounts (e.g. Plutarch *Theseus* 28) the motive for this murder was Th.'s desire to marry Pha. See also 398, 578f., 926ff., 1167.

Neither in Ovid *Her*. 4 nor in Eur. *Hipp*. is Hipp.'s mother married to Th.; in both (*Her*. 4.122, *Hipp*. 309, 962, 1083, 1455) Hipp. is a bastard (*nothus*). In *Pha*. on the other hand Antiope's status as wife is affirmed (226) and Hipp.'s legitimacy and right to the throne unquestioned (1112). Eur. in fact never mentions Hipp.'s mother by name; she is called simply "the Amazon" (*Hipp*. 10, 307, 351, 581). Nor is there any suggestion in Eur.'s play that she was killed by Th.

230 flees: *fugit*. For "flight" (or "shunning") and Hipp. see also 241, 243, 517, 566, 729, 736, 902, 1000, 1080, 1173, and esp. 1000n.

exosus: see 124n.

feminae: defining, appositional genitive. See 197n.

232 Amazon breed: the Amazons were female warriors who avoided permanent sexual unions, engaging in sexual activity with strangers for the purpose of reproduction. They killed their male offspring, keeping only the female. They are mentioned as early as Homer (e.g. *Iliad* 3.189). See 577, 909-12 below.

scias: potential subjunctive. See 120n.

233-35 A standard motif of Roman amatory poetry: cf., e.g., Propertius 2.26.29ff., Tibullus 1.4.41ff., and esp. Ovid *Am*. 1.9.9ff.

237 *Venere non casta:* ablative modelled on that found with *mutare*, which takes the accusative of the thing exchanged and ablative of the thing for which the former is exchanged. The ablative is perhaps best construed as instrumental in origin, i.e. the means by which something is changed. See Woodcock §43. Note the use of *non* here to negate an adjective, as often in the tragedies: see, e.g., *non miti*, 274 below, *non uirilem*, *HF* 470, *non indociles*, *Tro*. 82.

240-45 This kind of quick-fire verbal exchange between two speakers, involving divided verse-lines (*antilabai*), is common in Senecan tragedy: see, e.g., *HF* 426ff., 1186f., 1263f., *Med*. 168ff., *Oed*. 699f., 796f., *Ag*. 791ff., 956f., 967f., *Thy*. 257ff., 442ff., 1100ff. It is generally structured, as here, around key-words.

240 He is wild: *ferus est*. This phrase is assigned to the Nurse in A, Pha. in E. The A assignment seems more likely since it accords both with the Senecan practice of *Stichworttechnik* (the structuring of exchanges in dialogue around "key-words") and with the way Pha. uses the language of the Nurse and others (e.g. Hipp., as at 608, 645) to articulate and strengthen her position. Most recent editors (Giomini, Viansino, Woesler, Zwierlein) follow the A assignment.

242 Father: Minos, whose ships control the seas (see 85ff.)

243   Cf. the similar exchange between Oenone and Phèdre at Rac. *Phd.* 789f.

244   Pirithous: see 94n.

245   Ariadne: Pha.'s sister, who fell in love with Th., helped him to kill the Minotaur, and fled with him to Naxos, where he deserted her.

246ff.   An elaborate form of appeal; cf. Virg. *Aen.* 4.314ff., *HF* 1246ff., *Pho.* 535ff., *Med.* 1002ff., *Oed.* 1020ff., *HO* 925f., and 868-71 below. Normally accompanied by repeated *per*, "by...", it was known as the *figura iusiurandi* and was common in Roman declamation (see, e.g., Sen. Rhet. *Con.* 9.4.4, 10.1.7, *Suas.* 7.9).

249   A quasi-proverbial *sententia*: cf. *Ep.* 34.3: "a great part of goodness is the desire to be good" (*pars magna bonitatis est uelle fieri bonum*). Cf. also *Ep.* 71.36.
   fuit: gnomic perfect again, as appropriate to a *sententia*.

250-54   Cf. Pha.'s "resolve" to die at Eur. *Hipp.* 400ff., and the suicide "threats" of Amphitryon and Aegisthus at *HF* 1311ff. and *Ag.* 302ff. respectively—and their effect. See also 712, 871, 880, 1188ff. below. Suicide was a typically Roman, esp. Stoic, way of avoiding disgrace or coping with disaster, although Sen. warned against the death-wish as such (*libido moriendi*), which he defined as an unreflecting tendency towards death (*Ep.* 24.24f.).

250   Cf. the similar statements of Hercules at *HF* 1240 and Clytemnestra at *Ag.* 288. See also Pha.'s change of mind at 885b.
   animo ingenuo: ablative of separation.

252ff.   uincatur...sequamur...praeuertam: jussive subjunctives. See 24n.

255   child: *alumna*, lit. "nurseling", an intimate form of address used by the Nurse here and at 588, and by the Nurse in *Medea* at 158, 380.
   impulse: *impetus*. An important term in the Stoic account of the emotions (= Greek *hormē*). See, e.g., *Ira* 2.3.4f. Cf. the similar language of the appeals for restraint by the Nurse in *Med.* (157f., 381) and *Ag.* (203).
   moderare: imperative.

256   dignam: sc. *te.*

257   quod...autumas: noun clause in apposition to *hoc*, lit. "because of this, viz. that you assert...". This construction is common in both prose and verse. Cf. Cicero *Fam.* 3.8.6.
   temet: emphatic form of *te.*

258   Cf. Jocasta at *Oed.* 1031f.

259f.   finiam ... incubem ... cadam: deliberative subjunctives. See Woodcock §109. On the modes of suicide cf. Oedipus at *Pho.* 147-49.

259 noose's snare: *laqueo.* At 75f. *laqueus* is used of Hipp.'s own snares and at 1086 of the reins which in turn ensnare him.

260 Pallas' citadel: the Acropolis in Athens.

261 *proin:* an abbreviation of *proinde* found esp. in the comic and tragic poets. It is scanned here as one syllable through a device known as synizesis or vowel-coalescence. The device is used frequently in Roman verse from Catullus onwards, often enabling the poet to use words and forms which would otherwise be inadmissible on prosodic grounds.

castitatis uindicem: uindex is used here predicatively and finally, and governs the genitive *castitatis:* lit. "to be saviour/defender of my honour". The phrase *libertatis uindex* was a common political slogan, and is obviously echoed by Pha.

armemus: jussive (hortatory) subjunctive. See 24n.

262 *sinat:* potential subjunctive. See 120n.

264 This line is omitted in A and is metrically defective; it is deleted by Scaliger. The problem is the spondaic second foot. But see *Oed.* 386 where a spondaic second foot also occurs, and *Ag.* 934 where a spondaic fourth foot is found. On metre see Appendix II.

265f. Cf. Pha.'s later *sententia* at 878. See also *Ep.* 12.10, 70.24, and *HO* 922: "Who has decided on death is vainly held" (*frustra tenetur ille qui statuit mori*).

265 *periturum:* substantival use of the participle; lit. "can restrain one about to die". See 95n.

266 *qui:* indefinite pronoun, "anyone", as at Plautus *Rudens* 133, Caesar *De Bello Ciuili* 2.24.4.

267-73 Similarly Myrrha's Nurse at Ovid *Met.* 10. 423-30, initially horrified by her mistress' unnatural passion for her own father and concerned to expel it, collapses in the face of Myrrha's suicide resolution and decides to help.

267 sole comfort: *solamen unicum.* Cf. *Tro.* 703f., *Med.* 945f. See also *Tro.* 462, 960f.

269f. Cf. Virgil's famous description of *fama* at *Aen.* 4.173ff., esp. 188: "As tenacious of the false and crooked, as herald of the truth." See also Ovid *Met.* 7.137-39, 12.39ff. (the "House of Fame"). Cf. Eur. *Hipp.* 501f.

270 *merenti:* substantival use of the participle.

271-73 An important cluster of "Hippolytan" adjectives: "grim" (*tristis*), "intractable" (*intractabilis*), "wild" (*ferus*), "savage" (*saeuus*), "ungentle" (*immitis*). Cf. the description of Pasiph.'s bull at 116ff. See also 416 and n.

271 *temptemus:* jussive (hortatory) subjunctive. See 24n.

FIRST CHORAL ODE (274-357)

A reflective ode on the universal power of sexual love. As often in Senecan tragedy (see, e.g., *Tro.* 371ff., *Med.* 301ff., *Thy.* 122ff.) the Chorus examines moral and other issues relevant to the dramatic action. Also common Senecan practice is the commencement of the ode with an invocation: see 959ff. below and *HF* 524ff., *Med.* 56ff., *Oed.* 110ff., 405ff., *Ag.* 57ff., 808ff., *Thy.* 122ff., 789ff. As here, this opening invocation seldom leads to prayer. The absence of strophic corresponsion in this ode is typical of Senecan and Roman tragic practice. With this ode should be compared Eur.'s *Erōs* chorus at *Hipp.* 525ff. (see also *Hipp.* 443ff.).

The songs of the chorus in fifth-century Attic tragedy were delivered away from the stage. In the Roman theatre (certainly by Vitruvius' day—see Vitr. 5.6.2) this area had been given over to senatorial seating. Confined as it was to the stage, the Roman tragic chorus—at least of the imperial period—was probably much smaller than its classical Greek counterpart (some suggest a figure of between three and seven). The difference in size allowed for greater flexibility in the matter of choral entrances and exits (see 405n.) and in the number of choruses employed. *Ag.*, e.g., has two choruses, as does the non-Senecan *HO*, although *Pha.* adopts the Senecan norm of a single chorus. Choral odes were accompanied by music (the flute, see Act One introd. note).

The chorus of *Pha.* does not identify itself. Self-identification by the chorus is common in the parodos of fifth-century Greek tragedy, more rare in Sen. (*Tro.* 67ff., *Oed.* 124ff.). Senecan choruses, however, sometimes identify themselves (e.g. *Ag.* 310ff.) or are identified by others (e.g. *HF* 827ff., *Ag.* 586ff.) later in the plays, or identify themselves (in a general sense) implicitly by the content and dramatic function of their opening song (*Med.* 56ff., *Thy.* 122ff.). The chorus of *Pha.* neither identifies itself nor is identified by others. E has after *CHORVS* the word *GRESSAE*, which may be a corruption of *CRESSAE*, "Cretan Women". Others posit a chorus of Athenian citizens. I have followed E, taking *GRESSAE* as *CRESSAE*. It is worth bearing in mind that in all three Attic plays on the subject the chorus was of women (in Eur.'s extant *Hipp.* women of Troezen). The identity of *Pha.*'s chorus would have caused no problems in performance.

Metre: sapphic (274-324); anapaestic (325-57). See Appendix II.

274-329   Cf. Pha.'s account of Cupid's power at 185-94 above.

154

274 **Goddess:** sea-born Venus, goddess of sexual love. Cf. 85 above for other sea-powers.

ungentle: *non miti.* Cf. 226, 231, 273, and 334 later in this ode. *Non* qualifies *miti.*

ponto: ablative of source or agent. See Woodcock §41.

275 **dual Cupid:** Cupid, Venus' son, the mischievous archer-boy who fires the arrows of love, is often thought of as bitter-sweet, i.e. as dual-natured (like love itself, see Eur. *Hipp.* 348). Sometimes indeed two Cupids (Eros and Anteros) are envisaged, as at Ovid *Fasti* 4.1. Cf. also *Oed.* 500. With 274f. cf. Horace *Odes* 1.19.1: *mater saeua Cupidinum* ("Cruel/savage mother of Cupids").

276 *flammis...sagittis:* ablatives of respect with *impotens*, as at *Tro.* 266f. and *Med.* 143. The ablative of respect seems to combine the instrumental and local functions of the case. See Woodcock §39.

277f. Hyperbaton. Trans. either: *quam iste...*; or *quam certo arcu iste...*

278 **unerring bow:** Latin *certo arcu.* Cf. 56f., 72, 193.

279f. These two lines are omitted in A. Several editors delete them. With them cf. the Ovidian Pha.'s self-description at *Her.* 4.15, and earlier versions of this topos: e.g. Catullus 45.15f., 64.92f., Virg. *Aen.* 4.66f., 8. 388-90. See also 640ff. below.

280 **ravages:** *populante.* So at 377 care "ravages" Pha., at 1095 stones "ravage" Hipp.'s face.

282 Cf. Pha.'s self-description at 641f.

285-90 Cf. 66-72.

285 Hyperbaton of *ora.* The normal order: *ora quae nascentem solem uidet.*

286 **Hesperia:** originally a Greek name for Italy (Dionysius *Roman Antiquities* 1.35.3), which was later applied by Roman poets to Spain and more generally, as here, the west. *Hesperias* is scanned as three long syllables (through synizesis). See 261n.

goal: *meta* is strictly speaking a turning-post. The metaphor is from chariot-racing, the idea being that Hesperia (the west) is the end of the sun's path, where its chariot is turned around.

287f. *si qua...si qua....:* sc. *ora* in each case. *Qua* is the nominative feminine of *qui* as indefinite adjective (= *aliqua*).

287 **the burning Crab:** the constellation Cancer, the fourth sign of the zodiac, in which the sun is found at the summer solstice. Hence it is used generally for "the south". See, e.g., Virg. *Ecl.* 10.68.

288 **Parrhasian bear:** Callisto, the northern constellation of the Great Bear.

Parrhasiae: scanned as three long syllables (through synizesis—see 261n.).

glacialis: modifies *qua* (*ora*).

295 *uultibus falsis:* ablative of accompaniment, a type of sociative-instrumental ablative. See Woodcock §§43 and 46.

296-98 The reference is to the period when Apollo served Admetus, king of Pherae in Thessaly, for a year, looking after his herds. Sen. seems to be using a version of this myth in which Admetus was loved by Apollo. Apollo, as sun-god, is the father of Pasiphae (see 124ff., 654).

298 scaled reeds: the Pan-pipe, consisting of several reeds of different lengths.

299-308 The chorus alludes to various sexual liaisons of Jupiter. Disguised as a swan, he had an affair with Leda (301f.), and, disguised as a bull, with Europa, whom he carried off (303-08). From the latter union was born Minos, Pha.'s father. See Ovid *Met.* 2.833ff., 6.103ff., and Moschus *Europa* (esp. 99f.). Cf. *HO* 551ff., *Oct.* 201ff., 764ff.

300 A reformulation of the epithet *nephelēgereta*, "cloud-gatherer", used in Homer of Zeus (Jupiter).

302 *uocem:* this use of the internal accusative of respect with an adjective seems to have been introduced in Latin in imitation of Greek. It is found predominantly in verse (e.g. *nuda genu,* "her knee bare", Virg. *Aen.* 1.320) but does occur in prose (e.g. Tac. *Ger.* 17). See Woodcock §19.

moriente cygno: ablative of comparison. See 144n.

304 *ludo:* dative of purpose. See Woodcock §67.

305 brother's waves: the sea, allotted to Neptune, Jupiter's brother.

fraternos...fluctus: the arrangement here of two adjectives and two substantives in chiastic order (abBA) is common in Sen.: see, e.g., 113, 281, 329, 626, 1253, *HF* 367, *Med.* 722, *Ag.* 54, *Thy.* 113. Cf. other kinds of chiastic arrangement at 308, 952 (aBbA) and 908 (AabB) below.

noua regna: accusative in apposition to *fraternos fluctus.* Here the appositive phrase is enclosed by the noun and its modifier. Cf. 1105 below, where the noun is enclosed by the appositive phrase.

308 *timidus rapina:* with the oxymoronic juxtaposition here cf. Horace *Odes* 3.20.3f.: *inaudax...raptor,* "spineless rapist".

309-16 The reference is to Diana, goddess of the moon (and hunt), who fell in love with a mortal, Endymion, and arranged for her brother, Apollo the sun-god, to drive her chariot of the moon while she spent the night with her lover. Diana's affair with Endymion is alluded to again at 422. Cf. also 785ff. Note that the chorus-leader at 405 still accords Diana her traditional title of *uirgo*. See also 54n.

313 *flecti:* passive infinitive with intransitive sense.

316 **Tremble...**: because Apollo, not Diana, is driving the chariot. Contrast Ovid *Met.* 2.161f., where Phaethon, replacing Phoebus in the chariot of the sun, makes the chariot light.

317-29 The story of Hercules, "Alcmena's son", who served Omphale, queen of Lydia as her slave. In love with her, he wore effeminate dress and jewellery, and performed women's duties. The incident is used by Lycus at *HF* 465-71 in his attempt to dispute Hercules' bravery. See also *HO* 371ff. For another "labour" of Hercules—directly connected with the play's action—see 843ff. below.

Sen.'s preoccupation with the figure of Hercules in the tragedies (he is rarely mentioned in the prose works) is noteworthy. Here, as, e.g., at *Ag.* 808ff., there is no allusion to Hercules' status—among the Stoics—as long-suffering champion of mankind, universal benefactor and sage (*sapiens*), for which see *Ben.* 1.13.3, *Const.* 2.1f. See, however, *Med.* 637 and *HF* 249ff., 882ff.

317 **put quiver down:** cf. love's opposite effect on Pha. (396 below).

natus Alcmena: lit."born from Alcmena". The ablative is one of source. See Woodcock §41.

318 **lion's menacing spoil:** the skin and head of the Nemean lion, which Hercules traditionally wears.

minax: modifies *spolium*. For the arrangement of adjectives and nouns here (abAB) see 85n.

322 **slippers:** the *soccus* is the characteristic footwear of comedy. It has obvious associations of domesticity, and is inappropriate footwear for an epic hero (or for a Roman magistrate—see Cic.'s famous expression of outrage at the "slippered [*soleatus*] praetor", *Ver.* 5.86).

323 Postponement of the relative *qua*; trans.: *qua clauam...*

325 **Persia...Lydia:** both countries would suggest oriental effeminacy, luxury and voluptuousness.

325f. *diti...regno:* sociative ablative, perhaps even ablative of description. See Woodcock §§43 and 83.

328 **Once prop...:** Hercules took the place of Atlas in supporting the world, when the latter offered to fetch the apples of the Hesperides for him.

329 **Tyrian:** from the city of Tyre, a city on the Phoenician coast famous for finely woven fabrics of silk or linen and for a purple dye.

Tyrio stamine: ablative of description. See 50n. On the chiastic order here see 305n.

330-57 There are clear allusions in this passage to Virgil's account in the *Georgics* of the destructive power of sexual *amor* throughout all animal life. See *Geo.* 3.209-83, esp. 242-44:

> omne adeo genus in terris hominumque ferarumque
> et genus aequoreum, pecudes pictaeque uolucres,
> in furias ignemque ruunt: amor omnibus idem.

> Every tribe on earth both of men and of beasts,
> And the tribe of the sea, the cattle and dappled birds,
> Rush to this frenzied fire: love for all is the same.

See also 339-47n. Eur.'s *Erōs* chorus at *Hipp.* 525ff. restricts itself to human "love". *Hipp.* 447ff. is less restrictive.

330 cursed fire: *sacer ignis.* The phrase, used here of sexual passion, has strong connotations of disease. It is used in Lucretius (6.660, 1167) as a name for erisypelas or a disease akin to it. Virg.'s third georgic in fact closes on the *sacer ignis* brought by the Noric plague: *artus sacer ignis edebat,* "the cursed fire ate the limbs" (*Geo.* 3.566)—a description which Sen. borrows (and slightly remodels) for his own account of plague at *Oed.* 187f.: *sacer ignis/ pascitur artus,* "the cursed fire crops limbs". See also Pliny *NH* 26.121. Since the meaning of *sacer* as "accursed" is to be found in the Twelve Tables (*sacer esto*), drawn up in the fifth century B.C. (although only a relatively modernised text survives), to Sen.'s contemporaries the word (and this phrase) probably had archaic force.

laesis: substantival use of participle. See 95n.

336 Nereid: a daughter of Nereus, i.e. a sea-nymph.

339-47 Cf. Virg. *Geo.* 3.219-41, 265, 248f., 255f.

344 swarthy: *decolor.* The defining epithet of India and its inhabitants. Cf. *decolor Indus*, Propertius 4.3.10, Ovid *Ars* 3.130. The theory was that Indians were scorched by the sun (*Med.* 484, *Oed.* 122f., *Thy.* 602, *HO* 41). Sen. himself wrote an account (*commentatio*) of the country (Pliny *NH* 6.60).

351 Luca-bulls: elephants, first sighted by Romans in Lucania in southern Italy, brought there by the invading king of Epirus, Pyrrhus, in the early part of the third century B.C. (Pliny *NH* 8.16).

Lucae boues: nominative plural of *Luca bos.*

352 With this seminal line cf. the apocalyptic pronouncement of Virg. *Geo.* 3.244: *amor omnibus idem,* "love is the same for all." Cf. also Virg. *Ecl.* 10.69: *omnia uincit amor,* "love conquers all." The fusion here in *Pha.* of nature and *amor* has no role in Eur.'s *Erōs* chorus (*Hipp.* 525ff.), where love's operation is restricted entirely to man. On the meaning of "nature", *natura,* in Sen. see Appendix I. See also 173n. and 959n. For the thematic importance of this line see Introd. p. 20f.

claims: *uindicat* embraces both the notion of making a legal claim to something (as one's property) and that of exacting legal redress or simply vengeance. Here and at 1187 the former sense seems uppermost; at 125 the latter. See also 1209n. The theme of "vindication" is common in Sen. tragedy—but see esp. *Med.* 668 (*iam satis, diui, mare uindicastis*, "Redress enough, gods, have you claimed for the sea"), where the "redress" or "vindication" the chorus vainly seeks to avert is for a breach of natural law (*Med.* 605f., 614f.). For *uindicare* = "claim" in Sen.'s prose works, see, e.g., *Ep.* 45.4, and esp. 33.4: "We (Stoics) are not subject to a king; each of us claims his own freedom" (*sibi quisque se uindicat*, lit. "each claims himself for himself"). Note how *uindicat* at 352 is verbal climax to the opening words of the first two sections of the ode (*diua*, 274, *uidet*, 325).

355 Yield to fire: the association of fire with sexual love (see elsewhere in this ode: 276, 280, 309, 330, 337f.) is of course commonplace and not only in ancient literature. What needs noting here also is the association of fire with nature, which is among other things Stoic. Zeno (335-263 B.C.), the founder of Stoicism, in fact defined nature as a craftsmanlike fire (*ignis artificiosus*, Cic. *ND* 2.57; cf. Cic. *ND* 3.27, *Ac.* 1.39; Tertullian *Ad Nat.* 2.2; Diogenes Laertius 7.156); while others saw fire as "the element par excellence", the one that persisted forever and into which the rest dissolved (see Von Arnim *SVF* II.413). See also Sen. *NQ* 3.13.1: "For we say that it is fire which takes possession of the universe and changes all things into itself" (*dicimus enim ignem esse qui occupet mundum et in se cuncta conuertat*). The ending of *Pha.*'s first choral ode thus seems to fuse commonplace (love=fire) and Stoic physics (fire=nature) into a dramatically signal vision (love=fire=nature).

356f. Love: *cura* is almost a technical term in Roman elegy for passionate, anxiety-ridden love: see Propertius 1.8.1., 1.15.31. It is often also used of the object of love, the loved one: Virg. *Ecl.* 10.22, Propertius 1.1.35f., Horace *Odes* 1.14.18, Ovid *Am.* 1.3.16.

savage stepmothers: "savagery" or "cruelty" was a defining feature of the traditional stepmother figure, the *nouerca* (see Eur. *Alcestis* 309f.). The figure appeared often in declamatory exercises; see Sen. Rhet. *Con.* 4.6 and 9.5, and cf. also Jerome *Ep.* 54.15: "Every comedy, mime-writer and rhetorical commonplace will declaim against the savage stepmother (*in nouercam saeuissimam*)." To Sen.'s contemporaries, however, the figure was not simply a traditional or legendary one. Stepmothers (Livia, Messalina, Agrippina) had played—and perhaps at the time of this play (if it predates Agrippina's murder in A.D. 59) were playing—an important and notorious role in imperial politics. Tacitus wastes no time in his

Annales in casting Augustus' wife, Livia, as the *nouerca* (*Ann.* 1.3.3, 1.6.2, 1.10.5).

With the end of this choral ode cf. the ending of the third georgic's account of love's power, where again the focus is on stepmothers (*malae nouercae, Geo.* 3.282—cf. also *saeuae nouercae, Geo.* 2.128). But note that, whereas in Virg. the stepmothers are an adjunct to the picture of wind-pregnant mares dripping hippomanes, here they are presented as the climactic instance of love's conquests.

ACT THREE (358-735)

The third act of three other Sen. tragedies dramatises a confrontation between the play's major figures: *Tro.* (Andromache-Ulysses), *Med.* (Medea-Jason), *Thy.* (Thyestes-Atreus). Act 3 of *Pha.* has a double confrontation: the Nurse with Hipp., Hipp. with Pha. Only the aftermath of the former confrontation is dramatised in Eur.'s extant *Hipp.* and the latter not at all, although a confrontation between Hipp. and Pha. seems to have taken place in the earlier version now lost, the so-called *Hippolytos Kalyptomenos*. Rac.'s Hipp.-Ph. confrontation (*Phd.* 581ff.) owes much to Sen. The third act of the remaining "complete" Sen. plays (*HF, Oed., Ag.*) consists primarily of a narration of events outside—but relevant to—the dramatic action.

Metre: iambic trimeter (senarius). See Appendix II.

358f. Every choral ode in *Pha.* is followed by a bridge-passage in iambics spoken by the chorus or chorus-leader to introduce the following act (see 824ff., 989ff., 1154f.). This is not a standard feature of Sen. tragedy. In *Thy.*, for example, there are no such bridge-passages. Since such passages are always accompanied in *Pha.* by the entrance of a character, I have regarded them as belonging to the act which they introduce.

358 *profare:* an elevated word for "telling", found almost entirely in epic or tragedy: e.g. Ennius *Annales* 563V[3], Pacuvius 145R[2], Virg. *Aen.* 1.561. It occurs also at *HF* 1176 and *Thy.* 244.

360 *tantum...malum:* noun-clause in the accusative and infinitive after *spes* (sc. *est*).

362ff. Cf. the Nurse's description of Medea's rage or *furor* at *Med.* 382-96, and the "sickbed scene" of Eur. *Hipp.* 170ff. See also *HO* 233ff. Sen. was most interested in the physical effects of passion or anger (see *Ira* 1.1.4, 2.36.4f., 3.4.1-3).

362 **silent heat:** *aestu tacito.* Cf. Dido's "silent" (*tacitum*) wound at Virg. *Aen.* 4.67.

363 **traitored...face:** For this common belief that thoughts and feelings could be seen in the face, see, e.g., Cic. *Pis.* 1, Ovid *Ars* 1.574, *Met.* 2.447. Cf. *Ag.* 128, *HO* 704f., *Ben.* 6.12.1. Faces could also deceive: see 915ff. below.

365 **nil:** (=*nihil*) used as an adverbial accusative here ("in no respect").

367 **ut:** relative adverb, "as if". It modifies *moriens.* Cf. Publilius Syrus 624: *quod est uenturum sapiens ut praesens cauet.*

373 **mutatur habitus:** best construed perhaps with Pha. as subject. The phrase can be analysed either as a passive verb with an internal accusative of respect or as an attempt to imitate in Latin the Greek middle voice with an accusative of direct object. See Woodcock §19. Others take *habitus* as "dress", some as (singular) subject of *mutatur.*

373f. **No care...for food:** a recurring feature of Eur.'s presentation of Pha.'s love-sickness; see *Hipp.* 135, 275, 277.

Cereris: "for food". Ceres, the Roman goddess of agriculture, functions frequently as a metonym for corn (Virg. *Aen.* 1.177), bread (Virg. *Aen.* 1.701) or, as here, for food in general.

377f. These two lines are deleted by Leo. Most editors have not followed him.

377 **care:** *cura.* To the audience and reader—if not to the Chorus—the sense of "love" would also be present. See 356f.n.

ravages: *populatur.* Cf. 280, 1095.

378 **set:** *cecidit.* On the celestial metaphor here see 1270n.

379 **Phoebus' torch:** the sun. Phoebus, the sun-god, was the father of Pasiphae, Pha.'s mother.

380 **nihil gentile...patrium:** internal accusatives with the intransitive verb *micant.* Cf. [Virg.] *Culex* 222: *sanguinei micant ardorem luminis.* See Woodcock §13.

381ff. Cf. Ovid *Am.* 1.7.57f.

382 **Taurus' heights:** Taurus was a massive mountain-range in the south of Asia Minor.

384-86 These lines imply that the upper storey (*fastigium*) of the palace opens to reveal Pha. love-sick on her royal couch. Hence the stage-directions. The presence of a door or doors in the upper storey of the stage-building seems to have been a common feature of Hellenistic, Hellenistic-Italic and Roman republican theatres. Although a purely ornamental second storey became fashionable during the empire, there is no reason to suppose that all Roman imperial theatres jettisoned this facility. For other interior scenes—

involving the opening of the *regia* or central lower door—see 863ff. below and *Thy.* 901ff.

387-93 Cf. the choric diatribe on female luxury at *HO* 658-67.

388 Tyre: see 329n. above.

sit: jussive subjuctive. So too *constringat*, 390.

389 Serics: the *Seres* inhabited a region in eastern Asia beyond Scythia and India, identified with northern China. For the belief that they produced silk by combing off the white down of the leaves of certain trees, see, e.g., Virg. *Geo.* 2.121, *HO* 666f., Pliny *NH* 6.54. Pliny, however, knew that Coan silk was the product of a grub, *uermiculus* (*NH* 11.76). Silk dresses were often condemned by Roman writers as indecent (because transparent), extravagant and a symptom of moral and social decay: see esp. Sen.'s attack on "Seric dresses", *Sericas uestes*, at *Ben.* 7.9.5.

quae fila: hyperbaton. Trans. (*procul sint*) *fila quae...*

393 Assyrian nard: "Assyrian" is a frequent epithet of perfumes in the Roman poets: see, e.g., Catullus 68.144, Virg. *Ecl.* 4.25, Tibullus 1.3.7, Horace *Odes* 2.11.16. It is generally taken as a grandiose epithet for "Syrian" (see 87n.). Although the perfumes and spices used in Rome were from Arabia, they would have reached Rome via the Syrian ports. Assyria proper was part of Mesopotamia.

394f. Cf. Eur. *Hipp.* 202.

394 *sic temere:* modelled perhaps on the Greek phrase *houtōs eikēi*, "just anyhow". See Horace *Odes* 2.11.14.

396ff. Cf. the Ovidian Pha.'s passion for the hunt at *Her.* 4.41ff., and Eur. *Hipp.* 215ff.

397 Thessalia's spear: the light throwing-spear used in hunting and associated with Thessaly in north-eastern Greece. See also Eur. *Hipp.* 219ff.

398 Some editors delete this line.

399-403 See 181-83n.

399 Tanais or Maeotis: Tanais is a river to the west of Scythia, modern name the Don. It empties into lake Maeotis (the Sea of Azov), which itself adjoins the Black Sea.

400 Pontus: the Black Sea.

402f. *latus protecta:* the use of the internal accusative of respect with passive participles to denote a part of the body affected is primarily a poetic construction (probably in imitation of the Greek middle voice and/or the Greek accusative of respect). It does, however, also occur occasionally in prose: e.g. Livy 21.7.10, *femur tragula ictus*, "hit in the thigh by a spear". See Woodcock §19.

403 crescent shield: the light shield carried by the Amazons with a semi-circular indentation on one edge, giving it the appearance of a crescent moon. The phrase, *lunata pelta*, is Virgilian (*Aen.* 1.490, 11.663, of the Amazon, Penthesilea). See also *Med.* 214, *Ag.* 218.

  I will to the woods: cf. 82 above and Eur. *Hipp.* 215.

  It seems likely that the doors of the upper storey of the palace now close. Hipp. makes no reference either to the upper storey of the palace or to the distraught Pha. in the following scene with the Nurse.

404f. Correctly assigned by E to the Chorus, whose instructions to the Nurse signal the end of the Pha. scene and the beginning of the next one. See also 358f.n. above.

405 virgin goddess: the only reference in *Pha.* to Diana as *uirgo*. See 54n., 309-16n.

  rural power: *agreste* would perhaps suggest one of the Greek cult-titles of Artemis, *Agrotera*, "Lady of the Fields".

  The Chorus presumably exits at this point. Sen. seems to follow Hellenistic dramatic (tragic) conventions in his use of choral entrances and exits. In Sen. tragedy there is no reason to regard the Chorus, which was probably smaller than the classical Greek chorus, as present in any scene in which it is not compelled to speak. *Pha.* 599-601 make it clear that the Chorus is not present in the second part of this act, just as *HF* 827-29 make it clear that that play's chorus is absent from the act preceding those lines. One advantage of this increased flexibility in the use of the Chorus is that the Chorus does not have to be sworn to silence each time a plot is hatched or an intrigue conducted (see *Tro.* 203ff., *Ag.* 108ff., *Thy.* 176ff.). Contrast Eur. *Hipp.* 710ff., where Pha. has to extract a vow of silence from the Chorus before articulating her plot to destroy Hipp.

406ff. The second prayer to Diana in the play, more traditional in its structure than the earlier one of Hipp. (54ff.): appellation and general requests (406-12); specific requests (413-17); conditional prayer for the welfare of the goddess (417-22); concluding invocation (423). For the opening—and standard—invocation of Diana as queen of the forests and hills, see Catullus 34.9ff., Horace *Odes* 3.22.1. See also 54-80n.

407 *una:* best taken as nominative.

408 *in melius:* take with *conuerte.*

410f. The allusion is to Diana as goddess of the moon. Cf. Horace *Carmen Saeculare* 2, where both Diana and Apollo are invoked as "heaven's radiant splendour" (*lucidum caeli decus*). In Eur. *Hipp. Kalypt.* (according to a scholiast on Theocritus 2.10) it was the love-sick Pha. who invoked the moon.

412 Hecate triformed: Hecate was a primitive goddess, associated with the moon (Luna), Diana and the underworld, thus possessing heavenly, earthly and chthonic powers. Hence "triformed". She is generally identified with Diana and is particularly associated with witchcraft. Cf. her invocation by Medea at *Med.* 6f., 750ff. (in the latter passage she is called Phoebe, Trivia, Dictynna and Hecate). For the epithet *triformis*, "triformed", see also Horace *Odes* 3.22.4, Ovid *Met.* 7.94.

413 Tame...: so the Ovidian Pha. to Hipp.:"Tame your hard heart" (*duraque corda doma, Her.* 4.156).

414 *det:* jussive subjunctive. So too *discat* (415), *ferat* (415), *redeat* (417). See 24n.

416 Fierce, hostile, ferocious: *toruus auersus ferox.* Clusters of adjectives or nouns in asyndeton are common in the tragedies; see, e.g., 923, 939, *Med.* 21, *Ag.* 47. It was in fact a feature of the high tragic style of the republic (see, e.g., Pacuvius 53R^2, Accius 349R^2, 595R^2). The adjectives here are substantival in function (see 95n.). With the description of Hipp. here cf. that of the bull at 116-19, and of the sea-monster and Hipp. at 1063f.

417 Venus' law: cf. 125, 352, 910. See also Ovid *Am.* 1.2.20, where the elegiac lover submits to the "law" (*iura*) of Cupid (cf. also Propertius 1.9.3).

417ff. Turn...so may...so: this kind of conditional prayer for the welfare of the deity or person petitioned is a traditional feature of Greek and Roman petitions. Cf. Catullus 17.5ff., Virg. *Ecl.* 10.4ff., Horace *Odes* 1.3.1ff., Tibullus 2.5.121f. and *Tro.* 698ff.

sic: lit. "on this condition". It is followed by optative subjunctives (*ferant...eas*, etc.) to express the wish (see Woodcock §§113f.). The condition referred to is expressed either, as here, by a preceding imperative or, as at *Tro.* 698ff., by a succeeding one.

421 Thessaly's chants: the chants of witches, for which Thessaly was famous, were said to have the power to draw down the moon from the sky. See 791 below, and *Med.* 674, 789ff., *HO* 467f., 526ff. Cf. Aristophanes *Clouds* 749-52, Virg. *Ecl.* 8.69, Horace *Epode* 5.45ff., Propertius 1.1.19, Ovid *Met.* 7.207, Lucan 6.499ff.

422 A reference to Endymion, whom Diana loved. See 309-16 above.

423 *ades:* probably imperative, as at 54, 412, 1175.

424ff. Cf. Hipp.'s entrance in Eur. *Hipp.* 51ff., observed by Aphrodite and accompanied by a large crowd singing the praises of Artemis. Veneration of Artemis and her shrine follows. On "asides" in Sen. see 136-39n.

424 *intuor:* this third conjugation form is not uncommon in Roman drama. See, e.g., *Ag.* 917 and Plautus *Mostellaria* 836.

sollemne...sacrum: internal accusative with *uenerantem*, lit. "worshipping with due rites". See Woodcock §13.

427-30   Cf. the similar conflict between "orders" or "task" (*mandatum*) and "shame" (*pudor*) experienced by Pha. at 592ff.

428   Hyperbaton. Postponement of *qui*; trans.: *qui iussa...*

429   *deponat...pellat:* jussive subjunctives. See Woodcock §109.

433   *uultu:* ablative of respect. See Woodcock §55.

434   **two children:** Acamas and Demophon.

437   **more gently:** *mitior.* Cf. 226, 231, 273 (274, 334).
beatis...rebus: dative after *mitior.*

438   *anxiam:* proleptic adjective.
tui: objective genitive after *cura.*

440-43   A commonplace of popular wisdom: cf. Sophocles *Philoctetes* 1316-20.

442   **rack yourself:** *seque ipse torquet.* Cf. *Ep.* 5.4, where this is proclaimed to be "contrary to nature" (*contra naturam*).
perdere: the infinitive after *dignus* occurs in verse and postclassical prose.

443   *quis:* the alternative form of the dative/ablative plural of the relative pronoun (= *quibus*).

444   *noctibus festis:* ablative of time, a form of local ablative. See Woodcock §54.

445   *exoneret:* jussive subjunctive. So too *exultet* (448). See 24n.

446   **Enjoy...flies:** a Horatian commonplace; see, e.g., *Odes* 1.11.7f., 2.3.13ff., 2.11.5ff. Cf. 761ff. below and *HF* 177ff.

447   *nunc facile...:* sc. *est.*

450   **life's finest days:** *optimos uitae dies.* There is a clear allusion here to the general reflection (on cattle and horses) at Virg. *Geo.* 3.66f.: "life's finest days are ever the first to flee for piteous mortals" (*optima quaeque dies miseris mortalibus aeui/ prima fugit*). The Virgilian lines are quoted and discussed by Sen. at *Brev.* 9.2ff., *Ep.* 108.24ff.

456   *tenera:* predicative (adverbial) use of the adjective, lit. "when young". See Woodcock §88.

464f.   *ut...tolerent...domitent...gerant:* final noun-clause expressing indirect command (implied in *indictum*). Cf. Livy 1.52.5: *indictum... ut...adessent.* See Woodcock §139.

466-80   The order of these lines has often been changed. The order here is that of the manuscripts.

469   **Venus:** for Venus as the generative principle in nature see esp. the great proem to the first book of Lucretius. An analogous use is made of the notion of Cypris as goddess of all life by Eur.'s Nurse at *Hipp.* 447ff., but the target of the Nurse's rhetoric there is Pha., not Hipp. "Love" as a cosmic principle has a long philosophical and mythopoeic tradition (see, e.g., Hesiod *Theogony*, Empedocles *On Nature*, Aristotle *Metaphysics Lambda*). See also "Nero's" remarks at *Oct.*566ff.; Aeschylus fr.44N, Eur. fr.898N.

excedat: jussive subjunctive used in a concessive sense. So too *credas* (477), *probet* (478). See Woodcock §112.

475   For this topos cf. the Sen. Rhet.*Con.* 1.8.6, 7.1.9, Petron. *Sat.* 115.16.

477   *desse:* for *deesse.* Synizesis (see 261n.) is dictated by the metre.

477f.   **We seek...help:** cf. *HF* 185, "We seek the Stygian waves of our own accord" (*Stygias ultro quaerimus undas*). See also *HF* 870-74, *Tro.* 390, and Horace *Odes* 2.3.25.

480   *unius aeui:* genitive of description. See 208n.

semet: emphatic form of *se.*

481   **Follow nature...:** a central principle of Stoic ethics from Zeno and Cleanthes onwards—"to live in agreement with nature" (*homologoumenōs tēi physei zēn*, see, e.g., Diogenes Laertius 7.87). Cf. Cic. *Off.* 1.100: "If we follow nature as our guide, we shall never go astray (*quam [naturam] si sequemur ducem, numquam aberrabimus*). See also Sen. *Ep.* 41.9, 90.4, 90.16 ("follow nature", *sequere naturam*), and *Ep.* 5.6: "Our motto, as you know, is to live according to nature" (*nempe propositum nostrum est secundum naturam uiuere*). *Ep.* 5 also advocates sociability and the avoidance of excessive primitivism. Note the Epicurean principle, to which both idea and language here approximate: "life's guide" is "divine pleasure", *dux uitae dia uoluptas* (Lucretius 2.172).

sequere: imperative.

483ff.   Eulogies of the simple or "natural" life occur frequently in Roman poetry. With Hipp.'s defence here cf. esp. Lucretius 2.20ff., Horace *Epode* 2.1ff., Virg. *Geo.* 2.458-74, 493ff., and Ovid *Met.* 1.89ff. See also *HF* 159ff., *Thy.* 446-70, and the description of the primitive life according to nature at *Ep.* 90.36ff. Praise of poverty and the simple life and the condemnation of wealth and luxury were standard topics of declamation: see Sen. Rhet. *Con.* 2.1.11-13. Among later literature the speech of Henry VI in *Henry VI Part 3* ii.5.21ff. ("O God! methinks it were a happy life/ To be no better than a homely swain...") may be compared.

484   *colat:* generic subjunctive found in descriptive relative clauses. See Woodcock §155.

485   far from city walls: contrast Eur. *Hipp.* 1016ff., where Hipp. reveals himself no hater of the city.

492   Liberated...fear: so the Stoic sage "knows nothing of living in hope or fear" (*nescit nec in spem nec in metum uiuere, Const.* 9.2), nor does the true king (*Thy.* 348ff.). Cf. *Tro.* 399f., *Ep.* 5.7, 47.17, 82.18, 90.43, 110.4.

spei metusque: the genitive with *liber* seems to be an imitation of the Greek construction with *eleutheros* which takes a genitive of separation; cf. Horace *Ars Poetica* 212, *liberque laborum*, and Lucan 4.384, *curarum liber*. Contrast 601 below.

493   Gnawing envy: *edax liuor.* The phrase seems to be Ovidian: see *Am.* 1.15.1, *Rem.* 389. Cf. also Horace *Odes* 4.3.16.

494   Hyperbaton of *inter.* Trans.: *inter populos...*

**496-98   Cf. the description of the Tantalid palace at *Thy.* 646f. See also Horace *Odes* 2.18.1-4, Propertius 3.2.11f., Statius *Thebaid* 1.144-46, and *Ep.* 90.9.

**498-500   The slaughter of cattle (and the eating of animal flesh) featured in the mythopoeic tradition as a symptom of the moral decline which followed the Golden Age (see 525-39n.), an emblem of man's postlapsarian or "fallen" state: see Aratus *Phaenomena* 130ff., Virg. *Geo.* 2.536f., Ovid *Met.* 15.96-142. With Hipp.'s attitude here cf. 708f.

499f.   sprinkled...: Before sacrifices the victim was sprinkled with barley meal and thus consecrated to the gods.

500   *centena:* see 150n. With the arrangement of adjectives and nouns here (abAB) cf. 85 and n.

503   subtle traps: *callidas...fraudes,* lit. "crafty deceits/tricks". *Fraus* or "deceit" is generally not a feature of the Golden Age (525-39 below and n.); indeed according to Virg. *Ecl.* 4.31 *prisca fraus*, "primal deceit" (of Prometheus), was the cause of the Golden Age's disappearance. Cf. also *Oct.* 409ff., where hunting belongs to a degenerate age, *deterior aetas*, following the Golden Age proper. With Hipp. here cf. the usurer Alfius at Horace *Epode* 2.29ff. See also 828 below.

struxisse: perfect infinitives are often found in Latin verse where in prose one would expect the present: see, e.g., Virg. *Ecl.* 2.34, Tibullus 1.1.29f., 1.1.45f., Horace *Odes* 1.1.4, 3.4.51f. They are esp. common with verbs like *iuuat* (510, 519), *licet, pudet*, etc. So too *pressisse* (511), *duxisse* (512), *fugisse* (518), *captasse* (520). See also 977, 1184.

504   Ilissos: see 13(14)n.

505   Alpheus: the main river of the Peloponnese. It flows through Arcadia and Elis past Olympia into the Ionian sea. It was sacred to

Jupiter (Zeus)—see *Med.* 81, *Thy.* 116f.—and sometimes functions as a metonym for Olympia (and the Olympic games)—see Virg. *Geo.* 3.19.

507 Lerna: a river of the Argolid.

517-21 Cf. *Thy.* 449ff., *HO* 652ff., *Ep.* 90.41f. Contrast the attitude of the chorus at 777-84.

519 anxious gold: *sollicito auro. Thy.* 453 is more specific: "poison is drunk in (cups of) gold" (*uenenum in auro bibitur*).

520 *captasse:* syncopated form of *captauisse.* For the perfect infinitive here see 503n. Cf. *HO* 657.

522-25 The connection between the open sky and "good faith" was reflected in the Roman practice of swearing oaths by *Dius Fidius* (the god of faith) beneath the open sky. The roof of the temple of *Dius Fidius* was in fact pierced with holes so that the open sky could be seen (Varro *De Lingua Latina* 5.66). Note the focus on the "openness" of the lives of the primitives in *Ep.* 90 (*Ep.* 90.42f.: *in aperto, inter aperta*; cf. *aperto aethere,* 501 above) and the self-covering of Pha. at 886.

525-39 The myth of the Golden Age, a pre-urban (sometimes pre-technological) paradisical era of human innocence and man-god and man-nature harmony is by Sen.'s time well established in the Graeco-Roman literary tradition: it is often identified with the reign of Kronos (Greek) or Saturn (Roman). See Hesiod *Works and Days* 109-201, Plato *Politicus* 271cff., Aratus *Phaenomena* 96-136, Horace *Epode* 16.41ff., Virg. *Ecl.* 4, *Geo.* 1.121ff., 2.536ff., Tibullus 1.3.35ff., Ovid *Met.* 1.89-150, Statius *Thebaid* 1.144ff. (see also Catullus 64.384ff.). The account in *Pha.* owes much to several of the above but esp. to Virg. and Ovid (cf. 527 with *Ecl.* 4.15f., 528f. with *Geo.* 1.125ff., 530f. with *Geo.* 1.136ff. and *Met.* 1.94ff., 531f. with *Geo.* 2.539 and *Met.* 1.99f., 537f. with *Met.* 1.101ff.). See also *Med.* 329ff., *Ep.* 90. 36ff., which itself cites Virg. *Geo.* 1.125-28, and the account of the Golden Age and man's decline from it put into the mouth of "Seneca" by the author of *Octauia* (397-435).

525 *hoc:* ablative with *ritu* (526).

527f. blind desire/ For gold: cf. Aeneas' outcry at Virg. *Aen.* 3.56f.: "To what lengths do you not drive the hearts of men,/ accursed hunger for gold?" (*quid non mortalia pectora cogis, auri sacra fames?*).

528f. Hyperbaton: *nullus* and *sacer* modify *lapis,* to which *arbiter* is in apposition.

530f. Cf. Pha.'s opening lines (85-88).

531 *norat:* syncopated form of *nouerat.*

533 *saeua manu:* note the ablative with *aptabat* instead of the more usual dative.

535 *iussa nec: nec* is postponed *metri causa.*

538 *pauere:* perfect indicative; so too *rupere* (540).

540 **Impious rage for gain:** *impius lucri furor.* Similarly at Virg. *Aen.* 8.327 Evander speaks of "war's frenzy" (*belli rabies*) and "passion for gain" (*amor habendi*) as ending the Golden Age. Other accounts attribute man's "fall" to Prometheus' theft of fire (e.g., Virg. *Ecl.* 4.31, 6.42). With "rage for gain" (*lucri furor*) cf. the "rage for power" (*regni furor*) attributed to Thyestes by Atreus at *Thy.* 302. *Lucri* is objective genitive.

    covenant: *foedus.* See *Med.* 335 and 606,where man's breaking of "the sacrosanct covenants of the universe" (*sacro...sancta foedera mundi*) by venturing onto the seas brings devastation and death. See also 910 below.

542 *libido:* the final *o* is short. Shortening of the final *o* for the sake of metrical convenience increases in the post-Augustan poets and embraces nouns of the third declension (as here, cf. also *ratio,* 567), some first person singular verbal forms (e.g. *uiuo,* 880) and certain adverbs (e.g. *quando,* 673, *subito,* 1007, *uero,* 1082), as well as iambic dissyllables such as *modo* (1111).

543 *factus:* sc. *est. Minor* is the subject, *praeda maiori* the predicate.

544 *esse:* historic infinitive, frequent in excited narrative. So too *bellare* (545). See Woodcock §21.

546-49 Cf. the weapons of the hunt at 48-53. See also 706.

546 *uertere* = *uerterunt,* perfect indicative.

    cornel: defined by Virg. *Geo.* 2.447f. as "good for war" (*bona bello*) and used for spear-shafts: see, e.g., Virg. *Aen.* 9.698, 12.267.

548f. *crista procul...comantes:* a difficult expression, lit. "far crest-plumed", *procul* suggesting the visibility of the *galeae* from a distance. *Crista* seems best taken as instrumental ablative.

549 **grievance furnished arms:** as it did at Virg. *Aen.* 7.508 (*telum ira facit,* "anger furnishes arms") in the incident—the slaying of the pet stag of the family of Tyrrhus—which proves proximate cause of the war in Latium that occupies the second half of the *Aeneid.*

550 **Mavors:** Mars, god of war.

551f. Cf. the Fury's outburst at *Thy.* 44: "Let streaming blood irrigate every land" (*effusus omnes irriget terras cruor*)—as she urges the triumph of lust, *libido uictrix.*

555-58 Cf. Catullus 64.399ff., Ovid *Met.* 1.144ff. (the Iron Age), and *Ira* 2.8.9ff., in which the Ovid passage is cited and expanded. See also *Thy.* 40ff.

558 The attitude is commonplace (see 356n.); the silence less so. *mitius nil est feris:* the subject of *est* is *nouerca* treated as neuter. *Nil* is adverbial accusative of extent (see 119n.). *Feris* is ablative of comparison (see 143n.). Lit. "she is a thing to no extent more gentle than wild beasts".

559-64 Cf. Eur. *Hipp.* 616ff., where, however, Hipp.'s outburst against women follows rather than precedes the revelation of Pha.'s love. Cf. also the attitude to women at 824-28 below.

559 **Mistress of crime:** *scelerum artifex.* So Medea (see 563f.n.) is described by the Nurse at *Med.* 734.

560 *obsedit:* gnomic perfect. See 75f.n.
stupris: ablative of cause. See Woodcock §45.

563 *sileantur:* jussive subjunctive. See 24n.

563f. **Aegeus' wife,/ Medea:** daughter of Aeetes king of Colchis on the eastern shore of the Black Sea, and mistress of witchcraft. She helped Jason to carry off the golden fleece and fled with him. At Corinth, when Jason was about to desert her for Creusa, daughter of Creon king of Corinth, she killed both king and daughter and also her own children by Jason. She fled to Athens, where she married Aegeus, the father of Theseus. Later she tried to poison Theseus in order to secure the succession of her own son by Aegeus to the throne. See Ovid *Met.* 7.402ff. Hipp. refers to Medea again at 696f. On the stepmother figure generally—and its contemporary ramifications—see 356f.n.

567 *sit:* concessive use of the jussive subjunctive. See Woodcock §112.
ratio: the final *o* is short. See 542n.

568-73 **sooner...sooner...before:** the listing of impossibilities (*adynata*) in this manner is a common device of ancient rhetoric, used to underscore the proposition advanced. Cf. Virg. *Ecl.* 1.59-63, Propertius 2.15.31ff., Horace *Odes* 1.33.7ff., and *HF* 373ff., *Thy.* 476ff., *HO* 1582ff., *Oct.* 222ff. The device is often used to emphasise love or gratitude (but not so here nor in *HF* and *Thy.*). For its employment in declamation see Sen. Rhet. *Con.* 1.5.2.
ante...ante...quam: the conjunction *antequam* is often separated into two components as here, although in this case there is hyperbaton of *ante* in the first clause. Trans.: *ante ignibus..., ante ab.*

569 **Syrtis:** a notoriously dangerous sand-bank off the coast of north Africa.

571 **Tethys:** a sea-goddess, wife of Oceanus, envisaged here as dwelling in the west (Hesperia).

574f. Cf. 240, 353-55.

577 **the tribe's only son:** the Amazons usually killed their male offspring. See 232n.

578 **my mother's loss:** cf. 227, 926ff. Cf. also Eur. *Melanippe* fr. 500N: "Except for her who bore me I hate the whole female race."

579 *quod...licet:* noun-clause in apposition to *solamen*. There is hyperbaton of *quod* (trans.: *quod odisse...*).

580-82 On "asides" see 136-39n.

580 **Like some hard...rock:** *ut dura cautes.* The image is as old as Homer (*Iliad* 15.618ff.). But cf. esp. Virg. *Aen.* 6.470f., 7.586ff., 10.693ff. The present passage clearly also alludes to the famous oak-simile at Virg. *Aen.* 4.441ff., describing Aeneas' resistance to the appeals on Dido's behalf of her sister and confidante, Anna. In his prose works Sen. applies the image to the impregnable spirit of the *sapiens* or sage (*Const.* 3.5, *Ira* 3.25.3f., *Vit.* 27.3). Cf. Marcus Aurelius *Meditations* 4.49. See also *Ag.* 539: "like some steep rock", *ardua ut cautes* (of Ajax of Locris). For "epic" similes in Sen. dialogue see 181-83n.

impenetrable: *intractabilis* occurs in Sen. tragedy only in *Pha.*: at 229 and 271, where it is used of Hipp. ("intractable"), and here of the rock to which he is compared. It is one of a group of important "Hippolytan" adjectives. See 271-73n.

585ff. Cf. the fainting-spells of Hecuba at *Tro.* 949ff. and Cassandra at *Ag.* 775ff., and the collapse of Hercules at *HF* 1042ff. and *HO* 1402f.

585 *terrae:* the dative of goal of motion after compound verbs is common in verse. It is found in prose with certain verbs (e.g. *appropinquare*, *inferre*) and occurs more frequently in postclassical writers: cf. *genibus accidens*, Livy 44.31.13, Tac. *Hist.* 3.38. See Woodcock §62.

588 *temet:* emphatic form of *te*. Note the nervous alliteration of "t"s in this line.

590 *quam bene excideram mihi:* lit. "How nicely I had lost command of myself." For *excidere* and the dative cf. *Ira* 3.14.1, *NQ* 2.27.3.

591 *redditae lucis:* genitive of definition. See 197n.

592-99 Cf. 427-30 and n.

592 See 112n. Here the *anime* ("my soul") formula is used for self-exhortation; see 599 below and cf. *Tro.* 613, 662, *Med.* 41, 976, *Ag.* 192, *Thy.* 192.

593 *constent:* jussive subjunctive. So too *commodes* (599), *abeat* (600).

593f. **Who asks...denial:** a famous *sententia.*

171

594   Cf. Jocasta's words to Polynices at *Pho.* 542f.

596   *nefanda:* neut. plural, accusative of the internal object, often translated adverbially. See Woodcock §13.

596f.   Contrast the Ovidian Pha., for whom present kinship suffices to conceal the sin (*Her.* 4.138). Cf. also Virg.'s Dido (of her relationship with Aeneas): "She calls it marriage, covered her guilt with this name" (*coniugium uocat, hoc praetexit nomine culpam, Aen.* 4.172).

598   Cf. Eur.'s Nurse, *Hipp.* 700: "Had I succeeded I would have been thought wise."
   honesta: used predicatively.

601   This convention of looking around the stage and reporting on the absence of witnesses or eavesdroppers seems to derive essentially from Hellenistic drama. Compare Plautus *Miles Gloriosus* 955ff., 1137f. Cf. also *HO* 484, which repeats *Pha.* 601 except for the substitution of "safe", *tutus*, for "free", *liber*. See also 405n.

602   A similar difficulty is proclaimed by Ovid's Pha. (*Her.* 4.7f.). In Ovid the proclamation is transparent artifice. Not so Dido's behaviour at Virg. *Aen.* 4.76: "She begins to speak and stops in mid-voice", *incipit effari mediaque in uoce resistit*.

604f.   With the idea here cf. Atreus' demand of his subjects at *Thy.* 212: "Let them wish what they do not wish" (*quod nolunt uelint*).

605   Most editors delete this line. For other incomplete lines in Senecan tragedy, see *Tro.* 1103, *Pho.* 319, *Thy.* 100. In each case the line's truncation augments its rhetorical force.

607   The asyndeton here is typically Senecan: cf. *Tro.* 497, *Med.* 159. The Latin of this *sententia* is quoted (with a slight alteration) by Hippolito in Tourneur's *The Revenger's Tragedy*, i.4.22f.: "We have grief too, that yet walks without tongue—/ *Curae leues loquuntur, majores stupent.*"

608   mother: contrast 558.

609ff.:   Cf. Biblis' attempt to remove the names of brother and sister from her relationship with Caunus at Ovid *Met.* 9.466f. At *Her.* 4.1f. Pha. forestalls the incest objection in a rather different way. Cf. also Apuleius *Metamorphoses* 10.3.

609   *matris:* genitive of definition. See 197n.

610   fits: *decet*. Also at 618 ("befits"). See 216n.

612   servitude: "servant" (*famula*, 611, 612, 617), "servitude" (*seruitium*, 612) and "slave" (*serua*, 622) are words with evident sexual implications. The central concept of Roman elegy was precisely this "servitude of love", *seruitium amoris*. Cf. Ariadne's

request to be Theseus' slave, if she could not be his wife, at Catullus
64.158-63.

613-16   See 233-35 and n. Pha.'s protestation of love at 616 becomes
the reality of 1197f.

614   **Pindus:** a major mountain-range in Thessaly.

615   *si...:* sc. *me iubeas.*

617ff.   Cf. *Const.* 1.1: "One sex is born to obey (*ad obsequendum*),
the other to command (*imperio*)." On the "sceptre" see 217n.

618   Peiper deletes this line; most editors do not.

619   **to guard:** *tutari,* used only twice in Sen. (here and at *Ag.* 111), is
a formal, "elevated" word with overtones of public guardianship.
See Cic. *Rep.* 6.13, *Phil.* 4.2, Horace *Ep.* 2.1.2, Virg. *Aen.* 7.469.

621   *paterno imperio:* either sociative/causal ablative with *fortis* or
instrumental ablative with *rege*—or (more likely) both.

622   **slave:** *serua* is a more "lowly" word than *famula,* "servant"
(611, 612, 617), and occurs only here in Senecan tragedy.

623   **Pity a widow:** *miserere uiduae.* Cf. 636, 671. Compassion is an
important motif in this scene and elsewhere in Senecan tragedy: cf.,
e.g., the Andromache-Ulysses scene of *Troades* (esp. 694, 703, 762,
792) and the ending of *Medea* (1018). See also *HF* 1192, *Med.* 482. The
conventional Stoic classification of compassion (*misericordia*) was as
a milder "fault" or *uitium* (along with "love", *amor*, and "modesty",
uerecundia: Ira 2.15.3). Cf. Ovid's use of this motif at *Her.* 4.161f.

624   **omen:** Pha.'s use of the term "widow", implying Th.'s death. In
Senecan tragedy omens are nearly always of death or calamity: see
HF 688, *Tro.* 488, *Oed.* 359, 854f., and 408 above. But see *Ag.* 939.

  auertat: optative subjunctive used to express a wish or prayer. See
417ff.n. and Woodcock §§113 and 114.

625   **Lord of mute Styx:** Pluto, named at 628, Jupiter's brother and
king of the third realm, the underworld. He is also known as Dis. The
Styx was the main river of the underworld. Across it the souls of the
buried dead were ferried. It was invoked in the gods' most serious
oaths, and often functions metonymically for the underworld as a
whole.

626   Note the chiastic arrangement of adjectives and nouns again
(abBA). See 305n.

627   **ravisher:** see 94n.

628   **Pluto too:** i.e. as well as Jupiter, notorious for his indulgence to
lovers.

  sits: *sedet.* The image is perhaps that of the Roman magistrate in
his judicial chair. Cf., e.g., Catullus 52.2, Cic. *De Orat.* 2.196, Livy

3.46.9, Propertius 3.19.27, Tac. *Ann.* 11.11., where *sedere*, "sitting", is used in a technical, legal sense. See also *HF* 721, 731, *Ag.* 730, *HO* 1007f.

629 *Illum...reducem dabunt:* lit. "will render him returned". For this noun/pronoun plus adjective construction with *dare* see Sallust *Iugurtha* 59.3, Virg. *Aen.* 12.437.

631 **dear brothers:** see 434n.

633 On the dramatic function of the ambiguity here see Intro. p. 31.

634 *amantum:* substantival use of the participle. See 95n. This form of the genitive plural occurs frequently in verse for reasons of assonance and metre. So too *dolentum* (1109).

635 *admotis:* one of the uses of *admoueo* is as a quasi-technical term for the "moving up" of troops or siege-engines to or against a city: see, e.g., Cic. *Clu.* 36, Livy 29.23.10, *Thy.* 385. Some of this "military" sense may be latent in Pha.'s use of the word here.

636 **Pity me:** see 623n.

637 **long and loathe:** *libet...pigetque.* Lit. "It delights and disgusts me." A paradoxical manipulation of the *pudet/dolet pigetque* ("it shames/pains and disgusts me") formula: see, e.g., Terence *Adelphi* 392, Pacuvius 44R², Sen. *Ag.* 162.

639f. Cf. Th.'s words to the Nurse at 858f.

640ff. Cf. 279-82 above.

642 Some editors follow Heinsius in deleting this line, which is omitted in E.

644 With this simile cf. Lucretius 2.191f.

645 *nempe:* frequently used, as here, asseveratively to justify the sentiment expressed: "surely", "without doubt", etc. Contrast its ironic use at 244.

646-71 Pha.'s revelation speech alludes to and remodels the Ovidian Pha.'s revelations to Hipp. in *Her.* 4, esp. her sensuous appreciation of Hipp.'s physical attractiveness (67ff.): cf. *Her.* 4.72, 81, 77, 77f., with *Pha.* 652, 653, 657, 659f. See also 665f.n. and 666-69n. below. Other relevant texts include Pasiphae's declaration of her love for the bull in Eur.'s *Cretans* (Page *Select Papyri* III.11), and the description of Ariadne's infatuation with Theseus at Catullus 64.76ff. Sen.'s dramatisation of Pha. here impressed Racine, who modelled Phèdre's revelation speech upon it (*Phd.* 634ff.). See also Apuleius *Metamorphoses* 10.3.

648-50 *signaret...uidit...collegit:* to have both imperfect subjunctive and perfect indicatives in a temporal *cum* clause is unusual. The subjunctive perhaps characterises the time (i.e. is essentially generic); the indicative identifies it. See Woodcock §§231ff.

649 Cnossian monster: the monster of the Cretan palace at Cnossos, viz. the Minotaur (see 113n.). The "blind house" (*caecam domum*) is the Cretan labyrinth (see 122n.). Virg. describes it as "that house of toil and inextricable wandering" (*labor ille domus et inextricabilis error*, *Aen*. 6.27). See also Catullus 64.114f. and Ovid *Met*. 8.155ff.

650 long threads: Ariadne, daughter of Minos and sister of Pha., gave Th., with whom she had fallen in love, a spool of thread to enable him to find his way out of the labyrinth after he had killed the Minotaur. See Catullus 64.112-15, Virg. *Aen*. 6.28-30, Ovid *Her*. 4.59f., *Met*. 8.171-73, and 661f. below.

longa curua fila...uia: curua uia is ablative of place. Note the parallel arrangement of adjectives and nouns (abAB). See 85n.

651 shone: *fulsit*. Cf. 1112 and 1269.

Head-band: worn by sacrificial victims. An annual human offering to the Minotaur (on most accounts, seven young men and seven girls) had been imposed upon Athens by Minos as punishment for the murder of his son, Androgeos (Catullus 64.76ff., Virg. *Aen*. 6.20ff., Ovid *Her*. 10.99ff.). Th. joined the sacrificial contingent with the intention of killing the Minotaur.

quis: used here as equivalent to *qualis*, "how!", "in what condition!"

652 Golden shame: *flauus pudor*. Cf. Ovid *Her*. 4.72 (Pha. to Hipp.): "modesty's blush had painted your golden cheeks" (*flaua uerecundus tinxerat ora rubor*). In addition to gold (Ovid *Tristia* 1.5.25), *flauus* is used of honey (Lucretius 1.938), wheat (Virg. *Geo*. 1.73), sand (Virg. *Aen*. 7.31) and hair (Pliny *NH* 2.189). Its use here to qualify *pudor*, "shame", is most striking.

654 your Phoebe: Diana, *qua* moon-goddess, sister of Phoebus Apollo, the sun-god. The latter is called "my" by Pha. because she is descended from him through Pasiph., his daughter.

Phoebes: Greek genitive. *Erat ei* (possessive dative) are understood.

655f. like you...: cf. *Tro*. 464ff., where Andromache speaks of Hector's features imaged in those of Astyanax.

656 pleased his foe: i.e. Ariadne. See 650n. and 663-66n. Pha.'s language here ("pleased", *placuit*) is taken up by Hipp. at 684.

660 austere Scythian strength: *Scythicus rigor*. The Scyths were a nomadic tribe in south-east Russia (see 168), where the Amazons lived. Hipp.'s "austere strength", *rigor*, is praised too by Ovid's Pha. (*Her*. 4.77). See also 686n.

175

663-66 Ariadne fled with Th. to the island of Naxos, where Th. abandoned her. Bacchus then rescued and married her, and either (according to the most common version, e.g. Ovid *Met*. 8.176ff., *Fasti* 3.459ff.) set her gem-studded crown in the sky as the constellation Corona Borealis or transformed Ariadne herself into the constellation. See *HF* 18.

664 I call...: *inuoco ad causam*. The language is reminiscent of the law-courts.

665f. Cf. Ovid *Her*. 4.63-65, esp. 63: "A single house has pleased two women" (*placuit domus una duabus*).

666-69 Cf. Andromache's formal supplication of Ulysses at *Tro*. 691ff. See also the "supplication" of Ovid's Pha. at *Her*. 4.149ff., and of Antigone (described by Oedipus) at *Pho*. 306f.

667 at your knees: the knees were touched or invoked in supplication—cf. *Tro*. 691, *Pho*. 306, *Med*. 247. According to Pliny (*NH* 11.250) this was because the knees were thought to possess a vital principle (*uitalitas*). The practice is as old as Homer (*Iliad*. 22.338ff., 24.478; cf. Virg. *Aen*. 3.607).

668 untouched: *intacta*. I.e. a virgin. For this use of *intacta* cf. Catullus 62.45, Horace *Odes* 1.7.5 (of Pallas), Virg. *Aen*. 1.345 (of Dido before her marriage), Propertius 2.6.21 (of the Sabine women).

671a Pity a lover: *miserere amantis*. See 623 and n., and 636. Cf. Andromache's appeal, "Pity a mother" (*miserere matris*), at *Tro*. 694, 703.

671bff. Hipp. begins his appeal for cosmic justice by invoking Jupiter and the sun-god, both of them Pha.'s ancestors. See 888-90, where Pha. herself invokes these two deities, and 154-58. With Hipp.'s appeal cf. Thyestes' appeal for cosmic disruption and justice at *Thy*. 1068ff., the prayer of Hercules at *HF* 1202ff., that of Medea at *Med*. 531ff., and the complaint of "Octavia" at *Oct*. 245ff. Cf. also Hipp.'s invocation of Mother Earth and the Sun at Eur. *Hipp*. 601. Hipp.'s opening words (671f.) are repeated with a slight variation by Titus in Shakespeare's *Titus Andronicus* iv.1.81f. They were much imitated from Statius onwards (see *Thebaid* 1.79f.). On prayers in Sen. generally see 54-80n.

671b monarch of gods: Jupiter, from whom Pha. is descended through Minos. Cf. 903, where the same god is invoked by Th. at the opening of his speech.

deum: genitive plural. So too *diuum* (680).

672 See and not act: similarly Iarbas at *Aen*. 4.206ff., "Almighty Jupiter...do you behold these things?"

lentus: predicative (adverbial) use of the adjective. See Woodcock §88.

673 *et:* used to introduce an indignant or surprised question, as at *Tro.* 429, 598, *Med.* 525.

quando: for the shortening of the final *o* see 542n.

674ff. Cf. the Nurse's initial response to Pha.'s self-revelations at 173-77.

674 *ruat:* jussive subjunctive. So too *condat* (675), *agant* (676), *cremet* (682). See 24n.

677-79 Cf. Medea's indignation that the Sun can bear to look on her disgrace at *Med.* 28ff. At *Thy.* 776ff. the sun flees before the horror of the Thyestean feast.

678 **Titan:** a poetic name (used frequently by Ovid in *Met.* and Sen. in the tragedies) for the sun-god, Apollo, from whom Pha. is descended through Pasiph. The sun-god is generally imaged in art with rays of light emanating from his head ("crowned with a palisade of pointed rays", *radiis frontem uallatus acutis,* Ovid *Her.* 4.159): hence "radiate". The image appealed to Nero, who had a colossal, gilded bronze statue of himself as the sun-god with rays of light spurting from his head set up in the vestibule of his Golden House (A.D. 64-68).

679 *speculare:* present indicative, alternative form of second person singular (= *specularis*).

680 **Ruler of gods and men:** *diuum rector atque hominum.* The "epic" style is noticeable; cf. the standard Virgilian expression "father of gods and king of men", *(diuum pater atque hominum rex, Aen.* 1.65, 2.648, 10.2, 10.743), itself derived from Ennius *(Annales* V³ 175) and ultimately Homer *(Iliad* 1.544 *et al.).* Cf. also Virg. *Aen.* 8.572 *(diuum tu maxime rector),* Ovid *Met.* 2.848, *HF* 517.

681 **triple flame:** from the triple-pointed thunderbolts of Jupiter. See 189.

682 Cf. Pha.'s demand for self-destruction at 1159ff., and that of Thyestes at *Thy.* 1089f. Cf. also *HO* 847ff.

685 **matter:** *materia.* The word seems to be used in the quasi-philosophical sense of that which has the potentiality for something and is acted upon to produce it; see *Ep.* 65. Cf. *Med.* 914.

686 **austerity:** *rigor.* Here used without the physical implications of Pha.'s phrase at 660, "austere Scythian strength", *Scythicus rigor,* which suggests Hipp.'s rugged looks.

687-93 In Rac. *Phd.* it is Ph. who envisages herself as a monster (*un monstre,* 701, *ce monstre,* 703) from which the world needs to be delivered.

687 *scelere:* ablative of respect. See 276n.

688 **greater evil:** *maius malum.* This and similar phrases (*maius* *nefas, maius scelus*) and the associated motif of the enlargement or intensification of evil are common in Senecan tragedy: see, e.g., *Tro.* 45, 427, *Pho.* 286, 457, 531, *Med.* 50, 674, *Ag.* 29, *Thy.* 259, 745; and 142f. above, 697 below. See also Accius *Atreus* 200R². The present line is thought by some to be an interpolation inspired by *Ag.* 29.

monster-pregnant: *monstrifera.* Cf. the description of the sea, "monster-bellied", *tumidum monstro*, at 1016. *Matre monstrifera* is ablative of comparison; so too *genetrice* (689), *Colchide nouerca* (697).

690 *diu:* modifies *tacitum.*

691 *biformi...nota:* best taken perhaps as instrumental ablative. The subject of *exhibuit* is *partus.*

694 Another epic reminiscence: cf. Homer's Odysseus at *Odyssey* 5.306, and Virg.'s Aeneas at *Aen.* 1.94: "O thrice and four times blessed..." (*o terque quaterque beati...*), quoted by Sen. at *Ep.* 67.8.

697 Colchic stepmother: Medea. See 563f.n.

698 recognise the fate of our house: see 113 and n., and 124-28. Cf. Rac. *Phd.* 679f., where Ph. speaks of *le feu fatal à tout mon sang* ("the fire fatal to all my line"). Fate is extremely important in Senecan drama. Identified at times with nature and fortune (see 959n. and Appendix I), it is generally in the tragedies cyclic (see esp. *Tro.*, *Med.*, *Pha.*, *Ag.*, *Thy.*): an unimpedable revolution of human acts, motivation and events, of human tragedy and history. Past becomes present, becomes future. See Intro. p. 26f. For choric pronouncements on fate see *HF* 178-91, *Oed.* 980-97, *Thy.* 607-21.

699 With the sentiment here cf. 177ff.

mei: an objective genitive after *potens* is usual. Cf., e.g., *potens mentis*, *Thy.* 547.

700-02 Cf. 233-35, 241, 1179f.

701 Hyperbaton of *quos*; trans.:*quos unda...*

703 *aduoluor:* the passive in Latin is sometimes used, as here, to make a transitive verb intransitive. What results is something akin to the Greek middle.

704 *procul:* take with *amoue.*

705 *etiam:* used to indicate shock or surprise; lit. "does she really rush into my arms?" Cf. *Oed.* 678, *Ag.* 983.

706 sword: Sen.'s use of the sword motif—here, at 729f. as "proof of crime", at 896 as accuser, and even at 1197f. as instrument of Pha.'s death—may well be original. At any rate it is doubtful that the motif derives from Eur.'s lost *Hipp. Kalypt.* On Hipp.'s attitude to the sword, *ensis*, cf. 548.

stringatur...exigat: jussive subjunctives. So too *deserat* (714).

See 24n.

707-09 Hipp. addresses the enshrined Diana, "goddess of the bow" (709), to whom he offers Pha. as sacrifice—a fine example of Sen.'s emblematic and ironic use of theatrics (see also 578ff., 1247ff., and esp. *Thy.* 542-45). With Hipp.'s behaviour here cf. his earlier condemnation of sacrifice (498f.) and the sword (547f.). For both idea and language see Pyrrhus' slaying of Priam (*Tro.* 45-48) "at the very altars" (*ipsasque ad aras*), "the twisted hair in his left (savage) hand, the royal head bent back" (*laeua [saeua] manu/ coma reflectens regium torta caput*), and Virg. *Aen.* 2.550-53. Cf. also the self-righteous and self-deceived Aeneas' words at Virg. *Aen.* 10.530ff. as he "sacrifices" the suppliant Magus, and the description of the death itself: "So saying he holds the man's helmet with his left hand (*laeua*), bends back the suppliant's neck (*reflexa ceruice*) and drives home the sword (*ensem*) to the hilt."

711f. For death as healing see 249ff., *HF* 1262. For Pha. and death see also 871, 880, 1188ff. For death by the sword of the beloved (love-in-death) see esp. Dido at Virg. *Aen.* 4.642ff.; also Deianira at Sophocles *Trachiniae* 923ff. Cf. Rac. *Phd.* 704ff., and 1197f. below.

711 *uoto meo:* ablative of comparison. See 143n.

712 *saluo...pudore:* ablative (absolute) of attendant circumstances. See Woodcock §49.

715f. **Tanais...Maeotian lake:** see 399n. The same places and the same idea occur at the end of *HF*, where Hercules proclaims the impossibility of his own purification (*HF* 1323ff.). Contrast Eur.'s Hipp., who has no doubts about his ability to purify himself with running water (*Hipp.* 653f.).

barbaris...undis: perhaps ablative of description (see 50n.); if not, a more general sociative-instrumental ablative with *incumbens*, or instrumental ablative with *eluet*.

717f. **the great father:** Neptune, brother of Jupiter and Pluto, and god of the sea. Hipp.'s words are echoed in Th.'s prayer for his son's extinction at 958. With the general idea here cf. Shakespeare *Macbeth* ii.2.59ff. (Macbeth speaking): "Will all great Neptune's ocean wash this blood/ Clean from my hand?..."

Ocean: *Oceanus* is the great sea that surrounds the land mass of the known world.

718 *expiarit:* syncopated form of *expiauerit*. The perfect subjunctive is potential. Note that there is little perceptible distinction between the perfect and the present subjunctive in sentences of this kind, in which the perfect subjunctive usually refers to the future. See Woodcock §119.

sceleris: partitive genitive; lit. "so much of crime". Partitive genitives are esp. frequent in Latin after neuter adjectives and pronouns.

719ff. Contrast Eur. *Hipp.* 715ff., where it is Pha. who devises the plan to accuse Hipp. Similarly in Eur.'s first *Hipp.* (*Hipp. Kalyptomenos*) it seems to have been Pha. who cried for help after Hipp. had left, not the Nurse (scholiast on Homer *Odyssey* 11.321).

719   soul...: see 112n.

720f. *regeramus...arguamus:* jussive subjunctives. See 24n.

ipsi: dative after *regeramus* used in a figurative sense. The purely metaphorical use of *regero* here is rare; but cf. Horace *Satires* 1.7.29, *Ag.* 223f.

721   Crime...crime: for different formulations of this *sententia* see Clytemnestra's remark at *Ag.* 115, and *Clem.* 1.13.2. It became one of the commonplaces of Elizabethan and Jacobean tragedy.

scelere: instrumental ablative, not ablative of agent. The agent with the gerundive is usually expressed by the dative. See Woodcock §202.

726   *nefandi...stupri:* genitive of description or quality; lit. "a rapist of unspeakable filth". See 208n.

728   *pudicam:* substantival use of the adjective.

abit: abbreviated form of *abiit* as frequent in verse; e.g. Ovid *Met.* 7.487.

729f. On the use of the sword as "proof" see 706n.

731   revive her: cf. Cassandra's revival at *Ag.* 787ff.

733   *perferte:* sc. *haec*, "convey (the news of) these things..." For *perferre* in the sense of "deliver a message" or "take the news" see, e.g., Caesar *De Bello Ciuili* 2.37.2., Sen. *Ep.* 108.38, and *HO* 100. Cf. also *Tro.* 802.

734 Cf. Pha.'s behaviour at 886f.

735 With this *sententia* cf. Publilius Syrus 710: "The will, not the body, makes one impure" (*uoluntas impudicum, non corpus facit*), and *HO* 886: "He does not sin who sins without intent" (*haud est nocens quicumque non sponte est nocens*). See also the consolation offered (Livy 1.58.9) to Lucretia, who claims her purity, *pudicitia*, has been lost: "It is the mind that sins, not the body (*mentem peccare, non corpus*)." For the popularity of the *sententiae* of Publilius Syrus with the declaimers see Sen. Rhet. *Con.* 7.2.14, 7.3.8, 7.4.8.

SECOND CHORAL ODE (736-823)

As generally in Senecan tragedy (see *HF* 830ff., *Med.* 579ff., *Oed.* 709ff., *Thy.* 546ff.), the choral ode following the third act takes its impetus directly from the dramatic action. This ode on Hipp.'s beauty and its dangers begins with Hipp.'s flight at the end of Act Three and concludes with the focus still firmly on Hipp. Contrast the ode at *Med.* 579ff., where the chorus' initial focus is on Medea but their final focus is on Jason.

Metre: sapphic (736-52), asclepiadean (753-60, 764-82, 784-823), dactylic (761-63), glyconic (783). See Appendix II.

736 On the entry of the chorus here—as opposed to its presence on stage during the preceding act—see 405n.

737 Faster...Corus: cf. Horace *Odes* 2.16.23f.: "faster than cloud-driving Eurus" (*agente nimbos/ ocior Euro*). Corus is the north-west wind, renowned for its violence (see *Ag.* 484ff., and 1013, 1131 below).

Coro: ablative of comparison; so too *flamma* (738). See 143n.

738-52 With this association of star and planet with Hipp. cf. 1112, 1174, 1269f. See also 743-52n.

740 stars on the wind: shooting stars or meteors were commonly thought to be driven through the sky by the winds. See Sen. *NQ* 1.14.5; cf. Aratus *Phaenomena* 926ff., Virg. *Geo.* 1.365ff., Pliny *NH* 18.352.

741-60 Cf. the chorus' formal eulogy to Creusa's and Jason's beauty at *Med.* 75ff.

741 conferat: jussive subjunctive; see 24n. The subject is *fama*.

742 senioris aeui: objective genitive after *miratrix*. *Senioris* is comparative for positive as often in verse. The adjective is more usually used of persons or animals.

743-52 Comparison with the moon or Lucifer (or the sun) was commonplace in encomia: see, e.g., Sappho 34, Pindar *Isthmian Odes* 4.23f., Bacchylides 9.27ff., Ovid *Met.* 2.722ff. Sen.'s treatment and its dramatic and thematic relevance are not. See also *Med.* 95-98, and the comparison of the beauty of the doomed Polyxena to that of the setting sun at *Tro.* 1138ff.

743f. Hyperbaton. Trans.: *tanto pulchrior...lucet, quanto clarior micat...* Both *tanto* and *quanto* are ablatives of measure of difference, a form of the instrumental ablative (see Woodcock §82). The subject of *micat* is *Phoebe* (747).

744 *orbe pleno:* ablative (absolute) of attendant circumstances or instrumental ablative—or (more likely) both, with intentional syntactic ambiguity as often in Latin verse.

747 **Phoebe:** Diana, qua goddess of the moon.

749-52 Cf. Virg.'s description of the morning-star at *Aen.* 8.589-91.

749 **Hesperus:** the evening-star.

qualis est: sc. *tua forma talis est.*

750 *nuntius noctis:* "night's harbinger". Cf. *dux noctis*, "night's leader", *Med.* 878, *serae nuntius horae*, "the late hour's harbinger", *Thy.* 794—also of Hesperus/Vesper.

752 **Lucifer:** the morning-star. The evening-star and the morning-star, as was known from the fifth century B.C. onwards, are the same planet, viz. Venus. Hence "become" (*idem*). Poets played on the notion of the identity of the two stars with considerable ingenuity: see, e.g., Callimachus fr. 291Pf, Catullus 62.34f., Cinna fr. 8, Horace *Odes* 2.9.10-12. See also Cic. *ND* 2.53.

753-60 Cf. *Med.* 82-85, where, as here, Bacchus' beauty (*forma*) is compared unfavourably with that of a mortal (Jason). At *Oed.* 403-508, on the other hand, Bacchus' beauty receives a sustained choral eulogy.

753 **Liber:** another name for Bacchus, god of the vine and of wine, which "liberates". He was said to have conquered India, whose people were thus said to carry the thyrsus or Bacchic staff (a wand tipped with a fir-cone, tuft of ivy or vine-leaves, originally concealing a spearpoint—see 755) as a sign of their allegiance. Hence "thyrsed India"; cf. *Med.* 110, "thyrsed (*thyrsigeri*) Lyaeus".

754 *perpetuum:* adverb.

755 **Terror of tigers:** Bacchus rode in a chariot drawn by tigers, symbol of the east and of Bacchus' power to tame and to civilise. Cf. Virg. *Ecl.* 5.29f., *Aen.* 6.805f., Horace *Odes* 3.3.13-15, Statius *Thebaid* 4.656ff. It is an image used elsewhere in the tragedies: see *Med.* 84f. and *Oed.* 424ff. (where lions have replaced the usual tigers).

vine-clad spear: the thyrsus. See 753n.

756 In addition to his specific association with the vine, Bacchus was also a god of fertility, of nature generally and of animal power. He was sometimes thought of as a bull-god or goat-god and represented with horns on his head.

turban: *mitra.* Eastern head-gear traditionally associated with Bacchus because of his connections with the east. At *Oed.* 414 Bacchus' turban is "Tyrian" (*Tyria mitra*).

757 **stiff hair:** as opposed to the undulating locks of Bacchus. The Latin *rigidas comas* draws attention to one of Hipp.'s defining qualities, *rigor*, "hardness", "austerity", in both character (686) and physical appearance (660).

760 **Phaedra's sister:** Ariadne, whom Bacchus (= Bromius, "the noisy one"), rescued and married after her desertion by Theseus. See 663-66 and n.

praetulerit: subjunctive of indirect question.

761-76 The Horatian-Ovidian tone and language of these lines are noteworthy; cf., e.g., Horace *Odes* 2.11.5ff., and esp. Ovid *Ars* 2.113ff., 3.59ff. See also 446 above and n.

761 Cf. Ovid *Ars* 2.113: "Beauty is a fragile boon" (*forma bonum fragile est*). At *Oed.* 6 the "deceitful boon", *fallax bonum*, is "power", *regnum*.

762 **briefest gift:** on "gifts" in Sen. see 945n.

763 *ut...laberis:* = lit. "how...you slip away."

764-72 With the imagery of plundering and heat in this passage cf. similar imagery in the first choral ode at 279ff.

764 *non sic:* i.e. *non uelox celeri pede.*

766 Hyperbaton of *cum*. Trans.: *cum saeuit...*

768ff. A difficult passage, not helped by the hyperbaton of *ut* (768) and *qui* (770). Perhaps best construed: *ut lilia languescunt..., et fulgor qui radiat...*; lit. "as the lilies wither..., so the glow which radiates..." For this use of *ut...et*, "as...so (no less)", see Sen. *Ep.* 95.37.

768 **lily:** often associated with innocence as well as vulnerability: see, e.g., Virg. *Aen.* 12.68f., Propertius 1.20.37f., Valerius Flaccus 6.492ff.

769 Garlands of roses were regularly worn at the ancient symposium: see, e.g., Horace *Odes* 2.11.14f., Propertius 3.5.22, Martial 5.64.4, and *Thy.* 947. The withering of roses is a conventional symbol of the brevity of life; see, e.g., Horace *Odes* 2.3.13ff., Ovid *Ars* 2.116, and in later literature Spenser *Faerie Queene* 2.12.75, Herbert *Vertue*, Herrick "Gather ye Rosebuds while ye may", etc.

771f. Cf. *Ep.* 24.19f.: "We die each day. For each day a part of life is taken from us" (*cotidie morimur. cotidie enim demitur aliqua pars uitae*).

772 *formonsi:* this spelling is preferred to *formosi* because of its occurrence at 781 below in E and because the most plausible etymology for *-osus* is from *-onsus* (from ⋆*-o-unt-tos*).

773f. See 761n. At *Ep.* 1.3 it is time which is the "fleeting thing" (*res fugax*); cf. Horace *Odes* 2.14.1f.

774 **While you can:** *dum licet*. For this motif and phrase see, e.g., Propertius 1.19.25, Horace *Odes* 2.11.16, and esp. Ovid *Ars* 3.61ff.:

"While you can...you must use your time" (*dum licet...utendum est aetate*). See also *HF* 177ff.

utere: imperative.

775f. A reformulation of Ovid *Ars* 3.64 and 66.

777-84 Cf. Hipp.'s idealisation of country-life at 483ff., esp. 519-21, and Ovid *Her.* 4.169-74. On the impossibility of hiding even in "pathless places" (778) see Th.'s proclamation at 929ff.

778 *te:* accusative after *cingent* (780).

nemore abdito: local ablative (see 67ff.n.), lit. "in a secluded wood".

779 **Titan:** the sun-god. See 678n.

780 **Naiads:** nymphs of freshwater streams, lakes and fountains.

turba licens: in apposition to *Naides improbae.* Cf. 1105, 1174.

781 There is an allusion here to Hercules' favourite, the beautiful boy, Hylas, lost in Mysia during the Argonautic expedition. The boy was sent to fetch water and was dragged down into a spring by a Naiad enamoured of him. See Apollonius Rhodius 1.1207-72, Theocritus 13, Virg. *Ecl.* 6.43f., Propertius 1.20, Valerius Flaccus 3.596.

784 **Dryads:** wood-nymphs. *Dryades* is nominative in apposition to *lasciuae...deae* (783). There is hyperbaton; trans.: *Dryades quae Panas...*

Pans: Pan was god of woods and shepherds, imagined as half-man, half-goat. "Pans" suggests minor woodland deities.

785-94 Cf. the first choral ode's presentation of the moon's love for Endymion (309-16).

786 **The star...:** the moon, Diana. The Arcadians were thought to be one of the oldest people on earth and to have existed before the birth of the moon. See *HO* 1883f.

789 *sordidior:* probably comparative for positive again (see 742n.), although comparatives are also used in both prose and verse to suggest degree ("rather dull").

791 **Thessaly's chants:** see 421n.

tractam: sc. *eam* (the goddess) *esse.*

792 **Clashed the cymbals:** to counteract the witches' incantation ("Thessaly's chants", 791), which it was widely believed could be nullified by the loud clashing of bronze and the blaring of trumpets; see, e.g., Tibullus 1.8.21f., Livy 26.5, Tac. *Ann.* 1.28. And cf. *Med.* 795f.

labour: *labor,* the plural of which is used in Latin of lunar and solar eclipses (e.g. Virg. *Geo.* 2.478, *Aen.* 1.742, Lucan 7.4), as is the verbal form, *laborat.*

795 *Vexent:* optative subjunctive used with suppositional force: "Let the frost..." = "Provided that..." So too *appetat* (796).

797 Paros marble: marble from the Greek island of Paros was famous for its dazzling whiteness and featured frequently in the poets as a paradigm of brilliance. See, e.g., Theocritus 6.37f., Horace *Odes* 1.19.6, Petron. *Sat.* 126.17.

798 fierce...look: cf. 1063f.

800 Phoebus: Apollo.

801 *nescia colligi:* this adverbial, explanatory use of the infinitive with adjectives is esp. common in verse and postclassical prose. In classical Latin prose it tends to be restricted to participles used adjectivally. The extension of the construction may have been due to Greek influence. See Woodcock §26. For other instances of the infinitive with *nescius*, see, e.g., Virg. *Geo.* 4.470, *nescia mansuescere*, Lucan 1.17, *nescia remitti.*

804 *nulla lege:* ablative of manner (a type of sociative-instrumental ablative). See Woodcock §§43 and 48.

806 vast body's bulk: *uasti spatio corporis.* Cf. the "vast body" (*corporis uasti*, 1035) of the bull from the sea.

807 Hercules: the Greek hero famous for his twelve labours, a mythic paradigm of strength and brute force. Cf. 317ff., 843ff., 1217ff.

Herculeos: the adjective here instead of the genitive (so too *Castorea*, 810) is an "epic" touch suitable to the elevated tone of the eulogy. See also *cornipedis*, 809.

iuuenis: predicative adjective used concessively; lit. "although young".

808 Mars: god of war.

pectore: ablative of comparison (see 143n.); lit. "broader than the chest of war-mongering Mars".

809 *cornipedis:* an epic term not found before Virg. (*Aen.* 6.591, 7.779), although it is unlikely that he invented it. Virg. uses it as an epithet; later poets also as a noun—so Sen. here (see also Lucan 8.3, Silius 2.72).

810 Castor: son of Tyndareus (or Jupiter) and Leda, and brother of Pollux. Castor and Pollux were Spartan heroes, known as the Dioscuri or heavenly "twins". Pollux was famed as a boxer, Castor as a horseman. There was a temple dedicated to them in the Roman Forum.

811 Cyllaros: the horse given to Castor by Juno.

poteris: the indicative is normal with a verb of possibility (or duty) in the apodosis of an "ideal" or "unreal" condition; but note also

185

mittent (815), *descendent* (818), *afferent* (819), all future indicatives, used instead of the present subjunctive to express greater certainty. Cf. 123 above.

812-15 Javelins were fired from an *ammentum* or thong wrapped around the shaft to make the throw more accurate.

812 *tende:* imperative used to state a hypothesis. So too *derige* (813). See also 929f.

814 *dociles...figere:* see 801n. *Dociles* modifies *Cretes* (815).

816-19 With this praise of Hipp. as archer cf. that of Diana at 54ff. and of Cupid at 192-94, 277ff. See also *HO* 1652ff.

816 **Parthian style:** mass-shooting of arrows in an arc—generally from horseback while "fleeing" from the enemy (see, e.g., *Oed.* 118f., *Thy.* 382-84). Parthia was a large kingdom in western Asia to the south of the Caspian Sea, between the eastern borders of the Roman empire and India. It was a long-standing enemy of Rome and famous for its archers: see, e.g., Virg. *Geo.* 3.31, Horace *Odes* 1.19.11f.

819 **spoils:** *praedam.* Cf. 76, 543.

822 *praetereat:* optative subjunctive. So too *monstret* (823). See 417ff.n.

ACT FOUR (824-958)

The fourth acts of Sen.'s plays vary considerably. Here, as in *Tro.* (Helen) and *Ag.* (Agamemnon), a major character indirectly responsible for much of the dramatic action so far enters for the first time. The late entrance of Th. of course, as of Agamemnon (and probably of Helen too—cf. Eur.'s *Tro.*), derives from fifth-century Attic tragedy.

Metre: iambic trimeter (senarius). See Appendix II.

824-28 The chorus-leader is aware of Pha.'s passion and the plan to accuse Hipp. This need not surprise. Nor should the chorus' failure to inform Th. The chorus are Cretan women (see First Choral Ode), attendants of Pha. Knowledge of the accusation plan and loyalty to their mistress seem consistent with their dramatic "character". With the chorus-leader's attitude here cf. Hipp.'s earlier presentation of woman as "mistress of crime", *scelerum artifex*, at 559-64.

824 *sinat:* potential subjunctive. See 120n.
   inausum: predicative use of adjective as often with *sino*.

826f. Cf. 731f.
crine lacerato: best taken as instrumental ablative.

828 There is nothing odd in these remarks from a female chorus or chorus-leader. At *Ag.* 116 Clytemnestra says of herself: "Now devise in your heart a woman's traps *(femineos dolos)*." Implied self-criticism of this kind by women is common in Eur. (see *Medea* 408f., *Andromache* 181f., 272f., 943ff.), and contributed towards his reputation as a misogynist. See also the "male" comments at *Ion* 843ff.

830 *alto:* predicative, lit. "with the top (of his head) high".

831ff. *ut...gerit, ni...canderent...staretque:* imperfect subjunctives in the protasis of a present "unreal" condition are here preceded by an indicative in the apodosis expressing a fact independent of the condition; lit. "How he is like young P. in looks, if ashen pallor were not whitening..." The standard explanation for this kind of idiom is that the true apodosis—"or would be like him *(gereret)*"—has been suppressed.

831 **Pirithous:** see 94n.

834 **Look...now here:** *en...adest. Adesse* is often used in Sen. to announce the entry of a character; see, e.g., *Tro.* 522, *Oed.* 203, 205, *Ag.* 2, 411, 587. Cf. also the chorus' announcement of Ag.'s entry at *Ag.* 778f.: *en...adit.* With the chorus-leader's words here cf. Hipp.'s prediction of 624 *(aderit)*.

835 **I have fled:** *profugi.* An echo of Pha.'s initial description of Th. at 91: "fugitive lord", *profugus coniux.* See also 1000n.

837 Similarly Theseus at *HF* 653.
Hyperbaton: *uix* modifies *sufferunt.*

838 **Eleusis:** a city in Attica famous for the mysteries of Ceres (Greek Demeter), goddess of grain and fruits and mother of Proserpina (Greek Persephone)
Triptolemus: king of Eleusis and legendary inventor of agriculture. His "gifts" are the crops of the field. There have been four harvests since Th. entered the underworld.

839 **Libra:** a constellation and sign of the zodiac ("the Scales") under which the autumnal equinox occurs.

840 **doubtful lot:** *sortis ignotae.* A fate the outcome of which is unknown *(ignota)*; or perhaps "lot" in the strict sense with reference to the casting of lots which in some accounts of Th.'s descent to the underworld obligated Th. into helping Pirithous obtain a bride—see, e.g., Diodorus Siculus 4.63.3. In such accounts, however, Pha.'s death precedes the underworld expedition. The closest linguistic parallel in the tragedies to *sortis ignotae* is *sortis incertae* at *Ag.* 38, which means "uncertain oracle". But to translate *sortis* as "oracle" here would be difficult because of the absence of any reference to an oracle in the various accounts of Th.'s *katabasis*. Hyginus (*Fabulae* 79) is alone in suggesting an order from Jupiter, but even that order appears in a dream (*in quiete*). "Lot" with its wide range of meaning seems the best translation in this context. With Th. here cf. Rac.'s Th., who similarly (*Phd.* 959) claims reluctance (*à regret*) in serving Pirithous' amorous plan.

Postponement of *ut* (here = "since", "while"; cf. *Pho.* 372).

843 sense of pain: *sensus malorum*. Cf. *Thy.* 306.

Alcides: Hercules, descended through his mother, Alcmena, from Alceus. The last of his twelve labours was to descend to the underworld and bring back Cerberus, the dog that guarded the entrance to the underworld proper (or to the palace of Dis). Hercules so terrified Proserpina and Dis that they allowed him to take away Theseus as well as Cerberus. (See Th.'s own description of the event at *HF* 782ff.) With Th.'s attitude to Alcides' rescue of him here at 843ff. cf. that displayed at 1217ff. For Hercules see also 317-29 and 807.

844 Tartarus: strictly the part of the underworld devoted to the punishment of the wicked, but often used for the lower world as a whole.

848 Phlegethon: a river of the underworld, for which it often functions as a metonym.

849 *Alciden:* Greek accusative.

850 Cf. Pha.'s howl of grief (*uox flebilis*) at 1154, which begins the final act. See also Eur. *Hipp.* 790, where Th.'s first words on entering are "Women, what cry of grief is this in the palace?" (The cry is lamentation over the death of Pha.).

851 *expromat:* jussive subjunctive. See 24n.

853 Fit welcome: Sen. displays a fondness for this ironic use of *dignus* ("fit", "worthy"); see, e.g., *Tro.* 863, *Med.* 363, *Oed.* 979, *Ag.* 34.

854-62 The Nurse's lack of surprise concerning Th.'s presence and Pha.'s decision to commit suicide imply that Th.'s arrival is known to (and possibly has been observed by) the Nurse and Pha.

856 *reduce...uiro:* a good illustration of the ablative absolute functioning as what it essentially is, viz. an ablative of attendant circumstances (a special type of sociative ablative). See Woodcock §49.

858f. Cf. Hipp.'s words to Pha. at 639f. For the pattern of adjectives and nouns/pronouns in 858 (abAB), see 85n.

860f. In fact all Athens knows. See 725ff.

860 *haut:* an alternative form of *haud* found frequently in the mss.

861 *quo:* ablative of cause. See Woodcock §45. There is hyperbaton of *malum*; trans.: *malum quo moritur.*

862 *properato est opus:* this construction—*opus* with the ablative of the perfect passive participle—is common. Cf. Livy 3.27.7, *maturato esse opus.*

863 **the doors...:** the *regia* or *porte royale*, the large double door in the centre of the Roman stage-building—see Vitruvius 5.6.8, Suetonius *Augustus* 31.5. Grimal, following E, assigns 863 to the Nurse. Most editors assign it to Th.

864-958 With this whole scene between Th. and Pha. cf. Livy's account of the story of Tarquinius' rape of Lucretia, esp. the interchange between Lucretia and her husband, Collatinus, after the rape (Livy 1.58.6-12). Lucretia's reply and immediate suicide form one of the major paradigms in the Roman tradition of wifely chastity (*pudicitia*). The scene plays with this paradigm. Note how Sen. sexualises the "interrogation" itself: imagery of opening and concealment (859ff.), Pha.'s initial refusal (870ff.), Th.'s violence (882ff.), Pha.'s surrender (885ff.), Hipp.'s sword (896ff.). With Pha.'s "secret" (*secretum*, 860, *arcana*, 875) cf. 55f.

864f. Rac.'s Th. begins with tenderness, not reprimand (*Phd.* 913f.).

866 *quin:* used adverbially (= "why not?"). *Ense* is ablative of separation (see 176n.).

868-71 On this form of appeal see 246ff.n. On the "sceptre" see 217n.

869 **Noble:** *magnanime*, lit. "great-souled", occurs only here in *Pha.* Elsewhere in Sen. tragedy it is used (always with respect) of Hercules (*HF* 310), Oedipus (*Pho.* 182, *Oed.* 294), and again of Theseus (*HF* 647).

indolem: "lives". *Indoles* means strictly the children's innate potential or "promise"; cf. *Thy.* 492, *generis inuisi indolem*, "the hope of his hated race".

870 *reditus:* plural for singular as with *hospitia* (853), or just possibly genuine plural (this is not the first time that Th. has "returned").

871-81 To Th.'s requests Pha. replies with a series of *sententiae*. For analogous uses of *sententiae* in Senecan dialogue cf. the exchanges between Agamemnon and Pyrrhus at *Tro.* 325ff., Medea and the Nurse at *Med.* 155ff., Oedipus and Creon at *Oed.* 515ff., and Clytemnestra and Aegisthus at *Ag.* 284ff. Note the extended passage of single-line dialogue or stichomythia at 872-79. Stichomythia is both more frequent and more extensive in Greek tragedy than in Sen., where it is usually combative. The longest passage of Senecan stichomythia is a mere thirteen lines (*Ag.* 145-57).

878   Cf. the analogous *sententia* at 265f. and n.

desse: for *deesse* (through synizesis—see 261n.). Like most other compounds of *esse* (e.g.*obesse, prodesse, adesse*) and *esse* itself, it frequently takes a dative of the person interested, as here (*uolenti*, participle used substantivally). See Woodcock §59.

880   That I live: *quod uiuo.* A most important reply. Cf. Rac. *Phd.* 308: *J'ai pris la vie en haine et ma flamme en horreur* ("I view life with hate and my passion with horror"). For Pha.'s view of her life see 113ff., 698f., 1178; on life's inherent detestability see *Ag.* 589ff. See also Atreus' comment on his sons' inherited wickedness: "they are born so", *nascuntur* (*Thy.* 314); Aegisthus' self-indictment: "For one so born (*sic nato*) it is no penalty to die" (*Ag.* 233); and *Pho.* 243ff., *Oed.* 875ff. See Intro. p. 36f. Sen.'s predilection for the dramatic and potent use of a single word or short phrase is noteworthy: cf., e.g., *Med.* 166, 910, *Ag.* 1012, *Thy.* 100f.

uiuo: the final *o* is short; see 542n.

nonne: occurs only here and at *Ag.* 12f. in Sen. It belongs to the language of ordinary speech, and does not occur even once in the *Aeneid.*

881   See Solon fr. 22 Diehl, "quoted" by Cic. *Tusc.* 1.117: "Let not my death lack tears..." Cf. Rac. *Phd.* 837.

suis: dative of agent as usual with gerundives. In origin it seems to be the dative of the "person interested". See Woodcock §202.

882-85   In the Roman criminal procedure evidence was obtained from slaves by means of torture. The practice was common in republican times but generally restricted in the empire to serious crimes. With one or two exceptions (adultery being one) slaves were not tortured into giving evidence against their own masters. With Th.'s behaviour here cf. that of Ulysses at *Tro.* 578ff. and Oedipus at *Oed.* 852ff. See also *Ag.* 988ff.

884   *extrahat:* jussive subjunctive. See 24n.

885b   Cf. Pha.'s change of mind in Act Two (250ff.).

886f.   There may be some counterpoint here with Eur.'s first *Hipp.* (*Kalyptomenos*), in which apparently Hipp. veiled his head on hearing Pha.'s revelations. Cf. also 734.

888-97   Sen.'s dramatisation of Pha.'s accusation of Hipp. should be compared with Eur. *Hipp.* 856ff. and Rac. *Phd.* 1001ff. In the former the accusation is made by means of a writing tablet attached to the hand of the dead Pha.; in the latter the accusation is made by the nurse and confidante, Oenone. In both Eur. and Rac. the accusation is unambiguous. For analysis of the Sen. treatment see Intro. p. 31f.

888-90   Pha. appeals to her divine ancestors, Jupiter ("creator of gods") and Apollo, the sun-god ("bright flame"). Cf. Hipp.'s invocation of the same gods at 671ff. and nn. See also 124ff., which 890 esp. seems to recall.

890   *ex cuius ortu:* lit. "from whose source/rising our house hangs". There is verbal play on *ortus* = "rising" (of the sun) and "source", "origin".

891-93   On the ambiguities here see Intro. p. 31f.

891f.   Similarly (Livy 1.58.7) Lucretia claimed that "her mind was innocent" (*animus insons*), "only her body was violated" (*corpus est tantum uiolatum*).

895   *rere:* second person sing. present indicative of *reor* (= *reris*).

896   **This sword will say:** so too at Eur. *Hipp.* 877 it is the inanimate object (wax tablet) that "shouts, shouts" (*boai, boai*). Cf. Pha.'s reluctance to speak (602, 637, 872ff.). On the sword motif see 706n.

898   **what crime do I see:** *quod facinus...cerno.* Similarly Hercules on recognising his dead children and wife: "What sin do I see?" (*quod nefas cerno? HF* 1159).

899f.   Cf. Ovid *Met.* 7.422f., where the engraved ivory hilt of Th.'s sword enables him to be identified. In the Ovidian case the identification baulks the plans of the step-mother (Medea) and prevents the crime, *facinus* (*Met.* 7.423—cf. *Pha.* 898). See also Plutarch *Theseus* 12.

899   *paruis asperum signis:* lit. "rough with small marks". *Asperum signis* virtually = *caelatum*, "engraved"; cf. Virg. *Aen.* 5.267, 9.263, *aspera signis*, and Ovid *Met.* 12.235, *signis asper.* The ablatives are sociative-instrumental.

900   **Attic house:** the royal house of Athens. Attica was the district in central Greece which had Athens as its capital.

decus: in apposition to *ebur* (899). *Decus* with the genitive is almost a descriptive mannerism in Senecan tragedy; cf., e.g., *HF* 592, 619, *Tro.* 766, 876, *Med.* 130, 571, *Oed.* 250, 405, and 410 above.

902   **fearful flight:** *trepidum fuga* (901). Pha. here picks up and uses the Nurse's account at 729 (*trepida...fuga*).

903-58   With Th.'s long speech here cf. his reaction and words (esp. his exchange with Hipp.) in Eur. *Hipp.* 874-1089. Cf. also Hipp.'s reaction at 671ff. above.

903   **love:** *pietas* means specifically the love owed by one member of the family to another. So the choral ode following the apparent reconciliation of Thyestes and Atreus in *Thy.* proclaims: "There is no greater force than true *pietas*/love" (*Thy.* 549).

firmament's lord: Jupiter.

Pro: with the vocative (or accusative) is a standard formula for exclamations.

904   you whose billows...: Neptune, ruler of the sea, "the second realm" (cf. *HF* 599, *Med.* 598, and see 1212n.), and reputed father of Th., who is also of course the son of the preceding Athenian king, Aegeus. Double paternity, divine and human, if not common, was also not unique. Hercules was son of Jupiter and Amphitryon, the Dioscuri were sons of Jupiter and Tyndareus. In Th.'s case double paternity (originally he was son of Aegeus at Athens, of Neptune at Troezen) seems to have been sometimes explained by having the two fathers visit Th.'s mother, Aethra, on the same night.

905   *generis infandi:* perhaps best taken as an objective genitive, with *infandi* as either proleptic or transferred. Cf. the description of Lycus at *HF* 358 as *nostri generis exitium ac lues*, "the destruction and infection of our race".

906f.   Cf. Andromache's outburst on hearing the account of Astyanax' death at *Tro.* 1104-09.

906   Tauric Scyth: see 168n. *Scythes* is technically the adjective.

907   Colchic Phasis: Colchis was a country on the south-east of the Black Sea associated with Medea (see 563f.n.). Its chief river was Phasis.

908   Another type of chiastic arrangement liked by Sen.: noun-epithet-epithet-noun (AabB). Cf. 305n., 308.

909   warrior tribe: the Amazons, who avoided marriage (Antiope is an exception in this regard). See 232n.

armiferae: Sen. shows a fondness for compounds in *–fer*. There are about thirty such in the tragedies. See, e.g., *igniferi* (960) below.

910   Venus' covenants: *Veneris foedera.* Used by Th. apparently to describe legally sanctioned sexual relations, i.e., marriage. But Venus' "law" covers more than marriage: see 274ff., 417 and n. See also 540 and n.

913f.   At Ovid *Met.* 10.323ff. Myrrha, desiring intercourse with her father, argues precisely the opposite, viz. that animals do commit "incest" and this is "what nature allows" (*quod natura remittit*). Myrrha is of course right about animal behaviour. With Th.'s pronouncement here cf. the dead Laius' indictment of Oedipus at *Oed.* 638ff.

915-17   Th. makes a similar charge of hypocrisy to Hipp.'s face at Eur. *Hipp.* 948-54.

918-22   Cf. Th.'s outburst at Eur. *Hipp.* 924-31 and Rac. *Phd.* 1039f.

920ff. *impudentem...audacem....:* adjectives used substantivally. See 95n.

921 *probant:* probably "approve", "praise", as at 478 above, *Med.* 160, etc.

925 *uirum:* "manhood", as at Catullus 63.6, Ovid *Ars* 1.690, Lucan 10.134. For analogous uses of "concrete for abstract" cf. Horace *Epistles* 1.18.2 (*professus amicum*), Lucan 1.131 (*dedidicit...ducem*), Petron. *Sat.* 97.9 (*ut saltem ostenderet fratrem*).

926 Now, now: *iam, iam:* cf. *Med.* 692, 949, 982, *Oed.* 28, 668, *Ag.* 44, 1011—all passages of heightened emotion. The device occurs frequently in both prose and verse.

927 Antiope: see 227n.

928 Stygian caves: the caves of the river Styx, i.e. the underworld. See 625n.

929-41 On the impossibility of Hipp.'s concealment cf. the preceding choral ode, 777-84.

930f. *ultimo...mundo:* local ablative. See 67ff.n.

931 Ocean: see 717f.n.

dirimat: concessive subjunctive after *licet* ("although"); so too *colas* (932), *transieris* (934), *liqueris* (936).

plagis: instrumental ablative (Woodcock §43), lit. "separate you (from us) with Ocean's tracts".

936 Boreas: the north wind. Cf. 1130.

942 My father...: Neptune, reputed divine father of Th. See 904n.

943 three prayers: *uota terna.* At Eur. *Hipp.* 887-90 Th. has received from Poseidon (= Neptune) three "curses" (*arai*), with the first of which he curses Hipp. Cf. Rac. *Phd.* 1068. In Sen. it is the last of the three "prayers" or "curses" (*uota*) that Th. uses (949ff.).

ut...concipiam: final noun-clause. See Woodcock §§139ff.

944 Styx: chief river of the underworld. By it the gods swore their "greatest and most dread oath" (Homer *Odyssey* 5.185f.). For a full description of this aspect of the Styx see Hesiod *Theogony* 793-806. Cf. also Virg. *Aen.* 6.323f., Statius *Thebaid* 1.291.

945-47 So at Eur. *Hipp.* 887ff. Th. prays: "Father Poseidon...make an end of my son; let him not escape this day." Cf. also Pha.'s prayer to Neptune, "savage master of unplumbed sea", at 1159ff. below. On prayers generally in Sen. see 54-80n.

945 grim gift: *donum triste.* The motif of the deceptive, "fatal" gift is common in Senecan tragedy: see, e.g., *Med.* 642, 844, 882, *Ag.* 626ff., 1009, *Thy.* 536, 984, and 1217f., 1252 below. See also 762.

946 Hippolytus: the first and only mention of his name in this act.

cernat: jussive subjunctive; so too *adeat* (947). See 24n. The negative with *non* instead of *ne* occurs occasionally in postclassical verse (see, e.g., Juvenal 3.54, 16.28) and even in Sen. prose (e.g. *Ira* 3.43.5, *Tran.* 14.2).

951-53   Cf. Hercules' claim at *HO* 1293-95.

951   Tartarus: strictly the part of the underworld devoted to the wicked. See 844n.

Dis: Pluto, king of the underworld. See 222n.

954   *genitor:* a reverential term, "sire", here ironic. See 245 and 942 above.

955f.   Cf. Hipp.'s appeal at 675 above.

958   Ocean's floods: see 717f.n. Th.'s final words in this act seem to echo those of Hipp. earlier (717f.). See also previous note.

THIRD CHORAL ODE (959-88b)

A short ode on *natura*, nature, and *fortuna*, fortune. Quasi-philosophical odes of this kind are common in Senecan tragedy; see, e.g., *Tro.* 371ff. (on death), *Oed.* 980ff. (on fate), *Ag.* 57ff. (on fortune), *Thy.* 336ff. (on true kingship), and 1123ff. below (on fortune). Choral odes on stock themes seem to have been a feature of the plays of the late fifth-century tragedian, Agathon. Aristotle criticised them as "interludes" (*embolima, Poetics* 1456a29f.). Sen.'s choral odes have been similarly criticised.

Metre: anapaestic. See Appendix II.

959   nature: *natura*. Identified here, as elsewhere in Sen., with the ultimate power of the universe. At *Ben.* 4.7f. it is in fact identified with the gods or god—"What else is *natura* but god and divine reason, *diuina ratio*, inserted into the universe and its parts"—and with both fate, *fatum*, and fortune, *fortuna*. In the same passage it is called "author of our world", *auctor rerum nostrarum*, "the first cause of all things", *prima omnium causa*, and "mother of all", *omnium parens*. Cf. *Ep.* 90.38, *NQ* 2.45, and esp. *Ep.* 107.7-12, where nature, fate, god and Jupiter are again associated and Lucilius is advised: "Whatever happens, think that it ought to have happened, and refuse to rail against nature (*nec uelit obiurgare naturam*)." With the title accorded *natura* at 959 ("mother of gods", *parens deum*), cf. also the Virgilian formula "father of gods and king of men", *diuum* *pater atque hominum rex*, applied to Jupiter (*Aen.* 1.65, 2.648, 10.2, 10.743), whom Sen. identifies with *natura* at *Ben.* 4.8 (see 960n.), and Sen.'s translation of Cleanthes' hymn to Zeus (Jupiter), *o parens celsique dominator poli* (*Ep.* 107.11). Note also the words put into the mouth of "Seneca" by the dramatist of *Oct.* (385f.): "Mother nature ... architect of infinite creation", *parens/natura ... operis immensi artifex.* For *natura* in the play see 173n., and in Sen. generally Appendix I.

deum: archaic form of the genitive plural (= *deorum*) found often in verse.

960   fiery Olympus' lord: Jupiter, wielder of the thunderbolt (hence "fiery") and king of the gods, whose traditional home was on Mt. Olympus in Greece. At *Ben.* 4.7f. nature and Jupiter are presented as one and the same: "There is neither nature without god (*natura sine deo*), nor god without nature (*deus sine natura*), but each is the same thing; they differ only in function." See also *NQ* 2.45.

961   cito...mundo: local ablative; so too *celeri...cardine* (963). See 67ff.n. On the parallel arrangement of adjectives and nouns in 961 (abAB) see 85n.

962   wandering planet's course: cf. *HF* 126f., *Thy.* 834.

967   arbustis: dative of goal of motion. See 585n. *Arbustum*, a plantation or orchard, is often used by later poets instead of *arbor* where metrical convenience dictates.

968   summer lion: the constellation Leo, which returns in the northern hemisphere at the end of July, bringing hot summer days.

970   Ceres: goddess of grain and fruits. See 838n.

971   the year tempers...: autumn.

973f.   vast world's balanced/ Mass: *uasti pondera mundi/ librata.* Cf. *Med.* 401, "While the central earth upholds the balanced heavens (*caelum libratum*)." See also Ovid's picture of "the earth balanced by its own mass (*ponderibus librata suis*)", *Met.* 1.12f.

975   hominum: the so-called genitive of respect with *securus* is found in verse and post-Augustan prose. It may have been influenced by the genitive with *oblitus*, with which as here it is sometimes virtually synonymous. Cf. Virg. *Aen.* 7.304, 10.326, *Ag.* 638.

977   nocuisse: perfect infinitive for present. See 503n.

978-80   Cf. the maxim, "fortune, not wisdom, rules life", *uitam regit fortuna, non sapientia*, quoted by Cic. *Tusc.* 5.25. See also *Ep.* 16.4f.

979   Fortune: *fortuna*. Identified with nature at *Ben.* 4.8, (see 959n.) but not here. The notion of a capricious, amoral fortune (Greek *tychē*) emerges in fifth-century Greek literature, esp. late Euripides, and is commonplace in Hellenistic and post-Hellenistic literature, art, religion and thought. In the Roman world the goddess *Fortuna* was well established. At Praeneste in the Alban hills outside Rome was an enormous sanctuary to *Fortuna* built in the early first century B.C. by Sulla, her other great centre being at Antium on the Latin coast south of Rome. Originally an Italian fertility goddess, *Fortuna* quickly took on the identity of the Greek *Tychē*. Rome itself had several monuments to *Fortuna*, some of which were believed to go back to Servius Tullius (sixth-century B.C.). For capricious, blind Fortune in Republican tragedy see Pacuvius 366-75R² (cf. Accius 422f.R²), and in later literature Shakespeare *Henry V* iii.6.26ff. ("Fortune is painted blind..."). For a less blind *fortuna/Fortuna* than that envisaged in this ode see 1123ff. below and the opening chorus of *Ag.* (57ff.). To preserve the duality of *fortuna* and "fortune" (abstract force/goddess) I have avoided (except for the beginning of English verse lines) spelling either word with an initial capital.

sparsit: gnomic perfect; so too *tulit* (985). See 75f.n.

980   *caeca:* modifies *manu* (979).

981-88b   There are obvious allusions here to the Hipp.-Pha.-Th. situation. With the general sentiments cf. Hesiod's description of the "iron race" at *Works and Days* 190ff.

983   authority: *fasces* (only here in Sen.'s plays) refers to the bundle of "rods" carried by lictors before a Roman magistrate as a symbol of his power. The image is particularly Roman. The attitude here recalls Horace's description of the Roman people at *Odes* 1.1.7: "a mob of fickle Quirites", *mobilium turba Quiritium*. See 488f. above and *HF* 169ff. Cf. also *Oct.* 679, where the time when *fasces* were given to "worthy citizens" (*dignis ciuibus*) is proclaimed as "long gone" (*olim*).

turpi: substantival use of the adjective.

984   they serve...hate: *colit atque odit.* Lit. "they serve and they hate (the same)". For similar paradoxes involving *odit* cf. *Tro.* 1129, (of a crowd of onlookers) "they hate...and they watch", *odit...spectatque*; Lucretius 3.1069, "clings to and hates", *haeret et odit*; Juvenal 15.71, "laughs and hates", *ridet et odit.* Cf. also *Med.* 582, (of Medea) "she burns and she hates", *ardet et odit*, and *Ben.* 5.20.2.

987   Evil want: *mala paupertas.* The phrase (reminiscent of Hesiod's *kakē peniē*, *Works and Days* 638) and evaluation are anything but Stoic. Contrast the attitude to "poverty" at *Ep.* 2.5, 17.3f., 20.7, 85.30ff. But cf. "grim/base want", *tristis/turpis egestas* at *Thy.* 303, 924, *Oct.* 833.

uitio: ablative of respect. See 276n.

ACT FIVE (989-1122)

As in *Tro.* and *Oed.* the fifth act is taken up primarily with a messenger's account of tragic disaster. See further 1000-1114n.

Metre: iambic trimeter (senarius). See Appendix II.

989f. Cf. the entrance of Eurybates at *Ag.* 408ff. and of the Messenger at *Oed.* 911ff., both announced by the chorus. Cf. also *HO* 1603ff., *Oct.* 778f.

991-99 Tragic messengers are notoriously reluctant to deliver the disastrous news; cf., e.g., Aeschylus *Persians* 249ff., Sophocles *Oedipus Tyrannus* 1146ff., and Sen. *Tro.* 168, 1056ff., *Oed.* 509ff., *Ag.* 414ff. In Eur. (*Hipp.* 1166ff.) and Rac. (*Phd.* 1491ff.), however, the messenger does not hesitate; he is aware of Pha.'s accusation and Th.'s curse. Not so in Sen. On reluctance to speak see also Pha. at 602, 637.

993 *ne metue:* see 131f.n. *Metuo* is often followed by a prolative infinitive as here (*fari*).

996 *Proloquere:* imperative.
  aggrauet: subjunctive of indirect question.

1000-1114 Senecan tragedy shows considerable diversity in the handling of the messenger's speech. The long, unbroken messenger's speech is restricted to three plays: *Pha.*, *Oed.* and *Ag.* In *Oed.* there are two such speeches: Creon in Act Three (530ff.), the Messenger in Act Five (915ff.—the penultimate act as in *Pha.*); in *Ag.* there is, strictly speaking, only one such speech, Eurybates' in Act Three (421ff.)—but cf. Cassandra's "vision" in Act Five (867ff.). In *Tro.* (Act Five, 1068ff.) and *Thy.* (Act Four, 641ff.) the Messenger provides a discontinuous account broken up by questions; in *Pho.* (387ff.) and *Med.* (Act Five, 879ff.) his report is extremely brief and in the latter interleaved with questions. In *HF* there is no messenger's speech at all, although Theseus' long and discontinuous account of the underworld in Act Three (658ff.) might be said to replace it. Generally, as in Greek tragedy, the messenger is anonymous. With *Pha.* 1000-1114 cf. Eur. *Hipp.* 1173-1254 and Rac. *Phd.* 1498-1593. See also Ovid *Met.* 15.506-29.

1000 **hostile flight: *profugus...infesto gradu*.** An "echo" of Th.'s words at 929 (*profugus*) and 938 (*profugum*). Hipp.'s flight is not caused, however, as in Eur. (*Hipp.* 893ff., 973ff., 1065ff., 1084ff.) and Rac. (*Phd.* 1053ff., 1140ff.) by a decree of exile. For "flight" or "shunning" and Hipp. see the references at 230n. For "flight" and

Th. see 91, 835, 849, 1151. Th. and Hipp. alone are labelled *profugus* (91, 929, 938, 1000). Contrast Pha.'s comment at 699. For "flight" as "self-flight" see Oedipus at *Pho.* 216ff.

ut: "when", as at *Ag.* 421, where the speech of the messenger, Eurybates, opens in a similar manner.

1002f.   Cf. Hipp.'s earlier instructions on the control of the hunting-dogs at 32-37.

1002   *ocius:* probably comparative for positive, as at 130, although comparatives are also used to express degree ("rather quickly").

1005   **calls...on his father:** note that, unlike in Eur. and Rac., Hipp. seems ignorant of his father's curses (and indeed of Pha.'s accusation). So too the Messenger. Both Eur. and Rac. in fact make much of Hipp.'s knowledge (e.g., *Hipp.* 1190-93, 1239-42, 1348f., *Phd.* 1561-67).

1007ff.   Cf. the description of the storm at *Ag.* 466ff., where a "deep murmur" (*murmur graue*) and "moaning" (*gemunt*) precede the turmoil.

1007   **sea thundered:** cf. the seismic rumbling "like the thunder of Zeus" which precedes the appearance of the monstrous bull at Eur. *Hipp.* 1201.

1008   *salo:* dative after *inspirat.* See 585n.

1011   **Auster:** the south wind.

   Sicily's strait: the strait of Messina separating Sicily from Italy, notorious for its storms. Cf. *Ep.* 14.8.

1013   **Corus:** see 737n.

1014   **Leucate:** a promontory on the island of Leucadia in the Ionian Sea.

1016ff.   **Monster-bellied ...:** *tumidum monstro.* Cf. "monster-pregnant" (*monstrifera*) Pasiphae at 688. The imagery of pregnancy and birth here ("monster-bellied", "the wave...womb", "Is...born") seems Sen.'s own. It occurs neither in Eur. nor in Ovid *Met.* 15. 1016 is deleted by Leo; few editors have followed him.

1021   **Cyclad:** the Cyclades are a group of islands in the Aegean Sea. The "birth" of volcanic islands is discussed by Sen. at *NQ* 6.21.1. For "new Cyclads" see also Ovid *Met.* 2.263f.

1022-24   The places listed here feature in Eur.'s account (see esp. *Hipp.* 1207-09) and are generally thought to be inappropriate to the setting of Sen.'s play at Athens. Eur.'s play is set at Troezen. It should be noted however that the places mentioned cover the Saronic Gulf from Epidaurus to west of Megara and could not all have been visible even from Troezen. In both Eur.'s and Sen.'s messenger's speech rhetorical and dramatic considerations seem more important than topographical verisimilitude.

1022f. Epidaurus'/ God: Asclepius, god of medicine, who had a famous sanctuary at Epidaurus, a town on the south-west coast of the Saronic Gulf.

latuere: = *latuerunt.*

numine...scelere: both causal ablatives after *nobiles.* See 30n.

1023 rocks of Sciron's crime: Sciron was a robber renowned for making his victims wash his feet before kicking them over the cliff into the sea. See 1225. The Scironian rocks, *Scironides*, were west of Megara on the northern coast of the Saronic Gulf.

1024 The land too...: the Corinthian Isthmus, with the descriptive possibilities of which Sen., like many Roman poets, was clearly fascinated. Cf. *HF* 336, *Med.* 35f., *Ag.* 564f., *Thy.* 111ff., 124f., 181f., 628f., *HO* 83ff. It is of interest to note that one of Nero's engineering projects was the attempt to cut a canal through the Isthmus (Suetonius *Nero* 19.2).

Hyperbaton; trans.: *et terra quae...*

1026 Bellows...: cf. Eur. *Hipp.* 1215f., where however the "bellowing" (*phthegma*) is of the bull when it appears, not (as here) of the ocean before the actual appearance of the *monstrum.* See also Ovid *Met.* 15.510.

1029 whale: *physeter.* Described by Pliny *NH* 9.8.

Ocean: see 717n.

qualis: often used with or (as here) without its correlative, *talis* (or *sic*, etc.), to introduce a simile. Cf., e.g., Virg. *Geo.* 4.511, Statius *Thebaid* 9.532, *Med.* 382, *Thy.* 707, 732—and 102, 399, 749 above and 1072 below.

1032 *litori:* dative of goal of motion. See 585n.

1033 *timore:* ablative of comparison. See 143n.

1034-49 No detailed description of the "monster" is to be found in Eur. (*Hipp.* 1214) or Ovid (*Met.* 15.511ff.). Rac. offers a description of four lines (*Phd.* 1517-20).

1035 vast body: *corporis uasti.* Cf. 806 (of Hipp.).

quis: used as equivalent to *qualis.* Cf. 651 above.

1038 *orbibus:* possessive dative.

1039 leader of a wild herd: cf. 116-18.

quem...: the antecedent is *color.*

habuisset: generic subjunctive (potential in origin) indicating sort or type. See Woodcock §155.

1040 *natus:* substantival use of participle.

1046 *pone:* used here as a preposition (with the accusative). This is the only occurrence of the word in Senecan tragedy. Cf. Virg.'s description of the serpents from Tenedos in *Aen.* 2, which also came from the sea: *pars cetera pontum/ pone legit sinuatque immensa uolumine terga* ("the rest skims the ocean/ Behind and their huge backs sinuously coil", *Aen.* 2.208f.). Sen. may be alluding to the Virgilian passage.

1049 beast: *pistrix*. The Latin word is of wide meaning and connotes some kind of sea-monster. Cf. Virg. *Aen.* 3.427.

1050-54 Seneca's emphasis again. No detailed account of the effect of the bull on the countryside and Hipp.'s companions is to be found in Eur., Ovid or Rac.

1053 *frigido...metu:* ablative of cause with *exsanguis*. See Woodcock §45.

1054-56 Cf. Rac. *Phd.* 1526f.: *Hippolyte lui seul, digne fils d'un heros,/ Arrête ses coursiers...*("Hippolytus' self alone, a hero's worthy son,/ Reins in his horses..."). See also Eur. *Hipp.* 1218ff. and Ovid *Met.* 15.514ff., where, however, Hipp. does not gain even temporary control over his horses. Like Sen., Rac. accords Hipp. a kind of aristeia (*Phd.* 1527-34).

1057-59 The abrupt introduction of a short topographical description (*descriptio* or ecphrasis) which is then picked up (usually with a demonstrative word) was a device as old as Homer (see, e.g., *Iliad* 2.811ff., *Odyssey* 4.844ff.) and a regular feature of Roman declamation (see, e.g., Sen. Rhet. *Con.* 1.4.8f.). Sen. uses the standard formula: *est...hic*; cf. Virg. *Aen.* 5.124ff., 7.563ff. Ovid is esp. fond of the device (see, e.g., *Met.* 11.592ff.). Only here in Sen. is the ecphrasis so short; elsewhere—*HF* 709ff., *Tro.* 1068ff., *Oed.* 530ff., *Ag.* 558ff., *Thy.* 225ff.—a more elaborate description is usual.

1059-61 An echo of some famous Virgilian lines depicting a battle between two amorous bulls in *Geo.* 3 (232-34). For other important reminiscences of *Geo.* 3 in *Pha.* see 339-47 and n.

1061 *irae:* dative after *prolusit*, lit. "practised for wrath".

1063f. fierce stood...ferocious glare: cf. the Nurse's description of Hipp. at 416 and similar language used of him elsewhere. See Intro. p. 27. With Hipp.'s "ferocity" (*feroci...uultu*) and fearlessness (1054) here cf. the similar qualities attributed to Astyanax and Polyxena in the Messenger's account of their deaths at *Tro.* 1088ff. (esp. 1093, 1098, 1146, 1152). Cf. also *Thy.* 720f.

1063 *torua:* used predicatively. It is feminine because of *moles* (1059).

   currus: plural for singular and metonym for "team", as at Virg. *Aen.* 12.287, Lucan 7.570. So too at 1075.

1065 thunders: *intonat*. Cf. *Ag.* 544ff., where Ajax of Locris "thunders" (*intonat*) his defiant challenge to Pallas. His death follows immediately.

1066 See 47b and n.

1067 So Hercules to his opponent, Achelous (now transformed into a serpent): "It is my cradle's task to conquer snakes" (*cunarum labor est angues superare mearum*, Ovid *Met.* 9.67). Hercules, unlike Hipp., wins.

father's trade: a reference to Th.'s slaying of the Minotaur (see 113n.) and perhaps also to his slaying of the Marathonian bull, brought by Hercules from Crete (see Ovid *Met.* 7.434).

1069 *derrantes:* = *deerrantes* (through synizesis—see 261n.).

1072 **as a helmsman:** cf. Eur.'s comparison of Hipp. to "a sailor on the oar" (*Hipp.* 1221), as he attempts to control his horses. They immediately bolt.

1074 **steers:** *gubernat. Gubernator* is the technical term for a ship's helmsman, and both it and the verb *gubernare* are used only rarely in a transferred sense of the driver of a chariot or rider of a horse (e.g. Ennius *Annales* 486V³, Martial 9.22.14). Its use here drives home the Messenger's analogy. Cf. *Med.* 3 where *frenare* ("control with a bridle") is used of a helmsman controlling his ship. See also the important simile at 181ff. above.

1077 **relentless comrade:** *adsiduus comes.* Cf. 54 above, where Hipp. seeks a different kind of comrade in the hunt. See also 1111.

1081 *corniger:* used substantivally (as at Manilius 5.39) and modified by two adjectives, *obuius* and *horridus*, both of which I have translated predicatively, although the latter may be attributive.

1082-84 Contrast Eur. and Ovid, who have the chariot break upon a rock (*Hipp.* 1233) or a tree-trunk (*Met.* 15.523).

1085-87 With the language of this description cf. 36f., 46, 75f.

1088f. *curru leui,/ dominante nullo:* two ablative absolutes in asyndeton, the second explaining the first.

sensere: = *senserunt.*

1090 **Phaethon:** Another descendant of Phoebus Apollo, the sun-god, in fact his son. Phaethon tried to drive his father's chariot (the sun) but was thrown out and killed. The story is told in full at Ovid *Met.* 1.746-2.400 (see esp. 2.161ff.), and is cited by the chorus at *Med.* 599ff. as an example of reckless presumption and a breach of the "sacrosanct covenants of the world" (*sacro...sancta foedera mundi*). See also *HO* 677ff.

1093 Cf. Virg.'s description of the dismemberment of Orpheus at *Geo.* 4.522: "they scattered the torn youth over the wide fields", *discerptum latos iuuenem sparsere per agros.*

1095 ravage: *populatur*. Cf. the operation of love's fire and anxiety at 280 ("ravages", *populante*) and 377 ("ravages", *populatur*), and that of time or beauty at 764ff. ("despoiled", 765, 772, "ravished", 771). *lapis:* collective singular.

1096 wound on wound: *multo uulnere*. Cf. Ovid's final description of the torn Hipp.: "And all was one wound" (*unumque erat omnia uulnus, Met.* 15.529), taken up by Rac. *Phd.* 1550. *Multo uulnere* is ablative of cause (an off-shoot of the instrumental function of the case—Woodcock §45).

1098f. With the unambiguous sexual overtones of Hipp.'s violent death, cf. Hipp.'s latent sexualisation of the landscape and of Diana's kingdom and power in the opening monody (esp. 55ff.). See Intro. pp. 19 and 23.

1098 *ambusta sude:* ablative of description. See 50n.

1100 Axelson and Zwierlein delete this line.

1101 *biiuges:* substantival use of adjective.

1101f. break delay/ And master: zeugma, viz. the syntactical figure where one word is connected to two other words or phrases but in a different sense with each. Here "break", *rumpunt*, is used figuratively with "delay", *moram*, literally with "master", *dominum*. The phrase "break (off) delay", *rumpe moras*, is Virgilian (*Geo.* 3.43, *Aen.* 4.569, 9.13). Cf. *Tro.* 681, *Med.* 54.

1103 *acutis asperi...rubis:* lit. "rough with sharp brambles". The ablatives are sociative-instrumental. Cf. 899.

1105ff. Reminiscences here perhaps of the story of Actaeon killed by his own hunting-dogs (Ovid *Met.* 3.155-252). See *Oed.* 751ff.

1105 *famuli:* nominative plural with *funebris manus* in apposition. Sen. was obviously fond of this kind of appositional construction and "enfolding" word-order; see, e.g., *geminum Tyndaridae genus, HF* 552, *alta muri decora, Tro.* 15, *turba captiuae mea, Tro.* 63, *fortis armiferi cohors, Med.* 980, *fida famuli turba, Ag.* 800. Cf. the analogous device at 305 above, where the appositive phrase, instead of enclosing the noun as here, is itself enclosed by noun and modifier. Both mannerisms derive from earlier Roman poets, esp. Virg. (see, e.g., *Ecl.* 1.57, 2.3, *Geo.* 2.146, 4.168), and seem to have been common in Hellenistic Greek verse.

1106 Hyperbaton. The usual order: *per illa loca quae...*

1107 *longum...tramitem:* either internal accusative or adverbial accusative of extent (Woodcock §§3, 10 and 13).

1108 Cf. Hipp.'s own description of the dogs at 39-43, 77f.

1109f. Gathering together the remnants of a dismembered person's body and restoring them to their proper place (*concinnare corpus*) prior to cremation or burial was in the Roman tradition a duty owed to the dead. See Apuleius *Metamorphoses* 7.26; cf. Statius *Thebaid* 3.131f.

1109   *dolentum:* substantival use of present participle; see 95n. On the form of the genitive here see 634n.

1110   Some editors postpone the entry of Hipp.'s companions with fragments of the body until Act Six. The deictic question at 1110b, Th.'s outburst at 1114, Pha.'s cry of grief at the beginning of Act Six suggest this as the more appropriate moment for such an entry. The scene's dramatic power would perhaps be more effectively realised if Hipp.'s body were brought in on a covered bier.

beauty's glory: *formae decus.* Cf. the remarks of the chorus on "beauty", *forma*, at 761ff.

1112   Assured heir: *certus heres.* In both Eur. and Ovid Hipp. is a "bastard" and not an "assured heir". See 227n.

like the stars: *siderum...modo.* For this imagery and Hipp. cf. also 736ff., 1174, 1269f. See also Eur. *Hipp.* 1121; and *Oct.* 168: *modo sidus orbis*, "just now the world's star" (of the dead Britannicus).

1114-17   Cf. Th.'s reaction in Eur. (*Hipp.* 1260): "I am neither pleased nor distressed by this woe." See also Rac. *Phd.* 1571-73.

1115   Nature: see 173n., 959 and n., and Appendix I.

1118   Hyperbaton. Trans.: *haud quisque potest...*

1119f.   Ironic definitions, often introduced by *maximus*, "the greatest...", are a feature of Senecan dialogue; cf., e.g., *Tro.* 422f., *Ag.* 271f., *Thy.* 176ff.

1122   *quod....:* either noun-clauses standing as internal objects to *fleo*, or adverbial clauses of causation (or both). See Woodcock §241.

non: its position might suggest to the reader ambiguity as to what it modified. When spoken, however, it would have to be taken with either *quod interemi* or *quod amisi*. Th.'s remark at 1117, which this line echoes, dictates the former.

It seems clear from 1154ff. (see also 1143ff.) that no one exits at this point. Similarly at *HF* 1054ff. and *Tro.* 1009ff. all the characters remain on stage during the final chorus (cf. also *Ag.* 808ff., where possibly Cassandra stays on stage during the final chorus).

FOURTH CHORAL ODE (1123-53)

An ode on fortune's wheel. In only two other plays is the final choral ode, as here, one of general reflection: *Tro.* (on grief, 1009ff.) and

Oed. (on fate, 980ff.). In *Med.* (849ff.) and *Thy.* (789ff.) the final ode is one of fear; in *HF* (1054ff.) it is—in part—a prayer, in *Ag.* (808ff.) a eulogy. With this ode cf. the preceding choral ode at 959ff. and *Ag.*'s opening chorus on *fortuna fallax*, "fortune the deceiver" (*Ag.* 57ff.).

Metre: anapaestic (1123-27, 1132-39, 1141-48); asclepiadean (1128f.); glyconic (1130); aristophanean (1131); pherecratean (1140); sapphic (1149-53). See Appendix II.

1123-40 The central ideas of these lines—the tendency of the (jealous) gods or fortune to strike down the lofty, the comparative safety of the life of obscurity and moderation, fortune's wheel—are commonplaces of ancient literature: see, e.g., Pindar *Isthmian* 7.39ff., Aeschylus *Agamemnon* 772ff., 921ff., Eur. *Hipp.* 1013ff., Herodotus 7.10, Ennius *Annales* 312f.V[3], Cic. *Pis.* 22, Tibullus 1.5.70. For the standard analogy with mountain-peaks struck by lightning, see esp. Lucretius 5.1120ff., 6.421ff., Horace *Odes* 2.10.9ff., Ovid *Rem.* 369f. See also *HF* 192ff., *Tro.* 259ff., *Oed.* 8ff., 882ff., *Ag.* 87ff., *Thy.* 391ff., 596ff., 1081ff., and *Ep.* 19.9. The mutability of fortune was of course also a commonplace of Roman declamation: see, e.g., Sen. Rhet. *Con.* 2.1.1 and 9, *Suas.* 1.9. *Pha.*'s dramatisation of these topoi is, however, far from commonplace. On fortune see also 979n.

1125 lightly...little: the Latin, *leuius...leuiora*, plays on two senses of *leuis*, "light" and "trivial". With the idea here cf. esp. *Thy.* 1081f.

1128 roofs: One such recent "assault" came from Caligula's building activities on the Palatine, including an attempt to construct a temple to himself *qua* Olympian Zeus to rival the temple of Jupiter Optimus Maximus on the Capitoline hill. See Dio 59.28.2f., and below 1140.

aetheriis...sedibus: dative of goal of motion common with compound verbs. See 585n.

1129 Eurus: the south-east wind.
Notus: the south wind.

1130 Boreas: the north wind. Cf. 936.

1131 Corus: the north-west wind. Cf. 737, 1013.

1134 high-roaring Jupiter: *Iouis altisoni*. Jupiter is king of the gods and wielder of the thunderbolt. See 671ff., 960ff. "High-roaring", *altisoni*, is an epic compound first attested in Ennius (*Annales* 575V[3], *Andromache* 88 Jocelyn, *Iphigenia* 188 Jocelyn), probably devised in imitation of the Homeric epithet *hypsēchēs* (e.g. Homer *Iliad* 5.772) or *hypsibremetēs* (e.g. *Iliad* 1.354). See also Cic. *Div.* 1.106 (quoting Cic.'s own epic, *Marius*). Sen. uses the expression again at *Ag.* 582; cf. *HO* 530.

tremuit telo: gnomic perfect (see 75f.n.) followed by ablative of cause (see 30n.).

1135 Caucasus: the Caucasus mountains lie between the Black Sea and the Caspian Sea.

1136 Cybele: the great mother goddess of Asia Minor. Her traditional home was in the forests of Mt. Ida in Phrygia. See Catullus 63.

Cybeles: Greek genitive.

1139 plebeian: an expressly Roman term (opposed to "patrician") for the lower social orders, used also at *HF* 738, *Thy.* 400, and (in the substantival form, *plebs*) at *Tro.* 1077. Cf. Sen.'s use of *Quirites* (= "sons of Romulus") for "citizens" at *Thy.* 396.

humilis tecti: genitive of quality or description. See 208n.

1140 thunders: *tonat.* Cf. the line of Maecenas criticised by Sen. at *Ep.* 19.9: "For even the topmost height thunders", *ipsa enim altitudo attonat summa.* Some editors follow Fabricius in deleting 1140.

1141-48 Cf. the Messenger's focus on the reversal suffered by Hipp. at 1110-14. See also 1213-16.

1143b *iterum uidet:* a lacuna is assumed in E. See Selective Critical Apparatus.

1146f. *ipso...Auerno:* ablative of comparison. See 143n.

1148 Avernus: a lake near Cumae in Italy, deadly to birds (lit. "the birdless place"). It was thought of as one of the entrances to the underworld, for which, like the Styx and Acheron, etc., it often functions, as here, as a metonym.

1149 Pallas: Athena/Minerva, patron deity of Athens. Hence "your" Theseus (1150).

Actaeae...genti: dative of agent after the gerundive. See 881n.

1151 Stygian pit: the underworld. See 625n.

1152 your uncle: Pluto, brother of Minerva's father, Jupiter, and ruler of the underworld, "hell's king" (1153). The greed or rapacity of death/Pluto was proverbial; see, e.g., Callimachus *Epigram* 2.5f., Virg. *Geo.* 2.492, Horace *Odes* 2.18.30. Cf. the "rapacious hands of fate" at 467.

1153 tally: *constat.* As in Homer (*Odyssey* 10.552ff.) and Virgil (*Aen.* 6.149ff.) a visit to, and return from, the underworld are linked with the death of another. *Constat* is a metaphor from commerce; it is used of the balancing of an account. See also 455, *fenus,* "return" or "interest".

ACT SIX (1154-1280)

With the exception of *Tro.* the final act of each Senecan play devotes itself substantially to a confrontation between the play's major figures. In the only other six-act Senecan drama, *Oed.*, the confrontation, as here, is between male (Oedipus) and female (Jocasta) and results in the suicide of the latter.

Metre: iambic trimeter (senarius), apart from 1201-12; trochaic tetrameter catalectic (septenarius), 1201-1212. See Appendix II.

1154   Cf. the cry of lamentation which greets Th. at 850ff.

1155   **sword:** this does not have to be the sword of Hipp. But, given the preceding focus on this sword and Pha. (706-35, 864-901), it makes more dramatic sense if it is so. See esp. 711f. and n.

   frantic: *uecors.* Cf. the chorus' announcement of the "frantic" (*uecors*) Jocasta at *Oed.* 1004ff.

1157   *quidue:* –*ue* is used frequently in this way to link a series of questions with cumulative effect. No disjunction is implied. The use goes back to early Latin (e.g. Plautus *Asinaria* 636, Terence *Eunuchus* 304).

1159ff.   Cf. Jocasta's suicide speech at *Oed.* 1024ff.

1159   **Me, me...:** cf. Hipp.'s prayer for self-destruction at 682f.; also *Pho.* 443ff., *Oed.* 872ff. For the emotional duplication of *me* (rare in Sen. tragedy) see *HF* 110, *Tro.* 680; cf. Virg. *Aen.* 8.144, 9.427, 12.260. On the prayer-motif see 54-80n.

   master of unplumbed sea: *profundi...dominator freti.* The reference is of course to Neptune. There is also an echo here of Pha.'s opening words in the play at 85: "O mighty Crete, mistress of endless sea (*uasti...dominatrix freti*)." On *dominator* see 85n. Cf. also 945 and *Med.* 4.

1160-63   Cf. 1015-20, 1204f.; also 570f.

1161   **Tethys:** see 571n.

1162   **Ocean:** see 717f.n.

   quicquid: sc. *monstrorum* (partitive genitive).

1163   *complexus:* the perfect participle of a deponent verb is often used with a present sense. See 124, 230 above.

1164f.   *o numquam...reuerse:* this grandiloquent use of the vocative participle probably originated in hymnic contexts; cf. Catullus 36.11, Horace *Odes* 3.21.1ff.

1165   **son's and sire's death:** the deaths of Hipp. and Th.'s father,

206

Aegeus. Aegeus killed himself because Th., returning from Crete, forgot to change the purple sails for white (to indicate his victory over the Minotaur) as he approached Athens. See Catullus 64.207-48.

1166 *luere:* = *luerunt.*

1167 **love of wife or hate:** Pha. is the wife supposedly loved, Antiope the wife hated.

1168 **is this...I see:** so Euryalus' mother begins her lament at Virg. *Aen.* 9.481: "Is this you, Euryalus, I see?" (*hunc ego te, Euryale, aspicio?*).

1169-73 Pha. alludes to brigands and monsters slain by Th. (Plutarch *Theseus* 8 and 11). For a similar but more extensive list see Ovid *Met.* 7.433-50. In Ovid the list is a eulogy of Th. Cf. also Rac. *Phd.* 79-82.

1169 **Sinis:** sometimes called Pityocamptes ("Pinebender"). He was a brigand who killed his victims by fastening their limbs to bent pine trees which he then let go. See *HO* 1393.

1170f. **Procrustes:** a robber ("the Stretcher") who invited travellers to spend the night and fitted them to their beds either by stretching them or by chopping off their limbs. He is mentioned also at *Thy.* 1050, *Clem.* 2.41.

Cretan/ Bull: the Minotaur. See 113n., and 122, 174ff., 648ff., 688ff., 1067.

1171f. **Daedalean/ Jail:** the Cretan labyrinth. See 120n.

1172 *ore cornigero:* most naturally taken with *ferox* as causal/ instrumental ablative. Cf. *spectu proteruo ferox*, Pacuvius 147R².

1173 **beauty fled:** cf. 773, 1270. See also 230n.

1174 **stars:** for star imagery and Hipp. see 738-52n. There is perhaps also an association here of "stars" and destiny.

nostrum sidus: in apposition to *oculi* without the interlocking pattern of 1105.

1177 *nefando pectori:* dative of goal of motion common with compound verbs. See 585n.

1178 **life and sin:** for their identity in the case of Pha. see 879f. and 880n.

anima...scelere: "true" ablatives of separation. See 176n.

1179f. Axelson and Zwierlein delete both lines; other recent editors do not. For the important motif here see 233-35, 241, 700ff.

1179 **Tartarean:** see 844n.

1180 **Styx:** see 625n.

1181f. The offering of a lock of hair to the dead was a traditional act of mourning, here individualised. Cf. Eur. *Hipp.* 1423-27, where (with reference to the historical cult of Hipp. at Troezen—see Pausanias 2.32.1-4) Artemis promises that, in compensation for Hipp.'s sufferings, unmarried girls of Troezen will cut off a lock of their hair in his honour before the day of their marriage. Hipp. will thus reap "the deep mourning of their tears" (*Hipp.* 1427). Pha.'s "wounded brow" (1182) is also an index of mourning.

1183f. Cf. the union in death of Thisbe with Pyramus at Ovid *Met.* 4.151ff.

iunxisse: perfect infinitive for present. See 503n.

1184f. if chaste...love: *si casta es, uiro;/ si incesta, amori.* The rhetorical figure of the dilemma or *complexio* (see Cic. *Inv.* 1.45). Cf. *Tro.* 510-12, where similarly the elements of the antithesis are expressed in metrically parallel form. See also *HF* 1278, *Pho.* 76, *Med.* 194, *HO* 1027-29.

morere: imperative.

uiro: dative of advantage/disadvantage; so too *amori* (1185). See Woodcock §64.

1186 *derat:* = *deerat* (through synizesis—see 261n.).

1187 *ut...fruereris:* consecutive noun-clause in apposition to *nefas.* See Woodcock §168.

sancta: predicative and ironic (= "as if I were pure").

1188-90 O death...: for Pha.'s preoccupation with death see also 250ff., 711f., 871, 880, and Intro. p. 36f..

1191 Athens: with Pha.'s truthful public address cf. the Nurse's deceptive one (725).

1191f. *funesta...nouerca:* ablative of comparison. See 143n.

1195 pure...impurely: *castus...incesto.* With this word-play cf. "pure" Iphianassa "impurely" slain (*casta inceste*) at Lucretius 1.98. See also 1184f. above and Rac. *Phd.* 1623f. (*chaste...incestueux*).

crimine incesto: both accompaniment and causation seem involved in this ablative.

1197f. On death by the sword of the beloved and its fusion of love and death, see 711f. and n. In Eur. (extant) *Hipp.* (764ff.) Pha.'s suicide is by hanging. See also 706n.

1199f. Some editors, following A, assign these lines to Pha. The E assignment seems more plausible on dramatic grounds and because the change of verse-form at 1201 provides a satisfactory explanation of how the A assignment came about. Th.'s move from iambic trimeters (1199f.) to another metre (1201ff.) within the same speech is parallelled in Sen. by Cassandra's change of verse-form at *Ag.* 759ff. The E assignment is followed by (among others) Leo, Grimal, Giardina and Zwierlein.

1200 tomb yourself: cf. Eur. *Hipp.* 1290f., where it is Artemis who advises Th. to hide in Tartarus.

condere: passive imperative with a reflexive or "middle" sense: "hide/bury yourself".

plagis: ablative of place. See 67ff.n.

1201-12 The change in metre in the translation here is intended to reflect Sen.'s movement from the normal metre of verse-dialogue, the iambic trimeter, to the longer and more emotional line of the trochaic tetrameter catalectic. Only twice elsewhere in his tragedies does Sen. use the latter metre: Medea's invocation of the gods and spirits of hell at *Med.* 740-51, and Creon's chilling description of his visit to the Delphic oracle at *Oed.* 223-32. With Th.'s prayer for self-destruction and punishment cf. that of Hercules at *HF* 1221ff., of Oedipus at *Oed.* 868ff., 936ff., and of Thyestes at *Thy.* 1006ff., 1068ff. See also 54-80n.

1201 caverns of Taenarus: a cave at Cape Taenarus in the south-east Peloponnese was another traditional entrance to the underworld. Cf. Virg. *Geo.* 4.467.

1202 Lethe's stream: the river of forgetfulness, from which the dead drink and forget their sufferings.

Lethes: Greek genitive.

1203 *impium:* sc. *me.*

1204f. Cf. 1160-63.

1205 Proteus: a sea-god, the chief herdsman of Neptune's marine "herd". See Homer *Odyssey* 4.385f., Virg. *Geo.* 4.387ff. He had the power to transform himself into different shapes and knew all things.

Hyperbaton: postponement of *quodcumque.*

1207 father: Neptune.

1208ff. I deserve no easy end: so Oedipus (*Oed.* 936ff.) seeks an extraordinary punishment to match his extraordinary crimes.

1209 avenger: *uindex*, related to *uindicat*, "claims". See 352n. and Intro. p. 20f.

1211 stars: a reference to the abandonment of Ariadne, who gave rise to a constellation. See 663-666n. "Shades" most plausibly refers to his underworld expedition, "ocean" to the deaths of Hipp. and Aegeus. Others take "shades" as alluding to the deaths of Antiope and Hipp., "ocean" to that of Aegeus alone.

1212 three kingdoms: i.e. the three referred to in 1211, heaven, ocean and hell, which were allotted to the three brothers, Jupiter, Neptune and Pluto respectively. Ocean or the sea is the "second kingdom", hell the "third". The notion of the "three kingdoms" is often used by Sen.; see, e.g., *Tro.* 344ff., and 904 above.

norunt: syncopated form of *nouerunt.*

1213-16   Cf. the preceding choral ode's focus on this theme at 1141-48.

1214   *bina:* distributive numeral for cardinal as often in verse. See 150n.

1215f.   Hyperbaton: postponement of *ut.* Trans.: *ut caelebs et orbus...* With the thought cf. *Oed.* 55.
funebres: modifies *rogos.*

1217-19   Cf. *HF* 1338ff., where it is Hercules who begs Th. to restore him to the underworld.

1217   **Alcides:** Hercules. See 843ff. and 843n. On Alcides' gift see 945n.

1218   **boon:** *munus.* Cf. *HF* 806, where Th. is himself the "boon" or "tribute" (*munus*) exacted by Hercules from Dis. On "gifts" in Sen. tragedy see 945n.
Dis: Pluto, ruler of the dead. See 222n.

1222   *tibimet:* emphatic form of *tibi.*

1223-25   Th. refers to punishments which he has inflicted on others: on Sinis (1169n.) at 1223f., on Sciron (1023n.) at 1225. Contrast Eur. *Hipp.* 976-80, where Th. uses his slaying of Sinis and Sciron to illustrate his resolve to punish Hipp.

1224   *caelo remissum findat:* sc. *me. Caelo* is dative of goal of motion (see 585n.). *Findat* is a deliberative subjunctive; so too *mittar* (1225). See Woodcock §172.

1226   **Phlegethon:** the river of fire in the underworld which surrounds and imprisons the wicked. See *Thy.* 73, 1017f. and Virg. *Aen.* 6.550f.

1228   *maneat:* subjunctive of indirect question.

1229-37   Th. alludes to famous sinners in hell. The ones referred to—Sisyphus, Tantalus, Tityos, Ixion—form a canon of sinners here and at *Ag.* 15ff., *Thy.* 4ff., *HO* 1068ff., *Oct.* 621ff., and *Apoc.* 14.5. The list occurs with modifications at *HF* 750ff., *Med.* 744ff. and *HO* 938ff. Cf. also *Ep.* 24.18. The canon without Ixion is found as early as Homer (*Odyssey* 11.576ff.).

1230   *degrauet:* jussive subjunctive; so too *ludat* (1232), *transuolet* (1233), *accrescat* (1234), *ferat* (1236). See 24n.

1231   **old Aeolian:** Sisyphus, son of Aeolus, punished for disobedience to the gods by being made forever to roll uphill a stone that forever rolled back again.
seni Aeolio: dative of either possession or "disadvantage".
perennis labor: in apposition to *saxum.*

1232   **elusive streams:** a reference to the punishment of Tantalus, who cooked and served up his son's flesh at a feast for the gods and was condemned to eternal hunger and thirst. Tantalus was tormented by water which flowed near his lips but always disappeared when he tried to drink it, and by boughs of fruit which hung near him but always eluded his grasp. He is an important figure in Senecan tragedy; his ghost opens *Thyestes*.

1233 Tityos: a giant, whose punishment for attempting (on Juno's orders) to rape Latona was to have his liver eaten out by a vulture each day. The liver grew back every night.

1234 *poenae:* dative of purpose. See Woodcock §67.

1235 father of my Pirithous: Ixion, punished for an insult to Juno by being chained to an eternally spinning wheel.

1238 Gape earth: *dehisce tellus*. Thus Oedipus begins his prayer for self-destruction at *Oed.* 868.

1240 *ne metue:* see 131f.n.

1241 eternal house: *aeterna domo*. This phrase figures frequently in funerary inscriptions: see, e.g., *Corpus Inscriptionum Latinarum* 1.1930.

casti: used predicatively.

1242f. My prayers...: similarly Thyestes exclaims, when he sees that his (very similar) prayers are unanswered (*Thy.* 1020f.): "The earth lies all unmoved, an idle mass./ The gods have fled (*fugere superi*)." Cf. Jason's "atheistic" outburst at *Med.* 1027, and the bitter jibe of Rac.'s Th.: *Inexorables Dieux, qui m'avez trop servi* ("Inexorable gods, all too helpful", *Phd.* 1572). With all such passages contrast the providential attitude to the gods in Sen.'s philosophical works, e.g., *Ira* 2.27.1.

1243 *forent:* = *essent*.

1245 *ocius:* comparative for positive as at 130. See also 1002n.

1248 Cf. Eur. *Bacchae* 1216f.: "Follow me, bearing the wretched weight (*baros*) of Pentheus."

1249 I recognise: cf. esp. 113 and 698. See 113n.

1250 *neu:* commonly used (or *neue*), as here, to join two main clauses the second of which is preceded by a negative final clause (= "and lest"). No disjunctive force is implied. Cf. 131f., 1157 above.

1252 On gifts see 945n.

1253 On the chiastic order of adjectives and nouns here (abBA) often favoured by Sen., see 305n. The position of *orbitas* between the adjectives and nouns makes the arrangement approximate to that of the so-called "golden line" ("two substantives and two adjectives, with a verb betwixt them to keep the peace", Dryden).

1254 Embrace these limbs: *complectere artus*. Cf. Rac.'s Th. at *Phd.*

211

1649: *Allons de ce cher fils embrasser ce qui reste* ("Let us go and embrace my dear son's remains"); and Th.'s embrace of Hipp. at Eur. *Hipp.* 1431ff. *Complectere* is imperative.

1256ff. For the "religious" significance of Th.'s actions here see 1109f.n. Cf. Agaue's actions in the lost part of Eur.'s *Bacchae* (reconstructed by E.R. Dodds, second edition Oxford 1960, 234). Often criticised, the dramatic significance—and power—of Th.'s actions are clear. Some editors, following Leo, assign 1256-61 to the Chorus, to whom E assigns the whole of 1256-80. I have followed A's assignment of these lines to Th.; so too recently Giardina and Zwierlein.

1257 *loco:* syntactically ambiguous. Take as ablative of separation with *errantes* or as dative with *restitue*—or as both.

1259 An especially elaborate word-order (aBabA).

1262 *lugubri officio:* ablative of cause with *trepidae*; lit. "trembling from the sad service". See Woodcock §45.

1269 **starry fire:** cf. 738ff., 1110ff. and 1174, for other "star" imagery associated with Hipp. See also Andromache's description of Hector's face "radiating beams of fire" (*flammeum intendens iubar, Tro.* 448), and Bacchus' "starry face" (*uultu sidereo*) at *Oed.* 410.

1270 **beauty set:** *cecidit* is used of the "setting" of planets. Cf. 378, and *Tro.* 1140-42, where Polyxena's shining beauty is compared in its last moments (*extremus decor*) to the light of the setting sun (*Phoebi cadentis*). With 1270 cf. also 1173.

1271 Cf. Oedipus at *Oed.* 75.

1273 **final gifts:** *suprema dona*. The death-gifts offered to the spirit of the departed: see Catullus 101.3, Virg. *Aen.* 6.883ff., 11.25f. Here presumably flowers, garlands etc. (wine, milk and honey were also usual), taken by Th. from one of Hipp.'s companions or an attendant. On "gifts" see 945n.

1274 *ferant:* jussive subjunctive; so too *sonet* (1276) and *incubet* (1280). See 24n.

1275 **Open...:** the *regia* or *porte royale* is opened once again. Cf. the earlier opening at 863.

1276 **Attica:** the Latin here, *Mopsopia*, is an old name for Attica. See 121.

1277f. **You...You...:** *uos...uos...* Cf. Hipp.'s instructions to his companions in Act One at 17ff., 31ff., 48ff. See Intro. p. 24.

1279f. Whereas Hipp. is to be cremated (1277) in accordance with contemporary (first century A.D.) Roman aristocratic practice, Pha. is to be degraded by burial. Inhumation did not become popular with the Roman aristocracy until the second century A.D.

As always in Sen. tragedy the last words of the play are dramatic dialogue delivered by one of the central characters. There is a marked contrast here with Greek tragedy, which ends more frequently than not (it becomes the rule in Eur.) with a short ode or utterance from the chorus. It should be observed that both the "non-Senecan" plays of the *corpus*, *HO* and *Oct*., conclude with a short choral ode, which may well have been standard Roman practice. Complete avoidance of a lyric or choral ending may be Senecan innovation; certainly the dramatic power of the Senecan ending (cf. esp. the final lines of *Med.*, *Ag.* and *Thy.*) is Sen.'s own.

APPENDIX I

NATURE

Facilius natura intelligitur quam enarratur.

Nature is more easily understood than explained.

Seneca *Ep.* 121

The concept expressed by the term *natura*, "nature", in Latin is complex and indefinable. A.O. Lovejoy and G. Boas, *Primitivism and Related Ideas in Antiquity* (Baltimore 1935) 447-56, distinguish sixty-six senses of the term. In Seneca's philosophical and tragic writings *natura* seems to embrace (at least) all of the following: the created order and processes of the cosmos and its parts (*Helv.* 8), the laws that govern such order and processes (*Helv.* 6.8, 20.1f., *Pho.* 856), the power that created and directs them—Jupiter, Venus, Diana, Neptune, Pluto, Liber, Hercules, Mercury, god (e.g. *Pha.* 959ff., 274ff., *Thy.* 834, *Helv.* 8.4, *Ben.* 4.7f., *Ep.* 90.38, 107.7ff.); the laws that govern man, govern him as part of this ordained order, and govern him physically, psychologically, historically, morally (e.g. *Pho.* 478, *Oed.* 25, *Ep.* 4.10, 25.4, 30.11, 107.9); the determined and determinant properties of earth, air, water, fire, sea, wind, stars, planets, field, forest, river, thunderbolt, summer, winter, autumn, spring, and the states of affairs, *rerum condicio* (*Ep.* 107.7), parasitic upon those properties; the determined and determinant properties—individual, specific, generic—of everything; the innate appetites, needs, *desideria*, instincts of animal and human life, hunger, thirst (e.g. *Helv.* 10, *Tran.* 9, *Ep.* 4.10, 119.2ff.), sexual desire (e.g. *Pha.* 352, *Helv.* 13.3, *Tran.* 9), the instinct for survival, the fear of death (*Ep.* 82, 121.18-21), the human drive towards concord and love (*Ira* 1.5.2f.,

3.5.6); the guiding principle of human behaviour, the canon of human happiness and fulfilment (*Pha.* 481, *Brev.* 8.1, 24.3, *Ep.* 66.39ff.), exemplified in *Epistle* 90 (esp. 4ff., 15ff., 36ff.) in the primal state of man, a pre-technological existence of forest, beast, crag, meadow, earth, breeze, stream and fountain, in which both "nature's bounty", *beneficia naturae* (*Ep.* 90.36), and the ordained condition of things were uncontaminated by human art; the boundaries that separate sea from land, earth from sky, death from life, mother from son, father from daughter (e.g. *Pha.* 173, 176, *Oed.* 25, *Ag.* 34), and the bonds that join them (*uinclo, Pha.* 1115, *uincula rerum, Med.* 376)—the bonding connections and separating differentiations of things that give the present physical and experiential world its laws, structure, rhythm, reality and its terror; and the force too which in the periodic conflagrations that consume the world dissolves all differentiations and restores them (*Pol.* 1.1, *NQ* 3.30). Identified in *De Beneficiis* (4.7f.) with fate, *fatum*, fortune, *fortuna*, and divine reason, *diuina ratio*, less simple and less comforting in the tragedies and especially in *Phaedra, natura* in Seneca is inextricably entwined with the unimpedable movement of the universe.

APPENDIX II

METRE

Dialogue

The standard metre of Senecan dialogue is the iambic trimeter or (more loosely) senarius. This is a six-foot line based on the iambus (ᴗ–), for which several equivalents are allowed, primarily the spondee (––), tribrach (ᴗᴗᴗ), dactyl (–ᴗᴗ) and anapaest (ᴗᴗ–). All dialogue in *Pha.* is in this metre with the exception of lines 1201-12. Its schema is as follows:

1	2	3	4	5	6
ᴗ –	ᴗ –	ᴗ –	ᴗ –	(ᴗ –)	ᴗ ᴗ̱
– –		– –		– –	
ᴗᴗᴗ	ᴗᴗᴗ	ᴗᴗᴗ	ᴗᴗᴗ		
– ᴗᴗ		– ᴗᴗ		(– ᴗᴗ)	
ᴗᴗ –	(ᴗᴗ –)			ᴗᴗ –	
(ᴗᴗᴗᴗ)					

Bracketed feet occur rarely. Caesuras (word-divisions within feet) occur regularly after the first syllable of the third foot, less regularly after the first syllable of the fourth foot. It is clear from the schema that Sen. thought of his iambic line as consisting of three pairs (dipodies) of iambi rather than six independent feet, and thus that it is more accurate to call it an iambic trimeter rather than a senarius ("sixer"). Sen.'s line is much closer to the iambic dialogue lines of the Greek tragedians than to the senarii of his Republican predecessors, who allowed spondees, for example, in every foot of the iambic line. The most common form of Sen.'s iambic trimeter is in fact a systematic alternation of spondees and iambs: $-- \cup - \; -- \cup - \; -- \cup -$ (see 88n.).

The outburst of Theseus at 1201-12 is in a metre which Sen. uses only twice elsewhere in his tragedies (*Med.* 740-51, *Oed.* 223-32), the trochaic tetrameter catalectic (more loosely termed septenarius, "sevener"). This is a seven and a half foot line based on the trochee ($-\cup$), but allowing the same equivalents for the trochee as the trimeter allows for the iamb. The schema:

1	2	3	4	5	6	7	
$-\cup$	$-\cup$	$-\cup$	$-\cup$	$-\cup$	$-\cup$	$-\cup$	$\underline{\cup}$
	$--$		$--$		$--$		
	$\cup\cup-$		$\cup\cup-$		$\cup\cup-$		
$\cup\cup\cup$	$\cup\cup\cup$	$\cup\cup\cup$	$\cup\cup\cup$	$\cup\cup\cup$	$(\cup\cup\cup)$		
	$(-\cup\cup)$				$-\cup\cup$		

There is usually a diaeresis (word-division between feet) after the fourth foot.

Lyric

The main metres used in the lyric sections of *Phaedra* are:

Anapaestic (lines 1-84, 325-57, 959-88b, 1123-27, 1132-39, 1141-48), viz. lines based on the anapaest ($\cup\cup-$), but allowing the spondee ($--$) and the dactyl ($-\cup\cup$) as equivalents. A run of four short syllables (dactyl followed by anapaest) is avoided. The standard line is the anapaestic dimeter (four feet):

1	2	3	4
$\cup\cup-$	$\cup\cup-$	$\cup\cup-$	$\cup\cup-$
$--$	$--$	$--$	$--$
$-\cup\cup$	$(-\cup\cup)$	$-\cup\cup$	$(-\cup\cup)$

Occasional monometers (two feet) occur (e.g. 34b, 43).

Asclepiadean (lines 753-60, 764-82, 784-823, 1128f.). The line used is the minor asclepiad: $---\cup\cup--\cup\cup-\cup\underline{\cup}$

Sapphic (lines 274-324, 736-52, 1149-53). The sapphic line:
$$-\cup---\cup\cup-\cup-\underline{\cup}$$
is sometimes interspersed with an adonius ($-\cup\cup-\underline{\cup}$), as at 740, 752.

In addition there are three dactylic tetrameters (four foot lines based on the dactyl [–∪∪], with the spondee [––] as equivalent: 761-63), two glyconics (–––∪∪–∪–: 783, 1130), one aristophanean (–∪∪–∪––: 1131), and one catalectic pherecratean (–––∪∪–: 1140).

In developing his lyric metres, especially the asclepiad and sapphic, Seneca was obviously influenced substantially by Horace's *Odes*. His favourite lyric line was, however, the anapaestic dimeter, which is not found in Horace but was used in Greek tragedy for the entrance and exit odes of the chorus. Republican and Augustan tragedians had extended this use to choral odes anywhere in the play and to individual monodies. The absence of strophic corresponsion in Seneca's choral odes—in marked contrast to Greek choral lyric—seems to have been typical of Roman tragic practice. On the translation of the lyric metres see Intro. p. 38.

APPENDIX III

VARIANTS FROM THE OXFORD TEXT

Differences of text between this edition and the Zwierlein Oxford text of 1986 are as follows. The source of each reading—ms. or scholar—is given in italics.

	Boyle	Zwierlein
10	iacent *EA*	patent *Zwierlein*
11	qua *ES²*	quae *A*
28	Phyle *Frenzel*	flius *E*
48	uibretur *E*	libretur *A*
81	faues *recc*	faue *EA*
97	pudorque *EA*	pudorue *Bentley*
123	promittet *E*	promittat *A*
187	laesumque *E*	ipsumque *A*
208	tecta *EA*	texta *Cornelissen*
208	cibus *EA*	scyphus *Gronouius*
216	uides *EA*	uide *C²*
218	fero *A*	reor *Zwierlein*
241b	fugiet *E*	fugiat *A*
326	regno *EA*	harena *Zwierlein*
332f	aetherio...mundo *A*	per ipsum...mundum *E*
349	tum *EA*	tunc *recc.*
367	moriens *EA*	marcens *Axelson*
428f	iussa...regis	iusta...reges
	...omne et *Heinsius*	...omne *EA*

	Boyle	Zwierlein
452	duxit *EA*	ducit *recc.*
472	classibus *EA*	piscibus *Bentley*
477	ista *Leo*	fata *EA*
508	sedesque mutat *E*	solesque uitat *Axelson*
510	iuuat *EA*	iuuat et *Peiper*
521	uersantem *E*	laxantem *Axelson*
549	comantes *EA*	micantes *Axelson*
567	durus *EPCS*	dirus *T*
596	amauimus *EA*	admouimus *Axelson*
636	tacitae *EA*	pauidae *Axelson*
641	intimas saeuus uorat *A*	intimis saeuit ferus *Gronouius*
643	uenis *EA*	uenas *Bothe*
749	qualis *EA*	talis *Leo*
755	territans *EA*	temperans *Axelson*
768	ut lilia *E*	lilia *A*
770	et *Richter*	ut *EA*
774	confidit *EA*	confidat *recc.*
784	Panas quae Dryades montiuagos petunt *E*	montiuagiue Panes *A*
831	Pirithoo *E*	Pittheo *Damsté*
899	paruis *EA*	patriis *D. Heinsius*
965	uias *EA*	uices *Busche*
1012	furenti pontus...sinu *EA*	furens Ionius...sinus *Bothe*
1021	ostendit *EA*	ostendet *recc.*
1025	querimur *A*	sequimur *Axelson*
1057	agros *E*	Argos *A*
1069	currum *EA*	cursum *recc.*
1092	deuio *EA*	deuium *Axelson*
1099	erecto *Trevet*	ingesto *Heinsius*
1104	truncus *EA*	ruscus *Bentley*
1106	quae *EA*	qua *recc.*
1120	optata *A*	optanda *E*
1123	humana *EA*	heu magna *Axelson*
1204	uastum mare *EA*	uasti maris *Axelson*

Of the above fifty-one different readings printed in this edition thirty-three retain the readings of E and/or A in preference to the conjectures of scholars (27) or the testimony of later mss. (6), twelve offer other readings from the EA group, four are themselves scholarly conjectures, one is the reading of a later ms., one that of Nicholas Trevet (early fourteenth century).

Omitting matters of orthography and punctuation, other differences between this edition and that of Zwierlein include the latter's occasional transposition of lines (261 is placed after 266 and 344-50 completely rearranged), its two lacunae (after 509 and 1144—this edition has only one lacuna, after 1143 as Leo), its assignment of *precibus...potest* in 239 to Phaedra (which this edition assigns to the

Nutrix as in EA), and its bracketing of the following lines for deletion: 264, 279-80, 377-78, 398, 618, 642, 1016, 1100, 1140, 1179-80. This edition brackets no lines for deletion, but indicates in the Notes where authenticity is doubted. Colometric differences between the two texts are confined to anapaestic verse, in which Zwierlein's divergences from ms. colometry and from the prevailing scholarly consensus have not been followed. The colometry of this edition is (with a few exceptions and adjustments) that of E. It is also substantially the colometry of (among others) Woesler, Grimal, Viansino and Giardina.

SELECT BIBLIOGRAPHY

1. Editions, Translations, Commentaries

Costa, C.D.N. *Seneca Medea* (Oxford 1973).

Fantham, E. *Seneca's Troades: A Literary Commentary* (Princeton 1982).

Giardina, G.C. *L. Annaei Senecae Tragoediae* (Bologna 1966).

Giomini, R. *L. Annaei Senecae Phaedram edidit et commentario instruxit Remus Giomini* (Rome 1955).

Grimal, P. *L. Annaei Senecae Phaedra* (Paris 1965).

Lawall, G. and S. & Kunkel, G. *The Hippolytus or Phaedra of Seneca* (Univ. of Mass. Amherst 1976).

Leo F., *L. Annaei Senecae Tragoediae* (Berlin 1878-79).

Miller, F.J. *Seneca: Tragedies* (London & Cambridge, Mass. 1917).

Peiper, R. & Richter, G. *L. Annaei Senecae Tragoediae* (Leipzig 1902).

Tarrant, R.J. *Seneca: Agamemnon* (Cambridge 1976).

— *Seneca's Thyestes* (Atlanta, Georgia 1985).

Viansino, G. *L. Annaei Senecae Tragoediae* (Turin 1965).

Watling, E.F. *Seneca: Four Tragedies and Octavia* (Harmondsworth 1966).

Woesler, W. *Senecas Tragödien: Die Überlieferung der a-Klasse dargestellt am Beispiel der Phaedra* (Münster 1965).

Zwierlein, O. *L. Annaei Senecae Tragoediae* (Oxford 1986).

2. Works of Reference and Criticism

Ahl, F.M. "The Rider and the Horse: Politics and Power in Roman Poetry from Horace to Statius", *Aufstieg und Niedergang der römischen Welt* II.32.1 (1984) 40-124.

Anliker, K. *Prologe und Akteinteilung in Senecas Tragödien* (Bern 1960).

Barrett, W.S. (ed.) *Euripides Hippolytos* (Oxford 1964).

Bieber, M. *The History of the Greek and Roman Theatre* (rev. ed. Princeton 1980).

Bonner, S.F. *Roman Declamation* (Berkeley 1949).

Boyle, A.J. "In Nature's Bonds: A Study of Seneca's *Phaedra*", *Aufstieg und Niedergang der römischen Welt* II.32.2 (1985) 1284-1347.

— (ed.) *Seneca Tragicus. Ramus Essays on Senecan Drama* (Berwick, Victoria 1983).

Braden, G. "The Rhetoric and Psychology of Power in the Dramas of Seneca", *Arion* 9 (1970) 5-41.

Busa, R. & Zampolli, A. *Concordantiae Senecanae* (Hildesheim 1975).

Calder, W.M.III. "The Size of the Chorus in Seneca's *Agamemnon*", *Classical Philology* 70 (1970) 32-35.

— "Seneca, Tragedian of Imperial Rome", *Classical Journal* 72 (1976) 1-11.

Canter, H.V. *Rhetorical Elements in the Tragedies of Seneca* (Urbana 1925).

Coffey, M. "Seneca: Tragedies—Report for the Years 1922-1955", *Lustrum* 2 (1957) 113-86.

Costa, C.D.N. (ed.) *Seneca* (London 1974).

Croisille, J.M. "Lieux communs, *sententiae* et intentions philosophiques dans la *Phèdre* de Sénèque", *Revue des Etudes Latines* 42 (1964) 276-301.

Cunliffe, J.W. *The Influence of Seneca on Elizabethan Tragedy* (London 1893; repr. New York 1965).

Davis, P.J. "*Vindicat Omnes Natura Sibi*: A Reading of Seneca's *Phaedra*", in Boyle, *Seneca Tragicus* (above), 114-27.

Denooz, J. *Lucius Annaeus Seneca Tragoediae Index Verborum* (Hildesheim 1980).

Dingel, J. *Seneca und die Dichtung* (Heidelberg 1974).

Dorey, T.A. & Dudley, D.R. (edd.) *Roman Drama* (London 1965).

Eliot, T.S. "Seneca in Elizabethan Translation", *Selected Essays* (London 1951) 65-105.

Enk, P.J. "Roman Tragedy", *Neophilologus* 41 (1957) 282-307.

Fantham, E. "Virgil's Dido and Seneca's Tragic Heroines", *Greece and Rome* n.s. 22 (1975) 1-10.

Fitch, J.G. *Character in Senecan Tragedy* (Diss. Cornell 1974).

— "Sense-Pauses and Relative Dating in Seneca, Sophocles and Shakespeare", *American Journal of Philology* 102 (1981) 289-307.

Friedrich, W.-H. *Untersuchungen zu Senecas dramatischer Technik* (Borna-Leipzig 1933).

Garton, C. *Personal Aspects of the Roman Theatre* (Toronto 1972).

Giancotti, F. *Saggio sulle tragedie di Seneca* (Rome 1953).

Giomini, R. *Saggio sulla Fedra di Seneca* (Rome 1955).

Griffin, M.T. "Imago Vitae Suae" in Costa (above) 1-38.

— *Nero, The End of a Dynasty* (London 1984).

— *Seneca: A Philosopher in Politics* (Oxford 1976).

Grimal, P. "L'Originalité de Sénèque dans la tragédie de Phèdre", *Revue des Etudes Latines* 41 (1963) 297-314.

Heldmann, K. *Untersuchungen zu den Tragödien Senecas* (Wiesbaden 1974).

Henry, D. & Walker, B. *The Mask of Power: Seneca's Tragedies and Imperial Rome* (Warminster 1985).

— "Phantasmagoria and Idyll: An Element of Seneca's *Phaedra*", *Greece and Rome* 13 (1966) 223-39.

Herington, C.J. "Senecan Tragedy", *Arion* 5 (1966) 422-71.

— "The Younger Seneca", in Kenney E. & Clausen W. (edd.), *The Cambridge History of Classical Literature. II: Latin Literature* (Cambridge 1982) 511-32.

Hermann, L. *Le théâtre de Sénèque* (Paris 1924).

Herter, H. "Phaidra in griechischer und römischer Gestalt", *Rheinisches Museum für Philologie* 114 (1971) 14-77.

Jacquot, J. (ed.) *Les tragédies de Sénèque et le théâtre de la Renaissance* (Paris 1964).

Jocelyn, H.D. (ed.) *The Tragedies of Ennius* (Cambridge 1969).

Leeman, A.D. "Seneca's *Phaedra* as a Stoic Tragedy", *Miscellanea Tragica in Honorem J.C.Kamerbeek*, edd. Bremer, J.M., Radt, S.L. & Ruigh, C.J. (Amsterdam 1976) 199-212.

Lefèvre, E. "*Quid ratio possit?* Senecas *Phaedra* als stoisches Drama", *Wiener Studien* n.f. 3 (1969) 131-60.

— (ed.) *Senecas Tragödien* (Darmstadt 1972).

Liebermann, W.-L. *Studien zu Senecas Tragödien* (Meisenheim am Glan 1974).

Long, A.A. *Hellenistic Philosophy* (London 1974).

Lucas F.L. *Seneca and Elizabethan Tragedy* (Cambridge 1922).

MacGregor, A.P. "Parisinus 8031: *Codex Optimus* for the A-Mss of Seneca's Tragedies", *Philologus* 122 (1978) 88-110.

Marti, B.M. "Seneca's Tragedies. A New Interpretation", *Transactions of the American Philological Association* 76 (1945) 216-45.

Merzlak, R.F. "*Furor* in Seneca's *Phaedra*", *Collection Latomus* 180 (Brussels 1983) 193-210.

Oldfather, W.A., Pease A.S. & Canter H.V. *Index Verborum Quae In Senecae Fabulis Necnon In Octavia Praetexta Reperiuntur* (Urbana 1918).

Owen, W.H. "Commonplace and Dramatic Symbol in Seneca's Tragedies", *Transactions of the American Philological Association* 99 (1968) 291-313.

Paratore, E. "Originalità del teatro di Seneca", *Dioniso* NS 20 (1957) 53-74.

— "Sulla Phaedra di Seneca", *Dioniso* 15 (1952) 199-234.

Pratt, N.T. "Major Systems of Figurative Language in Senecan Melodrama", *Transactions of the American Philological Association* 94 (1963) 199-234.

— *Seneca's Drama* (Chapel Hill & London 1983).

— "The Stoic Base of Senecan Drama", *Transactions of the American Philological Association* 79 (1948) 1-11.

Raven, D. *Latin Metre* (London 1965).

Regenbogen, O. "Schmerz und Tod in den Tragödien des Seneca", *Vortr. Bibl. Warburg* (1927-28) 167-218.

Rist, J.M. *Stoic Philosophy* (Cambridge 1969).

Segal, C.P. "Boundary Violation and the Landscape of the Self in Senecan Tragedy", *Antike und Abendland* 29 (1983) 172-87.

— *Language and Desire in Seneca's Phaedra* (Princeton 1986).

— "Senecan Baroque: the Death of Hippolytus in Seneca, Ovid and Euripides", *Transactions of the American Philological Association* 114 (1984) 311-26.

Seidensticker, B. *Die Gesprächsverdichtung in den Tragödien Senecas* (Heidelberg 1969).

— & Armstrong, D. "Seneca Tragicus 1878-1978 (with Addenda 1979ff.)", *Aufstieg und Niedergang der römischen Welt* II.32.2 (1985) 916-68.

Skovgaard-Hansen, M. "The Fall of Phaethon: Meaning in Seneca's *Hippolytus*", *Classica et Mediaevalia* 29 (1968) 92-123.

Stähli-Peter, M.M. *Die Arie des Hippolytus. Kommentar zu Eingangsmonodie in der Phaedra des Seneca* (Diss. Zurich 1974).

Stamm, R. *The Mirror-Technique in Seneca and pre-Shakespearean Tragedy* (Bern 1975).

Sullivan, J.P. *Literature and Politics in the Age of Nero* (Ithaca & London 1985).

Tarrant, R.J. "Senecan Drama and its Antecedents", *Harvard Studies in Classical Philology* 82 (1978) 213-63.

Tobin, R.W. *Racine and Seneca* (Chapel Hill 1971).

Trabert, K. *Studien zur Darstellung des Pathologischen in den Tragödien des Seneca* (Diss. Erlangen 1953).

Walker, B. Review of Zwierlein (1966) (below), *Classical Philology* 64 (1969) 183-87.

Wilson, M. *Seneca's Agamemnon and Troades: A Critical Study* (Diss. Monash 1985).

Winterbottom, M. (ed.) *The Elder Seneca: Controuersiae, Suasoriae* (London and Cambridge, Mass. 1974).

Woodcock, E.C. *A New Latin Syntax* (London 1959).

Zehnacker, H. (ed.) *Théâtre et spectacles dans l'Antiquité* (Leiden 1983).

Zintzen, C. *Analytisches Hypomnema zu Senecas Phaedra* (Meisenheim am Glan 1961).

Zwierlein, O. *Prolegomena zu einer kritischen Ausgabe der Tragödien Senecas* (Wiesbaden 1984).

— *Die Rezitationsdramen Senecas* (Meisenheim am Glan 1966).

INDEX TO THE NOTES

(i) PASSAGES CITED FROM OTHER SENECAN PLAYS

References are to line numbers.

(ii) GENERAL

The following list is selective of subjects and references. Reference is to the main note or notes concerned. A full index of proper names may be found in Zwierlein.